PASSAGE TO ESL LITERACY

Instructor's Guide

Diane M. Longfield
ESL Instructor
ESL Consultant

DELTA SYSTEMS, INC.

Copyright© 1981 by Delta Systems Inc. 1981

ISBN 0-937354-03-1

First published 1981 by Delta Systems Inc.

All Rights Reserved. No part of this publication may be reproduced, stored in a retrieval system, or transmitted in any form or by any means, electronic, mechanical, photocopying, recording, or otherwise, without prior permission of the copyright owner.

Printed in the United States of America.

DEDICATED TO

my family, for all the sacrifices willingly and lovingly made.

learning, a life long process.

excellence, a goal always to strive for no matter how small or large the task.

PREFACE

The use of visual symbols to represent the sounds of a spoken language certainly goes back to prehistory. These symbols which translate into reading and writing are perhaps the most decisive and far-reaching achievement of the human mind. However, the spread of literacy has been a gradual process. In the most highly developed societies its extension to the mass of people is a fairly recent innovation. Actually, before the invention of the printing press, there was no need for literacy for the general population since there was nothing to read. Therefore, illiteracy was not a problem.

In today's complex society, the reasons for being literate are self-evident. On one end of the spectrum, it means being able to read a street sign or a box label. On the other end, it means eradicating disease and poverty, improving involvement in national citizenship and moving toward self-realization.

Until recently, the main thrust of most ESL programs has been to teach foreign students to speak English, and rightly so. Most ESL materials utilize the audio-lingual, situational reinforcement or notional-functional methods to foster communication skills necessary to meet the student's basic language needs. Little or no attention is given to the systematic development of reading and writing skills. In fact, most ESL materials introduce reading and writing exercises as a reinforcement to the listening and speaking skills, again, justifiably so. This technique is particularly successful with students who are literate in their own language and who transfer word attack skills from their language to English, even when their language does not use the Roman alphabet. However, we cannot disregard that percentage of ESL students who need literacy training. Literacy training is correctly a part of adult education. When the teaching of literacy is complicated by the fact that the learner is also a foreign speaker, an issue that is already complex is compounded. If we teach ESL students to speak English in a structurally sequenced manner in order to guarantee success, we can also teach them reading and writing systematically in order to guarantee success.

The general objectives of **Passage to ESL Literacy** are:

1. to develop pre-literacy/readiness skills in visual and auditory discrimination through sequential and progressively more difficult exercises.

2. to prepare ESL students for listening, speaking, reading and writing in English.

3. to build a strong foundation in sound-symbol transference.

4. to cultivate an understanding of the most basic phonetic components of the English language while students learn a vast number of survival sight words.

5. to prepare ESL literacy students to learn from core ESL materials.

6. to develop self-confidence and self-respect in those students who are preliterate or illiterate in their own language and/or English by familiarizing them with controlled vocabulary, basic expressions and sight words in English which they can comprehend, say, read and write.

7. to teach secondary and adult ESL students to survive in their new environment by teaching them literacy skills within authentic situations which duplicate everyday life.

The **selection of students who require ESL literacy training** can proceed in various ways:

1. At registration, some candidates will be immediately identified by their interpreters.

2. Others can be pin-pointed once they have been set at ease and tested orally. Can they complete the simple form?* Can they hold a pencil? Do they turn the form right side up when it's handed to them upside down? Can they sign their name easily? Can they read high exposure words which are isolated such as "address", "telephone", "last"? Can they respond "n" when asked what letter "name" starts with? Can they write "n" when requested to do so? Can they decode: name, same, fame? If not, they may be candidates for literacy training.

3. Another way of choosing participants for ESL literacy training is to arbitrarily decide that all beginning level ESL students (non-speakers) need literacy training, whether they are or are not literate in their own language simply because they must learn the English sound system.

4. Perhaps the best method of selecting students in need of literacy training is for the teachers in an ESL program to wait until a student has completed a month or two of ESL course work. At that time, those students in need of literacy training will "surface". Those students can be grouped into an ESL literacy course or can be tutored before, during or after class.

*for teacher convenience, a reproducable form is presented on p. iii of this guide.

REGISTRATION

Mr. ☐
Mrs. ☐   Name _____
Miss ☐   last   first   middle
Ms. ☐

M _____   Address _____

F _____   _____
                    city   state   zip code

Telephone number (_____) _____   _____
                                                            country

Social Security Number _____

_____   Signature _____
       Date

TABLE OF CONTENTS

Preface i
Introduction 1
General Notes, Workbook 4
        Instructor's Guide 5
Instructions for Part 1 - Pre-literacy 17
Instructions for Part 2 - Literacy 41
Instructions for Part 3 - Reading and Writing correlated to Lessons 1-10
    of **Delta's Effective ESL for the 21st Century** 163
Instructions for Part 4 - Transition to Cursive Writing 369
Appendix A, Visuals for Duplication 371
Appendix B, Visuals Corresponding to **Passage to ESL Literacy**
    from **Delta's Effective ESL for the 21st century, Volume 3** 389
Appendix C, Exercises for Duplication 395
Appendix D, Games for Duplication 405
Appendix E, Sight Words 417

INTRODUCTION

1. *Passage to ESL Literacy* can be used as a core text with an entire beginning level ESL class. It can also be used by a literacy tutor or paraprofessional as an ESL supplement for a small group or an individual in need of developing literacy skills.

2. *Passage of ESL Literacy* is divided into four parts. Each part is followed by a mastery test. The mastery tests can also be used as pretests to place students into or out of a particular part of the book. All tests are on blue pages. All pages are perforated.

   PART 1, Pre-literacy, contains two sections. The first, pages 1-9, provides practice in writing personal information including name (first and last), address, city, state, zip code, telephone number and social security number.

   Foreign adults cannot wait to learn how to read requests for personal information until a phonetically appropriate time. Nor can they wait to learn how to write this basic information until they have had extensive practice in letter formation. Therefore, the request for personal information is taught orally for listening comprehension and as sight words for reading. No regard is given at this stage for phonics or extensive practice in letter formation. The goal is simple: to learn to say and write personal information as quickly as possible.

   The test on page 28 of the student workbook can be used as a pre-test to place a student into or out of pages 1-9. It can also be used as a mastery test upon completion of PART 1. It is essential to note that throughout the workbook, students are taught to correctly respond in writing to additional requests for personal information. These requests are practiced and reinforced at the upper right hand corner of each page. When requesting personal information, forms use a variety of formats and an attempt to teach some of these various formats has been made. For this reason, the information is requested in lower case and capitals, in reverse (last, first), in abbreviation (M, F) and in variety (telephone number, home phone) whenever appropriate. By the end of the workbook, students should be able to complete a fairly complex application or identification form.

   The second section of PART 1 is on visual discrimination. It is intended for *pre-literates* and *double-illiterates*.[1] These are students who have never been introduced to the written language either in the native tongue or in English. These students may not perceive the relationship between oral and written language and may not know how to hold a pencil. The exercises on pages 10-22 begin by requiring the students to distinguish gross shapes from one another. Next, the students learn to distinguish like shapes that are different in size and direction. Directionality exercises are followed by exercises on discriminating letters from one another. At this stage the letters are merely treated as shapes with no phonetic considerations. Visual discrimination is based on the distinctive features of the letters and thus the letters are grouped according to their shapes.

   Not all ESL students require this practice. The tests on pages 23-27 of the student workbook can be used as a pre-test to place the student into or out of this section of PART 1. It can also be used as a mastery test upon completion of pages 10-22.

---

[1] McGee, Donna, "Pre-literacy Definitions". A paper presentation for the Literacy Symposium at the Ontario TESL Convention (Vancouver, B.C., 1978), p. 1.

3. **PART 2, Literacy,** provides instruction in sound symbol association, common blends and digraphs and beginning reading and writing. This section can be used with several types of students: the *semi-literates*, who have some mechanical writing skills and limited oral and graphic skills in two languages but who have no word attack skills such as decoding; the *functional illiterates*, who know the names of the letters in their first language, can copy and recognize some words by sight in English but who probably can not put sound and symbol together or read information words in English; the *functional literates*[2] who have basic literacy skills in their native language but who bring few, if any, word attack skills to learning English. They cannot read for enjoyment, express themselves in writing or learn new things from the printed word. This could very well be a large portion of beginning level ESL students.

   Activities in PART 2, include the visual discrimination of words, listening comprehension exercises, sight word recognition, beginning decoding and encoding, cloze and dictation exercises, word elimination games, and alphabetizing.

   A test of sound symbol association is provided on pages 59-60. Page 61 tests the student's ability to match lower case letters with their capitals and the name of the letter with its written form. Because the writing of personal information continues to be taught in PART 2, a mastery test is provided on page 62 via an identification form. Pages 71-72 contain a review of the blends and digraphs taught in PART 2. Thus pages 59-62 and 71-72 can be used as pre-tests or mastery tests depending on the instructor's goals and the student's ability. Lastly, for those instructors who feel it is essential for an adult to know how to alphabetize, PART 2 also includes a section on alphabetizing between pages 73-75.

4. **PART 3** is intended for all in need of literacy training in English. It is correlated to the first ten lessons of **Delta's Effective ESL for the 21st Century. Delta's Effective ESL for the 21st Century** is probably the most effective core ESL material on the market today. The 40 lessons take students from controlled and semi-controlled exercises to spontaneous production and transfer to real life communication. "The controlled ones (lesson plans) show the student a useful pattern and how to manipulate it. The less controlled ones allow him to make original sentences with it and to use it in appropriate social contexts."[3] In spite of this, lessons 1-10 are too difficult for students in need of literacy training. For this reason, PART 3 simplifies, amplifies and rehearses the components of the first ten lessons in small pieces for easy digestion.

   In PART 3, the lesson and section numbers correspond directly to the lesson and section numbers in **Delta's Effective ESL for the 21st Century.** However, it is essential to note that ***Passage to ESL Literacy can be used on its own as a literacy text prior to use with any core ESL text.***

   PART 3 reinforces and puts to use those skills learned in PART 2. Speaking English is the basis for the listening, reading and writing exercises which are varied in format to maintain a high interest level. Matching exercises, sentence scrambles and odd-man out word games add fun to the learning process. Pages 133-136 test skills and knowledge developed in

[2]McGee, p. 2-3.
[3]Selman, Mary. *An Introduction to Teaching English as a Second Language* (Vancouver, B.C., 1979) p. 38.

lessons 1-5 and pages 191-193 test skills and knowledge developed in lessons 6-10. A final test of the student's ability to write personal information is provided on page 194 via an application form.

5. **PART 4, Transition to Cursive Writing**, is for students who have no skills in cursive writing and perceive it as a necessary adult skill. Letters are learned according to similarity of the initial stroke. It seems logical that this method simplifies the task. There are many different styles, sizes and directions in cursive writing. The goal is legibility, not perfection. In the test on page 208, students demonstrate their ability to match letters in cursive writing with their capitals and to write the alphabet legibly in cursive.

    PART 4 can be introduced at any time the instructor feels the students are ready. It is recommended however to wait at least until all the letters have been learned for sound symbol association in PART 2.

6. Implementation of these materials can proceed in a number of ways. The following are two suggestions:

    a. *Passage to ESL Literacy* can be used exclusively for all beginning level ESL students. Upon completion, students can proceed either to *Delta's Effective ESL for the 21st Century*, using lessons 1-10 for reinforcement and review and continue with lessons 11-40 or to any other core ESL text for beginners.

    b. Lessons 1-10 in *Delta's Effective ESL for the 21st Century* can be taught orally from the visuals while Parts 1 and 2 of *Passage to ESL Literacy* are being taught. Upon completion of PART 2, the class can review Lesson 1 of *Delta's Effective ESL for the 21st Century* orally and begin to use PART 3 of *Passage to ESL Literacy* as the reading and writing aspect of the lessons.

7. Extraordinary difficulty in listening comprehension, speaking, reading and writing may indicate a learning disability. According to Chapman, Vaillancourt and Dobbs, "In general, the teacher should watch for the student who does not seem to be making any consistent progress in a particular skill area or areas and who does not seem to remember from one class to the next what went on in the previous class. Such behavior exhibited over a period of time may indicate a learning disability."[4]

Chapman, Vaillancourt, and Dobbs also suggest that extraordinary difficulties with one or more of the four language skills may also indicate visual or hearing impairment. Therefore, for these special students, vision and hearing tests, which are often free of charge from clinics, should be given.

---

[4] Jean B. Chapman, Beverly Vaillancourt and Caroline S. Dobbs, "Are Your Adult English as a Second Language Students Learning Disabled?" (Material developed as part of a Special 310 Project under the Federal Adult Education Act by William Rainey Harper College, Palatine, Illinois, 1980. Funds for this Project were provided by the Illinois State Board of Education, Adult and Continuing Education Section.)

GENERAL NOTES

WORKBOOK

1. **Required Student Materials:** In addition to workbooks, it is strongly recommended that students have:

    - pencils

    - 3 x 5 cards* in white for the numbers, pink for the alphabet, green for the blends and digraphs and yellow for the sight words. When colored cards cannot be purchased by the students, they can write on white 3 x 5 cards with colored markers.

    - a holding envelope, card file or rubber bands for the cards.

2. **Pencils:** Insist that students work with pencils. This will allow students to easily correct errors.

3. **Warmup:** It may be necessary to provide instruction on how to hold a pencil and how to place paper on an angle. In a group situation, this should be done as a general instruction, so as not to embarrass a specific student. When necessary, provide limbering exercises in form of lines (/ / / / / / / /) and circles (ℓℓℓℓℓℓℓ).

4. **Examples:** Throughout the workbook, examples to the students are generally in a box under the directions. Any box with a smiley face in the upper left corner is a sample indicating to the students that they should do the same in those exercises which follow. For example:

DIRECTIONS: CIRCLE THE LETTERS THAT ARE THE SAME.

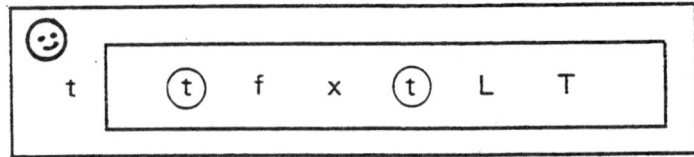

This format is particularly useful with students who cannot read the directions.

5. **Ambitious Students:** Some students have a tendency to work ahead in their workbooks prior to instruction. This may indicate the student is ready to learn at a more accelerated pace. If this is the case, the instructor might adjust the grouping or individualize. For other students, working ahead however can prove disastrous. We do not want to discourage independent work but it is imperative that students receive instruction prior to working on a particular concept. If this is the case, the instructor might collect the workbooks and hand out each individual page. This procedure may also facilitate correcting student work and minimize "loss" of student materials.

6. **Copying Exercises:** Several of the exercises throughout the workbook involve copying. While this may seem like a tedious task to both teacher and student, accurate copying is a new skill for many literacy students. This activity provides positive reinforcement for the

---

*White and colored 3 x 5 cards are available from Delta Systems Co., Inc.

placement of capitals and the use of punctuation. It instills a sense of word order and generates writing practice.

7. **Tests:** All tests are on blue pages. These may be used as pre-tests or mastery tests as previously indicated.

8. **Atmosphere:** As always with mature learners, the atmosphere must be warm, receptive, comfortable, and non-threatening.

INSTRUCTOR'S GUIDE

1. **Step by Step Instructions:** The step by step approach in this instructor's guide makes it possible for ESL teachers or paraprofessionals who are versed in ESL techniques and methodology but who are inexperienced in literacy training to successfully provide literacy instruction to ESL students.

2. **Grammar:** Syntactic structures are indicated by example and not by grammatical terms. Words which are underlined and put in parentheses are examples of vocabulary which can be substituted in the structure. For example:

    It's a (red) (dress).
    The (dress) is (red).

3. **Symbols:** Throughout the instructor's guide, T refers to teacher, St to student(s) and Gr to Group.

4. **Lesson Materials:** Instructional aids and visuals necessary to assist the instruction of each lesson are listed prior to the instructions for each lesson. When appropriate, sight words and new structures are also listed.

5. **Required Instructional Materials:** In addition to the student workbook and instructor's guide, teachers will need:

    - 5 x 8 cards* in white for the numbers, pink for the alphabet, green for the blends and digraphs and yellow for the sight words. When colored cards cannot be obtained, instructors can write on white cards with colored markers.

    - sentence strips for writing phrases, expressions and sentences.

    - markers.

    - the visuals listed prior to the instructions for each lesson are a separate component for this program, entitled ***Visuals for Passage to ESL Literacy***. These visuals have many details which can be used for extended vocabulary development when appropriate. Some instructors may already have a set of visuals entitled ***Delta's Effective ESL for the 21st Century, Volume 3***. Many of these visuals may be used to teach the lessons in ***Passage to ESL Literacy***. These are listed as "P" and followed by a number, such as P25 in Appendix B on p. 390 of this guide.

---

*White and colored 5 x 8 cards are available from Delta Systems Co., Inc.

6. **Optional Instructional Materials and Equipment:**

    - Language Master and blank cards

    - pocket chart or tack board for sentence strips

7. **Alphabet:** The entire alphabet is presented in PART 2. The letters are presented in random order, not in alphabetical order. The following is the order of presentation:

    Hh, Tt, Ss, Aa, Mm, Nn
    Bb, Pp, Ll, Ff, Ee, Dd
    Jj, Gg, Zz, Cc, Kk, Ii
    Rr, Oo, Vv, Ww, Xx, Yy, Uu, Qq

    The presentation of the letters follows this general format:

    a. The letter is identifed by name and located on an alphabet chart or written on a 5 x 8 flash card.

    b. The initial sound is modeled by the teacher and practiced by the students.

    c. The teacher shows visuals of words having the same initial sound. The name and the sound of each letter is identified and drilled. The names of common objects having the same initial sound are learned.

    d. Students practice writing the capital and small form of the letter in the workbook.

    e. Upon learning the name and sound of the letter and learning to write the capital and lower case letter, each student makes, with teacher assistance if necessary, a pink 3 x 5 flash card of the letter. The capital and lower case letter are written on one side. A magazine picture of an object with that initial sound can be stapled or taped on the other. When magazines are unavailable, the instructor may duplicate the visuals in Appendix A on p. 371 of this guide for this purpose.

    f. For further sound symbol association practice, the teacher models a variety of words with various initial sounds. When the students hear a word that begins with the letter being studied, they hold up their 3 x 5 card of that letter.

    g. Frequent review of sound symbol association is recommended.

    h. When several or all of the letters of the alphabet have been put on pink 3 x 5 cards, students can work in pairs taking turns in games. For example:

    Student #1 calls out a letter name or sound.

    #2 locates it from his set of 3 x 5 alphabet cards. If student #2 cannot identify the letter, it is isolated for study and review.

    Student #1 flashes a picture from the back of his 3 x 5 alphabet card or from the teacher's visuals.

#2 names the letter and/or sound the object begins with. (Variation: #2 writes the letter the object begins with.)

Student #1 turns all of the 3 x 5 cards to the side with the visuals.

#2 matches the letter side of the 3 x 5 cards to the visuals.

#1 and 2 check for accuracy.

8. **Phonics:** In addition to the sound symbol association of all consonants in the initial position, sound symbol instructions are also presented for at least one short vowel sound for each of the vowels, some long vowel sounds, and some common consonant blends and digraphs. Presentation of the blends and digraphs should follow the same format as the presentation of the letters of the alphabet. However, the color of the blend and digraph flash cards should be different from the color of the alphabet flash cards.

9. **Accumulating Phonetic Concepts:** Using the sight word flash cards, students can begin to learn about the following by instruction or discovery:

    a. letter patterns, such as consonant, vowel, consonant (hat, man, Sam).

    b. phonetic rules, such as that of the consonant, long vowel, consonant, silent "e" (hat-hate, man-mane, Sam-same).

    c. syllabication, and that all syllables require a vowel but that not all vowels indicate a syllable.

    d. alphabetizing.

    e. roots, synonyms suffixes, compound words and opposites.

10. **More on Phonics:** Words like "an, man, can, pan, fan" as part of a traditional phonic approach are a relatively insignificant part of the reading process, especially for the ESL literacy student. Meaning needs to be taught. Provide referrants through visuals or realia whenever possible. Occasionally, isolation of these activities is acceptable to solidify a concept. Do so only with the understanding that these types of exercises are strictly manipulative. Demonstrate the application of the concepts when engaged in other, more meaningful activities.

Suggestions:

a. Students get a list of words with initial letters blanked out. Instructor dictates words and students fill in initial sounds. Example:

(b) an	(b) ell	(k) in
(f) an	(s) ell	(p) in
(t) an	(sp) ell	(w) in

b. Students get a list of words with endings blanked out. Instructor dictates the words and students fill in the endings. For example:

ca (b)	fa (d)	f (all)
ca (n)	fa (n)	f (ell)
ca (p)	fa (t)	f (ill)
ca (t)	fa (st)	f (ull)

11. **Sight Words:** Sight words are listed in the upper right hand corner of this guide for each lesson. These should be put on 5 x 8 flash cards with bold markers by the teacher for frequent review with the class, small groups or individuals. It is strongly recommended that students maintain their own set of the sight words on 3 x 5 cards for frequent spelling and writing review. The sight words should be written on yellow flash cards so that the numbers, alphabet, blends and digraphs and sight word flash cards can be easily distinguished from one another for various activities. It is recommended that the sight word flash cards be numbered at the upper right hand corner as in Appendix E for easy retrieval and organization.

   a. With their own set of sight word flash cards, students can work on individual activities. For example:

   (1) student writes the sight words several times on writing paper. A master for lined paper is provided on p. 396 of this guide.

   (2) student looks at the card, looks away and spells the word. This activity is repeated until the word is learned for spelling.

   (3) capable students can find synonyms and antonyms for their sight words.

   b. With their own set of sight word flash cards, students can work in pairs, taking turns in games. For example:

   Student #1 reads a sight word.

   #2 locates it from his set. Those that cannot be identified should be isolated for study and review.

   Student #1 reads a sight word.

   #2 spells/writes it.

   Students #1 and #2 play "hangman's noose" with the sight words.

   Student #1 spells a sight word orally or simply holds it up.

   #2 identifies it.

   Students #1 and #2 play concentration.

c. With the set of sight word flash cards, the instructor can devise a number of activities. For example:

   (1) assign 5 to 10 words for study for a spelling test.

   (2) give students a list of sight words on a ditto. Have them circle the words having a specific sound such as /a/ as in hat: fall (tan) ate name

   (3) make a worksheet with 5 sight words in each numbered row. Read the row number and one sight word. Student circles the word:

1.	address	phone	zip	name	(last)
2.	hat	hot dog	(Hello)	Hi	ham
3.	(hat)	cat	fat	mat	pat
4.	can	(pan)	Nan	an	fan

   (4) ask the students to categorize words into food, color, furniture, personal information groups, etc.

   (5) instruct students to find the words having a particular beginning or ending sound.

   (6) instruct students to count out any 10 words and alphabetize them.

   (7) challenge students to find words that rhyme:

   | hat | cat |

   (8) whenever possible point out synonyms and antonyms:

   | father | dad |

   | wife | husband |

   (9) have students locate words containing a consonant blend or digraph.

   | March | chair | phone | birthdate |

   (10) encourage students to find words with 2 or 3 syllables:

   | doctor | telephone |

   (11) have students locate compound words:

   | housewife | birthdate |

(12) teach students how to make singular nouns plural:

| day | days | | man | men |
| dress | dresses | | city | cities |

12. **Suggestions for the Use of the Language Master:** Having a Language Master available in an ESL literacy class is a definite plus for vocabulary acquisition.

   a. Words can be introduced and reviewed by attaching a visual onto a blank Language Master Card* with a paper clip.

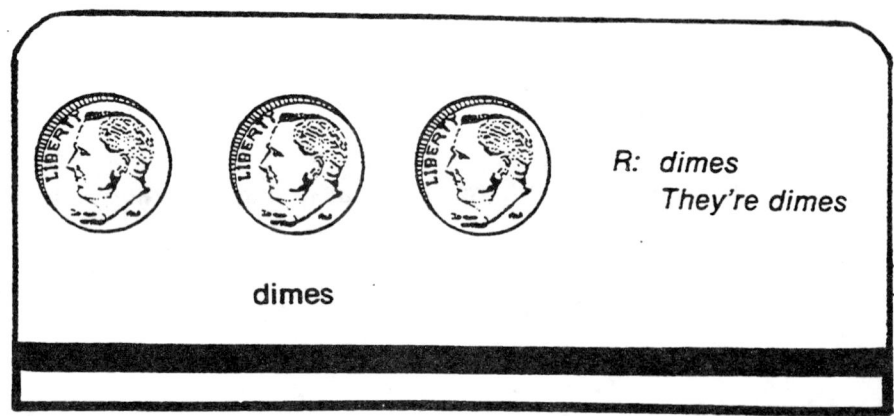

   Vocabulary can be presented in isolation and the student repeats it: "dimes". Vocabulary can be presented in a sentence and the student repeats it: "They're dimes." Student checks recording for correct response, pronunciation, stress and intonation.

   b. Words can be introduced in a yes-no question:

   After answering, student checks recording for correct response, pronunciation, stress and intonation.

*Blank Language Master Cards are available from Delta Systems, Co., Inc.

c. Words can be introduced in an either-or framework:

Is she at the supermarket or the laundromat?

R: *She's at the laundromat.*

After answering, student checks recording for correct response, pronunciation, stress and intonation.

d. Plurals can be practiced:

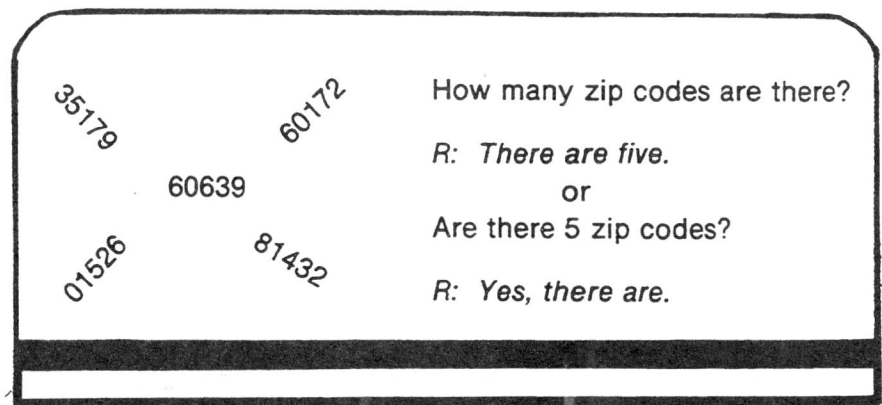

How many zip codes are there?

R: *There are five.*

or

Are there 5 zip codes?

R: *Yes, there are.*

After answering, student checks recording for correct response, pronunciation, stress and intonation.

e. Students can practice prepositions:

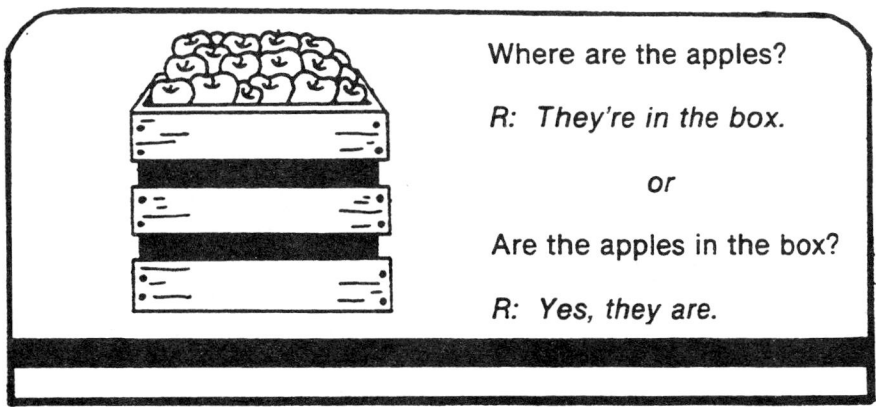

Where are the apples?

R: *They're in the box.*

or

Are the apples in the box?

R: *Yes, they are.*

After answering, student checks recording for correct response, pronunciation, stress and intonation.

f. Students can give easy solutions to problems:

After giving a solution, student checks recording for correct response, pronunciation, stress and intonation.

g. Students can simply read and check the recording for correct pronunciation, stress and intonation.

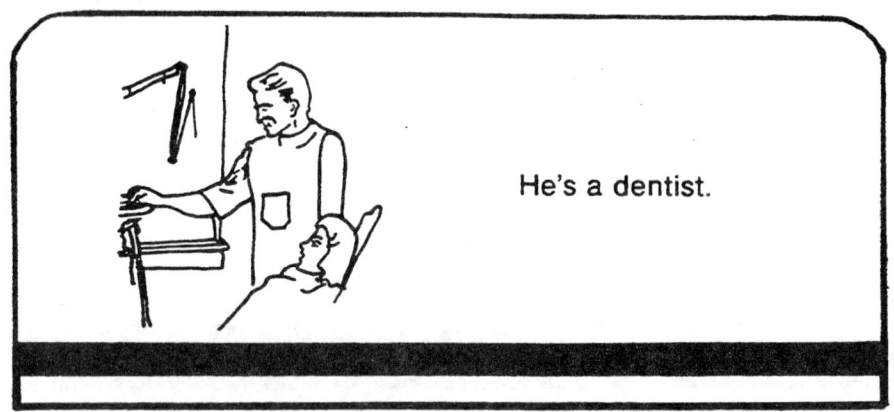

h. Using the same card as above, students can form questions:
"Is he a dentist?" or "What is he?" and check the recording for the correct structure, pronunciation, stress and intonation.

i. Students can complete sentences and check recording for accuracy:

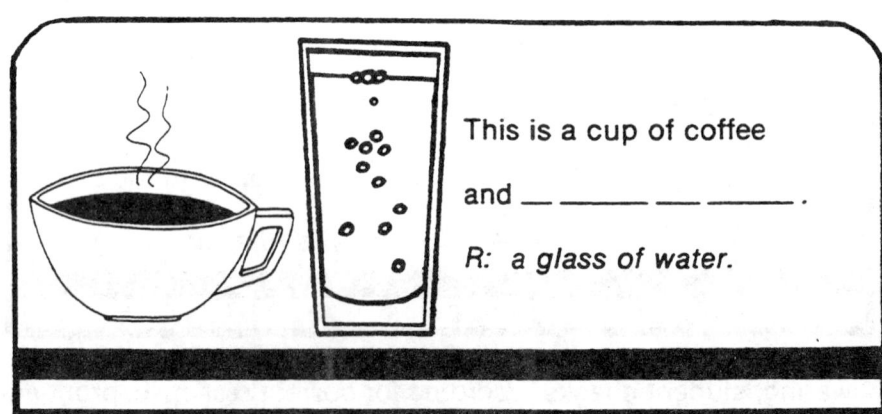

j. Students can practice subject pronouns and/or the present continuous:

After answering, student checks recording for correct response, pronunciation, stress and intonation.

k. Students can learn the days, months, dates and holidays:

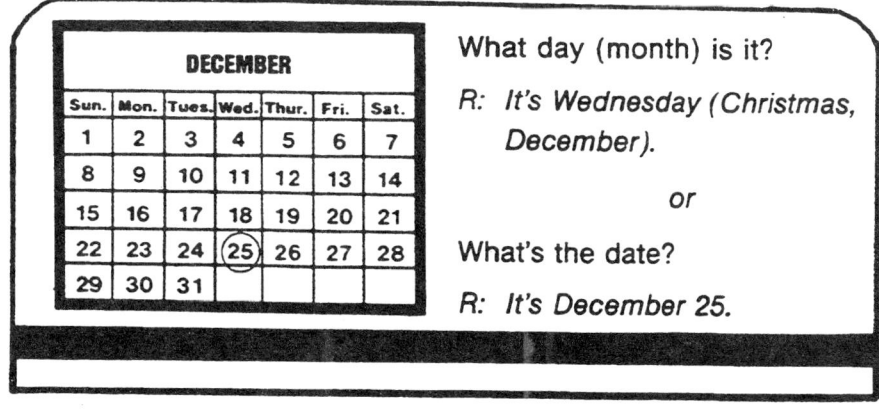

After answering, student checks recording for correct response, pronunciation, stress and intonation.

13. **Sentence Strips:*** Teachers should write key phrases, clauses, expressions and sentences on strips of paper to encourage students to read groups of words rather than to read word by word. The phrases, clauses, expressions and sentences should be modeled by the teacher, repeated and drilled by groups and individuals. The following are suggestions for the use of these strips once students have mastered the above objective.

   a. The strips can be cut into component parts, for example:

   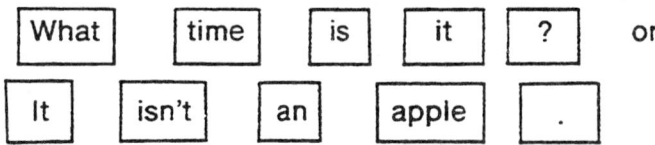

   The components can be:

   (1) read individually for sight word development.

   (2) used as spelling words.

   (3) alphabetized.

   (4) matched with a visual when appropriate.

   (5) phonetically manipulated, for example:

   "it" ⟶ <u>b</u> it
          <u>m</u> it
          <u>p</u> it
          <u>q</u> <u>u</u> it
          <u>s</u> it
          <u>w</u> it

   (6) scrambled and then reordered by a student in a pocket chart, on a tack board, on a table or on the floor. A variation of this activity would be to hand each component to a different student. Students would take turns correctly placing words to complete the sentence. This is an excellent exercise for getting a "feel" for word order.

   (7) manipulated:

   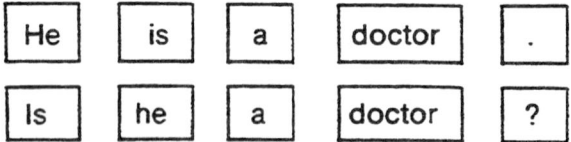

   Maintain a set of capital and small letters to interchange when necessary. A set of punctuation cards and plural "s, es, ies" are also necessary.

*Blank sentence strips are available from Delta Systems Co., Inc.

b. Once the components are correctly organized, keep them on display for frequent review.

c. The same activities can be done with mini-strips so that students get their own set and proceed with suggestions "a" and "b". On the other hand, students may wish to maintain their strips integral. This would be fine for frequent reading review.

d. Write each sentence of a paragraph or a story on sentence strips. Students sequence the sentences correctly. This can also be done on mini-strips for individual work.

e. The sentence strips can be matched to a visual.

14. **Review:** Each lesson should begin with a review of previously taught letters, sounds, sight words, phrases, sentences, structures and/or concepts. This review can be accomplished via flash cards, listening comprehension or visuals. If the students experience difficulty, reintroduce instruction.

15. **Feedback:** Throughout the instructor's guide, the teacher is instructed to check the student's written work. This feedback should be almost immediate whenever possible.

16. **Idea:** Whenever possible, label as many classroom objects as possible. Students are also encouraged to label objects at home.

17. **Extra! Extra!:** As a bonus, this guide includes Appendix C, Exercises for Duplication and Appendix D, Games for Duplication. These contain masters of exercises, ideas and games to extend and reinforce learning.

References

Chapman, Jean B., et al. *Are Your Adult English as a Second Language Students Learning Disabled?* Special project of Section 310 of the Adult Education Act, Public Law 91-230, Illinois State Board of Adult and Continuing Education Section. William Rainey College, Palatine, Illinois, 1980.

McGee, Donna. *Preliteracy Definitions.* A paper presentation for the Literacy Symposium at the Ontario TESL Convention, Vancouver Community College, Vancouver, B.C., Canada, 1978.

Selman, Mary. An *Introduction to Teaching English as a Second Language.* Vancouver, B.C.: Pampas Press, 1979.

Part 1 - Pre-Literacy

Writing Personal Information
Visual Discrimination

Part 1: PERSONAL INFORMATION
Student Workbook p. 1-9

OBJECTIVES

Listening Comprehension: The students will be able to:
1. Respond to the following classroom directions: Listen, Repeat, Write.
2. Comprehend the following vocabulary when spoken: name, first name, last name, numbers 0-10, address, city, state, zip code, telephone number, social security number.

Listening and Speaking: The students will be able to:
1. Respond correctly when asked their
   a. name, first and last.
   b. address, city, state and zip code.
   c. telephone number.
   d. social security number.
2. Say the numbers 0-10.
3. Perform the above with acceptable pronunciation.

Reading and Writing: The students will be able to:
1. Recognize and enunciate these sight words: name, first, last, address, city, state, zip code, telephone number (home phone), social security number (soc. sec. no.)
2. Hold a pencil properly in the hand and angle the paper correctly in order to write.
3. Demonstrate the understanding that reading and writing proceed from left to right, top to bottom.
4. Print their name (first and last), address, city, state, zip code, the number 0-10, telephone number and social security number on a form.

Student Workbook   p. 1
Writing Your Name

SIGHT WORDS
name, first, last

VISUALS
1 Hello. How are you?
2 What's your name?

INSTRUCTIONAL AIDS
yellow flash cards

STRUCTURE

1. What's your name?
2. What's your first name?
3. What's your last name?
4. How are you?
5. Hello.
6. Reception only: Listen, Repeat, Write.

RESPONSE

1. (My name's) (Ben Lee).
2. (My first name's) (Ben).
3. (My last name's) (Lee).
4. Fine, thank you.
5. Hi!

INSTRUCTION

(Note: Do *not* open books until oral skills are achieved and students are ready for reading and writing.)

1. My name's (Mrs. Renshaw).

2. Hello, class.

3. Hello, (Mrs. Renshaw).

4. Gesture and say "Repeat".

5. Divide class into groups.

6. My name's (Kay Renshaw).

7. What's your name?

8. Ask, "What's your name?"
   Answer, "My name's _____ ."

9. My first name's (Kay).
   My last name's (Renshaw).

10. What's your first name?
    What's your last name?

ACTIVITY/RESPONSE

1. T: Introduce yourself.

2. T: Greet students.

3. T: Greet yourself.

4. Cl: Hello, (Mrs. Renshaw).

5. Gr:
   St: ⟩Hello, (Mrs. Renshaw).

6. T: Write your full name on the board.

7. T: Elicit the name of each student.
   St: (My name's) _____ .

8. T: Have students do a repetition, question/response chain drill.

9. T: Point to first name.
       Point to last name.

10. T: Ask each student individually.
    St: My first name's _____ .
        My last name's _____ .

19

11. Ask each other:
    "What's your first (last) name?"

12. Her name's Ann.
    His name's Ken.

13. Listen and repeat:
    Hi, _____ !
    Hello, _____ !
    How are you?
    Fine, thank you.

14. You are Ann and you are Ken.

15. Listen and repeat:
    Ann: Hello, how are you?
    Ben Lee: Fine, thank you.
    Ann: What's your name?
    Ben Lee: My name's Ben Lee.

16. Let's talk.

17. Listen and repeat.
    "Hello, how are you?" and
    "Fine, thank you."

18. Listen and repeat.
    Hello.
    My name's (Kay Renshaw).
    My first name's (Kay).
    My last name's (Renshaw).

19. Let's read.
    My name's _____ _____ .
    My first name's _____ .
    My last name's _____ .

11. St: My first (last) name's _____ .

12. T: Point to Ann and Ken in Visual 1. Tape the visual above your head on the board. Stand under the character when modeling his/her line. Model the dialogue twice for comprehension and then model each line by line for repetition.

13. Cl:
    Gr: } Listen and repeat.
    St:

14. T: Pair students up.
    St: Role play the dialogue and reverse roles.

15. T: Tape the Visual 2 above your head on the board. Stand under the character when modeling his/her line. Model dialogue twice and then line by line.
    Cl:
    Gr: } Listen and repeat.
    St:

16. T: Practice by alternating lines:
    T - Cl, Gr - Gr, St - St assume roles.

17. T: Write the sentences on the board or on sentence strips.
    St: Listen and repeat. Read sentence strips in chorus and individually.

18. T: Write the sentences on the board or on sentence strips.
    St: Listen and repeat inserting their own names.

19. T: Model. Demonstrate right to left and top to bottom orientation.
    St: Read inserting their own names.

20. Listen and repeat:

| Name | First | Last |
| name | first | last |

My name's _____.

21. Hold your pencil.

22. Write lines and circles.

23. Open your books to p. 1.

24. Let's make cards.

25. Let's read.

20. T: Write the words on the board or make yellow 5 x 8 flash cards. Model each word.
    St: Read in chorus and individually.

21. T: Demonstrate how to hold a pencil in hand and how to angle paper.
    St: Observe and imitate.
    T: Continue this instruction throughout text as necessary.

22. T: Write / / / / / / / and ℓℓℓℓℓℓ on board.
    St: Write / / / / / / / and ℓℓℓℓℓℓ on lined paper. A master is provided on p. 396 of this book.
    T: Continue this practice prior to writing as necessary.

23. T: Read the directions to the students. Print student's name in the sample box. Explain where it says "name" only, first name is usually first.
    St: Observe T write their name in the sample box. Complete p. 1 in in pencil so errors can be erased and corrected.
    T: Observe students who have difficulty. Repeat instructions as necessary.

24. St: Take 4 yellow 3 x 5 cards and make cards identical to the instrutor's cards. On the back of "Name, name", students write their entire name, first name first. On the back of "First, first", students write their first name only, and on the back of "Last, last", students write their last name only.
    T: Assist as necessary.

25. St: Read sentence strips and flash cards.

21

Student Workbook p. 2, 3
Numbers 1-10

SIGHT WORDS
numbers 1-10, circle

INSTRUCTIONAL AIDS
10 rods, beans, pieces of paper, or any 10 objects for counting each student
white flash cards

INSTRUCTION

1. What's your name?

2. This is 1 (finger). 1.

3. This is 2.

4. 1, 2, 3, etc.

5. 5, 3, 7, etc.

6. Show me 6 (beans).

7. 1, 2, 3, etc.

8. Which one is 4?

9. Open your books to p. 2. See "NAME _____".

ACTIVITY/RESPONSE

1. T: Review vocabulary, flash cards, sentence strips and instructions from the previous lesson.
   St: Respond.

2. T: Hold up a finger, rod, bean or a piece of paper.
   St: Listen and repeat.

3. T: Hold up two fingers. Continue up to 10.
   St: Listen and repeat.

4. T: Teach the numbers 1-10 in order.
   St: Listen and repeat in chorus and individually.

5. T: Hold up 1-10 fingers randomly and say the numbers.
   St: Listen and repeat.

6. T: Give each student 10 (beans). Say 1-10 randomly.
   St: Count out that many (beans).
   T: Continue activity until students successfully identify the spoken number with the correct number of objects.

7. T: Call out the numbers consecutively as you write them on the board or on white 5 x 8 cards.
   St: Listen, repeat and read.

8. T: Call out 1-10 randomly.
   St: Point to the written number corresponding to the number they heard.
   T: Continue practice until students successfully identify the spoken number with the written number.

9. St: Open books and look at the upper right hand corner and write their full names, first name first.

10.	This word is "circle". This is a circle.	10.	T:	Demonstrate the direction word "Circle".
			St:	Listen and repeat "circle".
11.	This is a pencil.	11.	T:	Demonstrate how to hold a pencil in hand and how to angle paper.
			St:	Observe and imitate.
12.	Draw circles.	12.	St:	Observe and practice drawing circles on writing paper.
13.	1, 2, 3, 4	13.	T:	Count the four dots in the sample box and draw a circle around "4".
			St:	Count the dots and draw a circle around "4".
14.	Each box has a number.	14.	T:	Demonstrate that each box is consecutively numbered and that each exercise proceeds left to right.
			St:	Observe, then count the dots and circle the appropriate response in items 1-9 in pencil.
			T:	Correct student work.
15.	What number is this?	15.	T:	For review, show flash cards with dots printed on them and/or the numbers 1-10.
			St:	Count the dots or read the number.
16.	Let's write the numbers.	16.	T:	Demonstrate how each number is written on the board.
			St:	Observe and practice writing the numbers on the board.
17.	Turn to p. 3. Write the numbers.	17.	St:	Open books to p. 3 and practice writing the numbers.
			T:	Observe for correct formation and and legibility. Review as necessary.
18.	Let's make some cards.	18.	St:	Take 10 white 3 x 5 flash cards and write the numbers 1-10 on one side and a corresponding number of dots on the other if necessary.
			T:	Provide assistance where needed.
19.	Hold up the card when you hear the number "9".	19.	T:	Demonstrate activity.
			St:	Hold up card with number 9 on it.
			T:	Continue activity until students have made the sound symbol association.
20.	Put the numbers in order.	20.	St:	Place their 3 x 5 cards in order.
			T:	Check for accuracy.

Student Workbook p. 4
Review, Numbers 0-10

INSTRUCTION

1. Review previous learnings with the flash cards and sentence strips.

2. This number is zero.

3. Zero is before 1. It has no dots.

4. Zero is also called "0".

5. Let's make a card.

6. What's the name of this number?

7. Listen and write:
   9, 2, 0, etc.

8. Write the numbers in order.

9. Open your books to p. 4. Write your name.

10. Count the dots and circle the number.

11. Listen and write:
    3, 8, 1, etc.

12. Say the numbers 0-10 in order.

ACTIVITY/RESPONSE

1. St: Work in pairs on activities suggested on p. 8 of this guide.

2. T: Write "0" on the board.
   St: Listen and repeat.

3. St: Listen.

4. St: Listen and repeat.

5. St: Make a 3 x 5 white flash card of "0".

6. St: "zero" or "0"

7. T: Say the numbers 0-10 randomly.
   St: Write the numbers on the board.

8. St: Write the numbers in order.

9. St: Open books and complete the information at the upper right hand corner.

10. T: Review the directions and the sample box.
    St: Listen, count and circle correct responses.

11. T: For the bottom, dictate the numbers 0-10 randomly. Demonstrate activity on the board.
    St: Listen and write the numbers in the blanks.

12. T: Demonstrate.
    St: Count 0-10.

Student Workbook p. 5
Writing Your Address

SIGHT WORDS
Address, address

INSTRUCTIONAL AIDS
an envelope, yellow flash cards

STRUCTURE

What's your address?
Where do you live?

RESPONSE

(My address is) or (It's) _____ .
(I live at) _____ .

INSTRUCTION

1. What's this number?

2. My address is _____ .

3. My address is _____ .

4. Your address is _____ .

5. What's your address?

6. What's your address? My address is _____ .

7. A: Where do you live?
   B: I live at _____ .
   A: Where do you live?

8. Let's read this word.

9. Open your books to p. 5. Write your name.

10. Write your address.

ACTIVITY/RESPONSE

1. T: Review previous learnings via flash cards.
   St: Respond.

2. T: Draw an envelope on the board with your address on it or draw a house and write your address on it.
   St: Listen.

3. St: Listen.

4. T: Model each student's address.
   St: Lister. and repeat their address.

5. St: Repeat.

6. T: Initiate a chain drill.
   St: Ask and respond.

7. T: Model question and response.
   St: I live at _____ .

8. T: Write "address" "Address" on a yellow 5 x 8 flash card. Model.
   St: Listen and read.

9. St: Open books and write their name at the upper right hand corner.

10. T: Write the student's address in the sample box.
   St: Observe T write address in sample box and practice writing their address in pencil.
   T: Observe for legibility and correct letter formation.

11. Let's make cards.

11. St: Make a yellow 3 x 5 card with $\boxed{\begin{array}{c}\text{Address}\\\text{address}\end{array}}$ on one side and their address on the back.

Student Workbook p. 6
Writing your City and State

SIGHT WORDS
City, city, State, state

INSTRUCTIONAL AIDS
an envelope, a map of your state, yellow flash cards

STRUCTURE

What's your city? state?
Where do you live?

RESPONSE

(It's) _____ .
(I live in) _____ , _____ .

INSTRUCTION

1. My city's (Chicago). I live in (Chicago). What's your city?

2. Let's read.

3. My state's (Illinois). I live in (Illinois). What's your state?

4. I live in (Chicago, Illinois). My city's (Chicago). My state's (Illinois).

5. Let's read.

6. Read these words.

ACTIVITY/RESPONSE

1. T: Point to the envelope with your address on it or to a local map. Model the name of the learner's city.
   St: (My city's) (Chicago). I live in Chicago. Repeat as often as necessary.

2. T: Write "city", "City" on a 5 x 8 yellow flash card. Show card to students. Model.
   St: Listen and repeat.

3. T: Point to envelope or to a local map.
   St: Listen and respond.

4. St: Repeat, inserting their city and state.

5. T: Write "state" "State" on yellow 5 x 8 flash cards. Model.
   St: Listen and repeat.

6. T: Review all flash cards: name, last, first, address, city, state.
   St: Read in chorus and individually.

7. Read the card and give
your answer.

7. T: Game: Show the flash card.
Students read silently and
give the information orally.
Demonstrate:

| state |

St: (I live in) (Illinois).

8. Open your books to p. 6.
Write your name and address.

8. St: Open books and write their name and
and address in upper right hand
corner.

9. Write your city and state.

9. T: Write the student's city and state in the
sample box. Demonstrate the comma.
St: Observe and write.
T: Observe for legibility and correct use of
the comma.

10. Let's make cards.

10. St: Write yellow 3 x 5 cards

for | city / City | and and | state / State |

on one side. Students write the name
name of their city and state
respectively on the back of the cards.

Student Workbook p. 7
  Writing Your Zip Code

SIGHT WORDS
Zip Code, zip code

INSTRUCTIONAL AIDS
an envelope, yellow flash cards

STRUCTURE

What's your zip code?

RESPONSE

(My zip code's) or (It's) _____ .

INSTRUCTION

1. My zip code is (60119). What's your zip code?

2. This is "zip code".

3. Open your books to p. 7. Write your zip code.

4. When there are two lines for address, write your address on the first line and city, state and zip code on the second line.

5. Let's make cards.

6. Let's read.

7. Optional: Let's play a game.

8. Optional, listening comprehension: Listen and write.
   Variation: Students read zip codes from a directory or say their own zip codes and teacher listens for acceptable pronunciation, stress and intonation.

ACTIVITY/RESPONSE

1. T: Point to the envelope. Model each student's zip code.
   St: Repeat as often as necessary. (My zip code's) or (It's) _____ .

2. T: Write "zip code" and "Zip Code" on a 5 x 8 yellow flash card.
   St: Listen and repeat.

3. T: Write student's zip code in sample box if necessary.
   St: Observe and write zip code.

4. T: Demonstrate on board.
   St: Write their entire address in box #4 on page 7.
   T: Check for accuracy and legibility.

5. St: Make a yellow flash card with
   | zip code |
   | Zip Code |
    on one side and write their zip code on the other.

6. T: Model all flash cards.
   St: Repeat in chorus and individually.

7. T: Teach students to play games in item 11b p. 8.
   St: Play.

8. T: Dictate a variety of zip codes.
   St: Listen and write.

Student Workbook   p. 8
   Writing Your Telephone Number

SIGHT WORDS
telephone number,
Telephone number;
Home Phone, home phone;
phone number,
phone no.; number

VISUAL
3   telephone

INSTRUCTIONAL AIDS
yellow flash cards

STRUCTURE

What's your (tele)phone number?

RESPONSE

(It's) ____ - _____ .

INSTRUCTION

1. This is a telephone.

2. My telephone number is
   ____ - _____ .

3. My telephone number is
   ____ - _____ .

4. What's my telephone number?

5. What's your telephone number?

6. What's your telephone number?
   Variation: Repeat the drill.
   This time the student requesting
   the number writes it down and
   repeats it to the partner.

7. This is "telephone number".

ACTIVITY/RESPONSE

1. T: Hold up visual 3.

2. T: Make up a number.
   St: Listen.

3. T: Write the number on the board.
       Demonstrate the dash.

4. St: (It's) ____ - _____ .
   T: Observe for correct pronunciation,
       stress and intonation.

5. T: Model student's number or model
       "I don't have (a telephone) one."
   St: Repeat.

6. T: Initiate a chain drill.
   St: Respond and ask the next person.

7. T: Write "Telephone Number",
       "telephone number" on a 5 x 8
       yellow flash card.
   St: Listen and repeat in chorus and individually.

8. What's your home phone?
   What's your phone number?
   What's your number?
   What's your telephone number?

9. Let's read.

10. Open your books to p. 8.
    Write your name.

11. Write your telephone number.

12. Let's make some cards

13. Optional, listening comprehension:

14. Optional: Read the numbers.

15. Optional: What is your business phone?

8. T: Ask the question in its various forms.
   St: "It's ___-_____ " or "I don't have (a telephone) one."

9. T: Write "Home Phone, home phone" and "phone no." and "number" and "phone number" on yellow 5 x 8 cards. Model.
   St: Listen and repeat in chorus and individually.
   T: Repeat and review as necessary.

10. St: Open books and write their name at the upper right hand corner.
    T: Check for correct response.

11. T: Write the student's number in the sample box if necessary. Write "None" or a dash in box if they don't have a phone.
    St: Write their telephone number, "None" or a dash.

St: Make a yellow 3 x 5 card for the following:

Telephone Number telephone number	Home Phone home phone
phone no. phone number	number

St: Write their telephone number on the backs, "None" or a dash.
T: Assist when necessary.

13. T: Dictate a variety of phone numbers.
    St: Listen and write.

14. St: Students read telephone numbers from a local directory.
    T: Observe for pronunciation, stress and intonation.

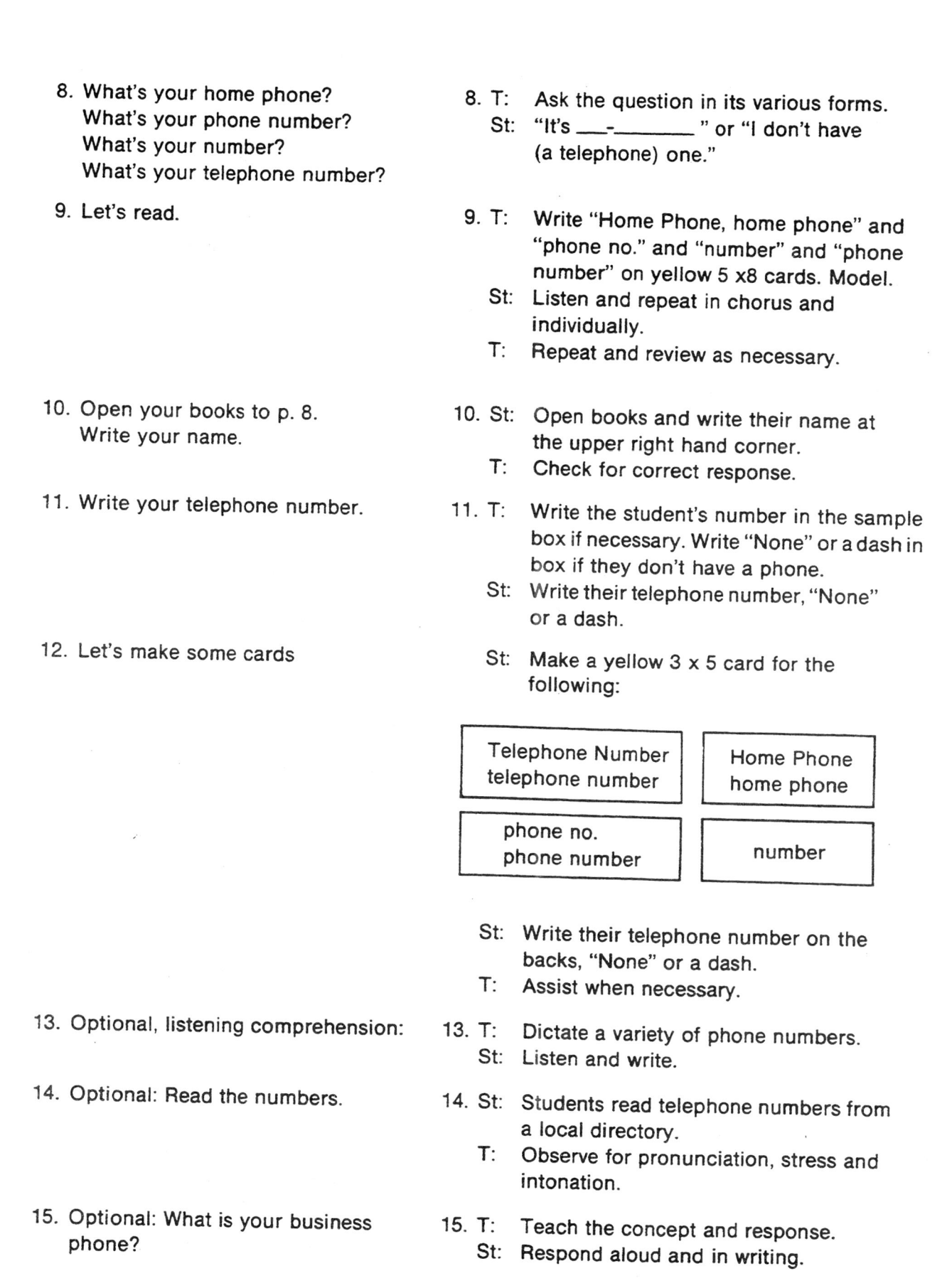

15. T: Teach the concept and response.
    St: Respond aloud and in writing.

Reminder: Review previous learnings from flash cards and sentence strips frequently.

Student Workbook   p. 9
Writing Your Social Security Number

SIGHT WORDS
social security number
soc. sec. no.

INSTRUCTIONAL AIDS
yellow flash cards.

STRUCTURE

What's your social security number?

RESPONSE

(It's) ___ - ___ - ___ .

INSTRUCTION

1. My social security number is
   ___ - ___ - ___

2. My social security number is
   ___ - ___ - ___

3. What's your social security number?

4. What's your social security number?
   Variation: Repeat the drill.
   This time the student requesting the number writes it down and repeats it to the partner.

5. Let's read.

6. Let's write.

7. Open your books to p. 9.
   Write your telephone number.

ACTIVITY/RESPONSE

1. T: Show your social security card.
   St: Listen.

2. T: Write the number on the board. Demonstrate the dashes.
   St: Listen and observe.

3. T: Model number for each student.
   St: "(It's) ___ - ___ - ___ " or "I don't have one."

4. T: Initiate a chain drill.
   St: Respond and ask the next student.

5. T: Write "social security number" and "soc. sec. no." on 5 x 8 flash cards. Model.
   St: Listen and repeat in chorus and individually.
   T: Repeat and review as necessary.

6. T: Demonstrate on the board various ways of requesting one's social security number as given on p. 9 of the student book.

7. St: Open books and write their phone number at the upper right hand corner.

8. Write your social security number.

8. T: Write the student's number in the sample box if necessary. Write "None" if they don't have one.
St: Write their social security number in the blanks or "None."

9. Let's make some cards.

9. St: Make a yellow 3 x 5 card for the following:

| social security number |

| soc. sec. no. |

St: Write their social security number on the back.
T: Assist when necessary.

10. Reinforcement and review: What is your _____ ?

10. T: Request personal information as per flash cards.
St: Respond orally or in writing on board or paper.

11. Optional, listening comprehension.

11. T: Dictate a variety of social security numbers.
St: Listen and write in proper form.

12. Optional: What is it?

12. T: Dictate various numbers such as 3256, 325-56-7719 and 325-5677
St: It's an address, a social security number, a telephone number.

13. Optional: Let's read.

13. T: Review all flash cards for p. 1-9.
St: Read.

33

Part 1: VISUAL DISCRIMINATION

Student Workbook p. 10-22

OBJECTIVES

Listening Comprehension:

The students will be able to:
1. Respond to the following classroom directions:
   Put an X on the shape(s) that is (are) different (the same).
   Circle the letter(s) that is (are) different (the same).
2. Identify numbers 11-30.
3. Demonstrate auditory discrimination related to reading readiness.

Listening and Speaking:

The students will be able to:
1. Respond correctly when shown several items and are asked if they are different or the same.
2. Say the numbers 11-30.
3. Perform the above with acceptable pronunciation.

Reading and Writing:

The students will be able to:
1. Read requests for personal information at the upper right hand corner of each page and correctly print the response.
2. Comprehend the directions on each page after the teacher reads and explains them.
3. Read "same" and "different" by sight word recognition.
4. "Read" the pictoral information provided in the sample boxes and put an X on or circle the shape that is different (the same) according to the printed directions which the teacher has read and explained.
5. Read and write the numbers 11-30.
6. Demonstrate visual and motor skills related to reading readiness.
7. Continue to demonstrate comprehension of the left to right, top to bottom orientation.

Student Workbook   p. 10
Visual Discrimination

SIGHT WORDS
same, different

INSTRUCTIONAL AIDS
yellow flash cards

INSTRUCTION

1. This is a (desk) and this is a (desk). They're the same.

2. This is a _____ and this is a _____. They're the same.

3. Are these the same?

4. This is a (pen) and this is a (pencil). They're not the same. They're different.

5. This is a _____ and this is a _____. Are they the same or different?

6. This is a (pencil) and this is a (pencil). They are (pencils) but they are different.

7. This is "same" and this is "different".

8. Let's make cards.

ACTIVITY/RESPONSE

1. T: Point to two identical objects.
   St: Listen.

2. T: Point to two other identical objects.
   St: Listen.
   T: Repeat step #2 several times.

3. T: Hold up, point to or draw identical items on the board.
   St: "(They're the) same" or "Yes."

4. T: Point to two different objects.
   St: Listen and repeat, "(They're) different."

5. T: Point to two different objects.
   St: "(They're) different" or "No."
   T: Practice "same" and "different" as many times as necessary until gross discrimination is achieved.

6. T: Hold up different color or size pencils. Practice "same" and "different" until fine discrimination is achieved.

7. T: Write "same" and "different" on the board or on a yellow 5 x 8 flash card.
   St: Read in chorus and individually.

8. St: Make a card with "same" on one side and two like objects on the other. For example, draw two horizontal parallel lines. Make another card with "different" on one side and two unlike objects on the other. For example, draw a circle and a horizontal line.

9. Hold up "same" when two things are the same. Hold up "different" when two things are different.

10. Are these the same or different?

11. Open workbooks to p. 10. Write your state and zip code.

12. "Put an X" means to write X on the one that is different.

9. T: Demonstrate activity.

10. T: Hold up a variety of items moving from gross discrimination to fine discrimination.
    St: Hold up "same" when the items are identical and "different" when the items are unlike.

11. T: Point to upper right hand corner.
    St: Write their state and zip code.

12. T: Demonstrate and do sample box together.
    St: Follow directions and do items 1-5.
    T: Correct student work and review as necessary.

Student Workbook p.11-22
Visual Discrimination

SIGHT WORDS
numbers 11-30

INSTRUCTIONAL AIDS
beans, rods or dots for counting, white flash cards

INSTRUCTION	ACTIVITY/RESPONSE
1. Let's count these (beans).	1. T: Gather students around a desk on which there are 10 (beans). Activity can proceed with dots on the board. St: Count in chorus. T: Add a (bean).
2. How many are there?	2. St: 11 T: If no one can respond, model eleven and elicit response. T: Add another (bean).
3. How many are there?	3. St: 12 T: If no one can respond, model twelve and elicit response.
4. Continue activity up to the number 30.	4. St: Respond. T: Model when necessary and elicit response.
5. Let's count.	5. T: Write the numbers on the board or on 5 x 8 cards. St: Count, say and read the numbers. T: Repeat instructions as often as necessary until students can count and identify numbers 0-30.
6. Let's write 11-30.	6. T: Demonstrate on board how to write each number. A master for a writing page is provided on p. 396 of this guide for duplication. St: Write.
7. Let's make cards.	7. St: Make a white 3 x 5 flash card for each number 11-30.

8. Additional activities:
   a. Show white 5 x 8 flash cards 0-30 in random order.
   b. Dictate numbers 0-30.
   c. Teach pronunciation contrast between 13 and 30.
   d. Have students count 0-30 in order.
   e. Have students put their flash cards in numerical order.
   f. Have students play games in #11b on p.8 of this guide.
   g. Teach capable students to spell the numbers 0-30.

9. Open your workbooks to p. 11.

10. Let's read the directions.

11. Repeat steps 9-10 for p. 12-22. (NOTE: Every letter, lower case and capital, is reviewed for visual discrimination between p. 13-22. Proceed slowly, review numbers, sight words and sentence strips strips frequently.)

8. St:
   a. Read in chorus and individually.
   b. Write.
   c. Pronounce and identify 13 vs. 30.
   d. Respond.
   e. Arrange cards.
   f. Play.
   g. Spell and write.

9. T: Point to the upper right hand corner.
   St: Fill in requested personal information.

10. T: Review the sample box together with the students.
    St: Listen to directions and proceed with the exercise.
    T: Correct student work. Review as necessary.

11. St: Listen to directions and proceed with the exercises. on p. 12-22.
    T: Correct student work. Review as as necessary.

Student Workbook   p. 23-28
TEST of Part 1*

OBJECTIVES

Listening Comprehension: To determine if the students can:
1. Follow simple oral directions.
2. Comprehend the numbers between 0 and 30.

Reading and Writing: To determine if the students can:
1. Demonstrate knowledge of the left to right top to bottom orientation.
2. Hold a pencil and make circles and X's.
3. Complete the personal information requested at the upper right hand corner correctly without being reminded.
4. Understand and follow the directions as exemplified in the sample box.
5. Visually discriminate all the letters in the alphabet, both small and capital, from other letters having similar shapes.
6. Complete a simple identification form.
7. Write the numbers between 0-30.

NOTES TO INSTRUCTOR:

1. There are too many test pages to administer in one sitting. Student fatigue may affect results. It is suggested that p. 23-24, 25-26, 27-28 be completed at different sittings. Allow students as much time as necessary to complete work.

2. Between p. 23 and 27 students will sometimes find 1, 2 or 3 letters that are the same.

3. Each letter is tested twice, once for the lower case letter and once for the capital. Note which letters are missed and give proper review where necessary.

4. On p. 28, item #3, dictate any 11 numbers between 0-30. It is suggested that 0, 13 and 30 be included.

5. A large number of errors may indicate a full review of p. 10-22, vision testing or a learning disability. Refer to p. 3 in the Introduction for further discussion.

*This post-test may also be used as a pre-test to place a student *into* Part 1 if test results are poor OR *out of* Part 1 if test results are good as determined by the instructor.

Part 2 - Literacy

Sound Symbol Association
Beginning Reading and Writing
Consonant Blends and Digraphs
The Alphabet
Personal Information, continued

Part 2: LITERACY
Student Workbook p. 29-76

OBJECTIVES

Listening Comprehension:

The students will be able to:
1. Understand that our alphabet has 26 letters and and that each letter has a name and at least one sound.
2. Identify all the consonants by name and sound.
3. Identify the vowels by name and by at least one short vowel sound.
4. Distinguish words beginning with a particular initial sound from words with other initial sounds.
5. Identify sh, sm, gl, fl, sp, sk, ch, wh, th, st, cl, ph, qu, bl, gr, sw, br, pl, dr, sn, sl, tr, cr, fr, pr, kn, and tw when spoken.
6. Comprehend the following personal information vocabulary when spoken: age, Mr., Mrs., Miss, Ms., male, female, color of hair and eyes.
7. Identify the numbers 31-76.
8. Recognize the sounds of English that correspond to vocabulary introduced.

Listening and Speaking:

The students will be able to:
1. Name the letters.
2. Make at least one sound for each letter.
3. Say various words beginning with each of the letters.
4. Identify the letter a particular word begins (or ends) with and identify other words having the same (or final) sound.
5. Identify some consonants with variant sounds (city, cat).
6. Recognize and enunciate basic sight words.
7. Make the sound of all of the consonant blends and digraphs listed above.
8. Say various words beginning with those consonant blends and digraphs.
9. Say the alphabet in order.
10. Provide a correct response when asked their age, color of hair and eyes. Female students will be able to say if they are Miss, Mrs. or Ms.
11. Say the number 31-76.
12. Perform the above with acceptable pronunciation.

Reading and Writing:

The students will be able to:
1. Associate the lower case letters with their respective capitals.
2. Write the letters and the capitals.
3. Use capitals for proper nouns and at the beginning of sentences.
4. Visually discriminate some words from others.
5. Read and write various sight words.
6. Demonstrate comprehension of specific vocabulary by matching pictures with words, filling in blanks, choosing the odd man out and doing sentence completion exercises.
7. Spell selected sight words.
8. Decode and encode new words and sentences as they relate to the ESL component of the lessons.
9. Read and spell the consonant blends and digraphs listed above.
10. Read and write various words beginning with the with the consonant blends and digraphs listed above.
11. Copy sentences.
12. Write sentences which have been dictated.
13. Compose basic sentences from sentence parts.
14. Punctuate with a period at the end of a sentence, a comma in a short answer and an apostrophe for contractions.
15. Demonstrate comprehension of controlled reading selections by answering what, who and what color questions.
16. Recognize and write word forms and endings such as the plural -s and verbal -s.
17. Write the alphabet in order.
18. Alphabetize words by first letter and maybe second and third.
19. Write the following personal information correctly when requested on an application or identification form: age, Mr., Mrs., Miss, Ms., color of hair and eyes.
20. Read and write the numbers 31-76.

Part 2, Introduction

SIGHT WORDS
numbers 31-76

INSTRUCTIONAL AIDS
white flash cards

INSTRUCTION

1. Let's count up to 30.

2. Let's go on.

3. This is 31.

4. This is (32).

5. This is 15. This is 50.
   This is 16. This is 60.
   This is 17. This is 70.

6. Let's write 31-76.

7. Let's make cards.

8. Additional activities:
   a. Show white 5 x 8 flash cards 31-76 randomly.
   b. Dictate the numbers 31-76 randomly.
   c. Have students count 31-76 in order.
   d. Have students put all their flash cards in numerical order.
   e. Have students play games in #11b on p. 8 of this guide.
   f. Play Bingo with numbers up to 76. (Bingo cards will have to be teacher or student made.)
   g. Teach capable students to spell the numbers 31-76.

ACTIVITY/RESPONSE

1. St: Respond in chorus and individually.

2. T: Continue counting up to 76. Review and repeat as often as necessary.

3. T: Write 31 on the white 5 x 8 flash card.
   St: Read and repeat.

4. T: Continue to show written numbers up to 76.
   St: Read and repeat.

5. T: Write the numbers on the board.
   St: Repeat.
   T: Observe for proper pronunciation contrast.

6. T: A master for a writing page is provided on p. 396 of this guide for duplication.
   St: Write.

7. St: Make a white 3 x 5 flash card for each number 31-76.

8. St: a. Read in chorus and individually.

   b. Write.

   c. Count.

   d. Arrange cards.

   e. Play.

   f. Play Bingo.

   g. Spell and write.

Student Workbook   p. 31
Sound Symbol Association, Hh /h/

VISUALS*

4 hat	7 hot dog
5 hand	8 house
6 hamburger	9 housewife

*or any visuals providing practice in the sound /h/

INSTRUCTIONAL AIDS

an alphabet wall chart or alphabet flash cards
old magazines or a copy of the hamburger on p.372 of this guide
a pink flash card

INSTRUCTION

1. This is the alphabet.

2. What is this?

3. This is a letter, this is a letter, etc.

4. What are these?

5. There are 26 letters in the alphabet. Let's count.

6. How many letters are there in the alphabet?

7. Each letter has a name. What does each letter have?

8. This is a letter.

9. What is it?

10. The name of this letter is "h". What's the name of this letter?

11. This is a capital "H". We use capital "H" for names.

ACTIVITY/RESPONSE

1. T: Spread the alphabet flash cards in hands or point sweepingly across an alphabet chart.

2. St: (This is) the alphabet.

3. T: Pick up several individual flash cards or point to individual letters on the chart.

4. St: (They're) letters.

5. T:⏝
   St:⏝ Count them together.

6. St: 26

7. St: a name

8. T: Hold up the letter "Hh" or print it on the board.

9. St: (It's) a letter.

10. St: "h"

11. T: Point to or write a capital "H". Say and write on board a student's name beginning with "H" or provide a name.

45

12. What's the name of this letter?	12. St: "H" or "capital H"
13. What is the capital "H" used for?	13. St: names
14. This is a small "h".	14. T: Point to or write "h" on the board.
15. What's the name of this letter?	15. St: "h"
16. The sound of the letter "h" is /h/ as in the word "hat". This is a hat.	16. T: Show visual 4. Hint: pretend to jog, demonstate breathlessness, hold palm up to mouth and feel breath on hand. St: Listen and hold palm up to mouth and feel breath on palm. Repeat "/h/ hat" three times.
17. Listen and repeat: /h/ hat /h/ hand (hamburger, hot dog house, housewife) Also, /h/ (hi, hello, he, his, how)	17. T: Show visuals. Teach students to make sound /h/. Model each word separately. St: Listen and repeat. T: Elicit words students may know beginning with /h/.
18. What is the sound of the letter "h"?	18. St: /h/ T: If students have difficulty, repeat steps 16-18.
19. Let's write.	19. T: Draw writing lines on the board: ══════ ══════ Demonstrate how to write "Hh". St: Practice on the board.
20. Open your book to p. 31.	20. St: Open book to p. 31. T: Be certain the social security number is filled in accurately.
21. Capital "H" is for names and the first word of a sentence.	21. T: Point to capital "H" in the strip "Hello, how are you?"
22. Let's write capital "H".	22. T: Demonstrate on the writing lines. St: Write a row of capital "H" in the workbook.
23. Let's write the small "h".	23. T: Demonstrate on the writing lines. St: Write a row of "h" in the workbook.
24. What is the name of this letter?	24. T: Point to "Hh". St: "h" T: Prompt if necessary.

25. Listen and repeat some words beginning with /h/:
hat, hand, hamburger, hot dog, house, housewife.
Also, (hi, hello, he, his, how and other words students provide)

26. Let's make a card.

27. Hold up the "Hh" card when you hear a word that begins with /h/:
June, Hello, goodbye, hamburger, Hi, etc.

28. What is the name of this letter?

29. What is the sound of "h"?

25. T: Model each word separately. Show the visuals.
    St: Listen and repeat.

26. St: Take a pink 3 x 5 card. Write "Hh" on one side. Staple or tape a picture from a magazine with the initial sound /h/ or a copy of the hamburger on p. 372 of this guide to the back of the card.
    T: Assist, if necessary. Make a corresponding 5 x 8 flash card.

27. T: Demonstrate activity. Model each word.
    St: Hold up "Hh" card when words beginning with /h/ are modeled.

28. T: Point to "Hh".
    St: "h"

29. St: /h/

REMINDER: Review flash cards, sentence strips and previously learned concepts frequently.

Student Workbook p. 31
Sound Symbol Association, Tt /t/

VISUALS*
  3 telephone   12 tea
10 table   13 ten dollars
11 teacher   14 truck
*or any visuals providing practice in the sound /t/

INSTRUCTIONAL AIDS
an alphabet wall chart or alphabet flash cards
old magazines or a copy of the telephone on p. 372 of this guide
a pink flash card

INSTRUCTION

REVIEW

1. What is this?

2. What are these?

3. How many letters are there in the alphabet?

4. What's the name of this letter?

5. What is the sound of the letter "h"?

6. What is this?

7. Capital "H" is for names and the first word of a sentence.

8. Write capital "H".

9. Write small "h".

NEW LESSON

1. This is the letter "Tt".

2. What's the name of this letter?

3. This is a capital "T".

ACTIVITY/RESPONSE

1. T: Spread the 26 alphabet cards in hand or point sweepingly across an alphabet chart.
   St: (It's) the alphabet.

2. St: (They're) letters.

3. St: 26

4. T: Point to or write "Hh".
   St: "h"

5. St: /h/

6. T: Show visuals from the previous lesson.
   St: It's a house, hat, hamburger, etc.

7. T: Point out a name beginning with "H". Point to capital "H" in "How are you?"

8. St: Write "H" on the board or on paper.

9. St: Write "h" on the board or on paper.
   T: Review/reinforce as necessary.

1. T: Print "Tt" on the board.

2. St: "t"

3. T: Point to or write capital "T".

4. We use capital "T" for names.

5. What's the name of this letter?

6. This is a small "t".

7. What's the name of this letter?

8. The sound of the letter "t" is /t/ as in the word "telephone". This is a telephone.

9. Listen and repeat:
   /t/ telephone /t/ table
   (teacher, tea, ten dollars, truck)

10. What is the sound of the letter "t"?

11. Let's write.

12. Open your book to p. 31.

13. Capital "T" is for names
    Let's write capital "T".

14. Let's write the small "t".

15. What is the name of this letter?

16. Listen and repeat some words beginning with /t/:
    telephone, table, teacher, tea, ten dollars, truck and other words students provide.

---

4. T: Say and write on board a student's name beginning with "T" or provide a name.

5. St: "T" or "capital T".

6. T: Point to or write "t".

7. St: "t"

8. T: Show visual 3.
   St: Listen and repeat "/t/ telephone" three times.

9. T: Show visuals. Teach students to make the sound /t/. Model each word separately.
   St: Listen and repeat.
   T: Elicit words students may know beginning with /t/.

10. St: /t/
    T: If learners have difficulty, repeat steps 8-10.

11. T: Draw the writing lines on the board:
    ─────────── Demonstrate how to write "Tt".
    St: Practice on the board.

12. St: Open books to p. 31.

13. T: Demonstrate on the writing lines.
    St: Write a row of capital "T" in the workbook.

14. T: Demonstrate on the writing lines.
    St: Write a row of "t" in the workbook.

15. T: Point to "Tt".
    St: "t"
    T: Prompt if necessary.

16. T: Model each word separately. Show the visuals.
    St: Listen and repeat.

17. Let's make a card.

17. St: Take a pink 3 x 5 card. Write "Tt" on one side. Staple or tape a magazine picture with the initial sound /t/ or a copy of the telephone on p. 372 of this guide to the back of this card.
    T: Assist if necessary. Make a corresponding 5 x 8 flash card.

18. Hold up the "Tt" card when you hear a word that begins with /t/: ten, door, Tom, Kay, time, table, house, Hi, telephone, etc.

18. T: Demonstrate activity. Model each word.
    St: Hold up "Tt" card when words beginning with /t/ are modeled.

19. What is the name of this letter?

19. T: Point to "Tt".
    St: "t"

20. What is the sound of "t"?

20. St: /t/

Student Workbook   p. 31
Sound symbol Association, Ss /s/

VISUALS*

15 student   18 sink
16 stop (street)   19 soft drink
17 stove   20 secretary

*or any visuals providing practice in the sound /s/ as in "student"

INSTRUCTIONAL AIDS

old magazines or a copy of
 the student on p. 372 of this guide
a pink flash card
yellow flash cards

INSTRUCTION

REVIEW

1. What's the name of this letter?

2. What's the sound of "h"?

3. Capital "H" is for names. Write capital "H".

4. Write a small "h".

5. Name some words that begin with "h"/h/.

6. Repeat 1-5 for "Tt"/t/.

7. Let's read.

NEW LESSON

1. This is the letter "Ss".

2. What's the name of this letter?

3. This is a capital "S".

4. We use capital "S" for names.

5. What's the name of this letter?

ACTIVITY/RESPONSE

1. T: Point to or write "Hh".
   St: "h"

2. St: /h/

3. St: Write "H" on the board or on paper.

4. St: Write "h" on the board or on paper.

5. St: Respond.
   T: If learners are unable to respond, review visuals listed on p. 45 of this guide.

6. T: If learners are unable to respond, review lesson and visuals on p. 48.

7. T: Review numbers, sight words and sentence strips.
   St: Respond.

1. T: Print "Ss" on the board.

2. St: "s"

3. T: Point to or write capital "S".

4. T: Say and write on board a student's name beginning with "S" or provide a name.

5. St: "S" or "capital S"

6. This is a small "s".

7. What's the name of this letter?

8. One of the sounds of the letter "s" is /s/ as in "student"
   This is a student.
   You are a student.

9. Listen and repeat:
   /s/ student   /s/ stop, street
   (stove, sink, soft drink, secretary)
   Also (six, seven)

10. What is one of the sounds of the letter "s"?

11. Let's write.

12. Open your book to p. 31.

13. Capital "S" is for names.
    Let's write capital "S".

14. Let's write the small "s".

15. What is the name of this letter?

16. Listen and repeat some words beginning with /s/: students, stop, street, stove, sink, soft drink, secretary. Also, (six, seven and other words students provide).

17. Let's make a card.

6. T: Point to or write "s".

7. St: "s"

8. T: Show visual 15.
   St: Listen and repeat "/s/ student" three times.

9. T: Show visuals. Teach learners to make the sound /s/. Model each word separately.
   St: Listen and repeat.
   T: Elicit words students may know beginning with /s/.

10. St: /s/
    T: If students have difficulty, repeat steps 8-10.

11. T: Draw writing lines on the board:.
    ─────────────── Demonstrate how to write "Ss".
    St: Practice on the board.

12. St: Open books to p. 31

13. T: Demonstrate on the writing lines.
    St: Write a row of capital "S" in workbook.

14. T: Demonstrate on the writing lines.
    St: Write a row of "s" in the workbook.

15. T: Point to "Ss"
    St: "s"
    T: Prompt if necessary.

16. T: Model each word separately. Show the visuals.
    St: Listen and repeat.

17. St: Take a pink 3 x 5 card. Write "Ss" on one side. Staple a magazine picture with the initial sound /s/ or a copy of the student on p. 372 of this guide to the back of the card.
    T: Assist if necessary. Make a corresponding 5 x 8 flash card.

18. Hold up the "Ss" card when you hear a word that begins with one of the sounds of the letter "s":
    hat, sister, son, table
    secretary, hello, sink, etc.

19. What's the name of this letter?

20. What is the sound of "s"?

18. T: Demonstrate activity.
       Model each word.
    St: Hold up "Ss" card when words beginning with /s/ are modeled.

19. T: Point to "Ss".
    St: "s"

20. St: /s/

Student Workbook   p. 31
Sound Symbol Association, Aa /a/

SIGHT WORDS
at, hat, hats, sat

VISUALS*
21 apple   4 hat
22 afternoon

*or any visuals providing practice in sound /a/ as in "apple"

INSTRUCTIONAL AIDS
an alphabet chart or
 alphabet flash cards
old magazines or a copy of
 the apple on p. 372 of this guide
a pink flash card

INSTRUCTION

REVIEW

1. What's this?

2. What's this?

3. How many letters are there in the alphabet?

4. Each letter has a name. What's the name of this letter.

5. How do you write capital "H"?

6. Write small "h".

7. What's the sound of "H"?

8. Say some words beginning with "Hh".

9. Repeat instructions 4-8 for "Tt" and "Ss".

10. Let's read.

ACTIVITY/RESPONSE

1. T: Point to the alphabet chart or spread the 26 flash cards in the hand.
   St: (It's) the alphabet.

2. T: Hold up individual letters.
   St: (It's) a letter.

3. St: 26
   T: Recount together if necessary.

4. St: "h"

5. St: Write "H" on board or paper.

6. St: Write "h" on board or paper.

7. St: /h/

8. St: Respond.
   T: Review respective lessons and visuals as needed.

9. St: Respond.

10. T: Review sight words, numbers and sentence strips.
    St: Respond.

NEW LESSON

1.	This is the letter "Aa".	1.	T:	Print "Aa" on the board.
2.	What's the name of this letter?	2.	St:	"a"
3.	This is a capital "A".	3.	T:	Point to or write capital "A".
4.	We use capital "A" for names.	4.	T:	Say and write on board a student's name beginning with "A" or provide a name.
5.	What's the name of this letter?	5.	St:	"A" or "capital A"
6.	This is the small "a".	6.	T:	Print "a" on board.
7.	What's the name of this letter?	7.	St:	"a"
8.	One of the sounds of the letter "a" is /ă/ as in the word apple. This is an apple.	8.	T: St:	Show visual 21. Listen and repeat "/ă/ apple" three times.
9.	Listen and repeat: /ă/ apple, /ă/ afternoon. Also, /ă/ address /ă/ avenue	9.	T: St: T:	Show visuals. Teach students to make the sound /ă/. Model each word separately. Listen and repeat. Elicit words students may know beginning with /ă/.
10.	What is one of the sounds of "a"?	10.	St: T:	/ă/ If learners have difficulty, repeat steps 8-10.
11.	Let's write.	11.	T: St:	Draw writing lines on the board: ═══════════ Demonstrate how to write "Aa". Practice on the board.
12.	Open your books to p. 31.	12.	St:	Open books to p. 31.
13.	Capital "A" is for names. Let's write capital "A".	13.	T: St:	Demonstrate on the writing lines. Write a row of capital "A" in the workbook.
14.	Let's write the small "a".	14.	T: St:	Demonstrate on the writing lines. Write a row of "a" in the workbook.
15.	What is the name of this letter?	15.	T: St:	Point to "Aa". "a" Prompt if necessary.

16. Listen and repeat:
/ă/ apple, /ă/ afternoon.
Also, (address, avenue, and other words students provide).

17. Let's make a card.

18. Hold up the "Aa" card when you hear a word that begins with /ă/ as in apple:
avenue, sister, table, animal, hello, ankle, hi, how, afternoon.

19. What's the name of this letter?

20. What's one of the sounds of "a"?

21. These are the letters "h", "t" and "s"

22. What's the sound "h", of "t", of "s"?

23. Let's make some words: This is "at". We are at school.

24. Read this word.

25. This is "hat". He has a hat.

26. Read this word.

27. This is "hats". Here are two hats.

28. Read this word.

29. This is "sat". I sat in a chair.

30. Read this word.

---

16. T: Model each word separately. Show the visuals.
    St: Listen and repeat.

17. St: Take a pink 3 x 5 card. Write "Aa" on one side. Staple or tape a magazine picture with the initial sound /ă/ or a copy of the apple on p. 372 of this guide.
    T: Assist if necessary. Make a corresponding 5 x 8 flash card.

18. T: Demonstrate activity. Model each word.
    St: Hold up the "Aa" card when words beginning with /ă/ are modeled.

19. T: Point to or write "Aa" on the board.
    St: "a"

20. St: /ă/

21. T: Write "h", "t" and "s" on the board.

22. St: /h/, /t/, /s/

23. T: Print "at" on board.
    St: Listen.

24. St: Read "at" in chorus and individually.

25. T: Print "hat" on board. Show visual 4 and point to one hat.
    St: Listen.

26. St: Read "hat" in chorus and individually.

27. T: Point to both hats in visual 4. Print "hats" on board. Point to the plural "s".

28. St: Read "hats" in chorus and individually.

29. T: Print "sat" on the board. Draw a stick figure on a chair or sit down.

30. St: Read "sat" in chorus and individually.

31. Read these words.

32. Let's write these words.

33. Let's make cards.

31. St: "at", "hat", "hats", "sat"

32. St: Write row of "at", "hat", "hats", and "sat" on lined paper. A master for lined paper is provided on p. 396 of this book.

33. St: Make a yellow 3 x 5 flash card of at, hat, hats, sat.*
    T: Assist when necessary. Make corresponding 5 x 8 cards of the sight words. Whenever possible, have students staple a visual of the sight word to the back of the card.

*See p. 8 for suggested uses of the sight word flash cards and p. 10 for suggested uses of the Language Master.

Student Workbook p. 31
Sound Symbol Association, Mm /m/

SIGHT WORDS
Sam, mat, mast, ham

VISUALS*
23 man   26 map
24 morning   27 mop
25 money   28 market
*or any visuals providing practice in the sound /m/

INSTRUCTIONAL AIDS
old magazines or a copy of the man on p. 372 of this guide
a pink flash card
yellow flash cards

INSTRUCTION	ACTIVITY/RESPONSE

REVIEW

1. What's the name of this letter?

2. What's the sound of "h"?

3. Write a capital "H".

4. Write a small "h".

5. Name some words that begin with "h".

6. Repeat instructions 1-5 for "t", "s" and "a" as necessary.

7. Let's read.

8. Let's write.

9. Let's read.

NEW LESSON

1. This is the letter "Mm".

2. What's the name of this letter?

---

1. T: Point to or wirte "Hh" on board.
   St: "h"

2. St: /h/

3. St: Write "H" on the board or on paper.

4. St: Write "h" on the board or on paper.

5. St: Respond.
   T: If learners are unable to do so, review "h" visuals.

6. St: Respond and write.

7. T: Write "at", "hat", "hats", "sat" on board.
   St: Read in chorus and individually.

8. T: Dictate: at, hat, hats, and sat.
   St: Write on paper or board.

9. T: Show all previous flash cards and sentence strips as necessary.
   St: Read.

1. T: Print "Mm" on the board.

2. St: "m"

3. This is a capital "M".	3. T: Print capital "M" on board.
4. We use capital "M" for names and for the first word of a sentence.	4. T: Say and write on board a student's name beginning with "M" or provide a name. Point to the capital "M" in "My name's _____ ."
5. What's the name of this letter?	5. St: "M" or "capital M"
6. This is a small "m".	6. T: Print "m" on board.
7. What's the name of this letter?	7. St: "m"
8. The sound of the letter "m" is /m/ as in the word "man". He is a man.	8. T: Show visual 23. St: Listen and repeat "/m/ man" three times.
9. Listen and repeat: /m/ man, /m/ morning (money, map, mop, market) Also, (my, Mr., Mrs., Miss, much)	9. T: Show visuals. Teach learners to make the sound /m/. Model each word separately. St: St: Listen and repeat. T: Elicit from students, words they know beginning with /m/.
10. What's the sound of "m"?	10. St: /m/ T: If learners have difficulty, repeat steps 8-10.
11. Let's write.	11. T: Draw writing lines on the board: ═══════════════ ═══════════════ Demonstrate how to write "Mm". St: Practice on the board.
12. Turn to p. 31 in the student workbook.	12. St: Open books to p. 31.
13. Capital "M" is for names. Let's write capital "M".	13. T: Demonstrate on the writing lines. St: Write a row of capital "M" in the workbook.
14. Let's write the small "m".	14. T: Demonstrate on the writing lines. St: Write a row of "m" in the workbook.
15. What's the name of this letter?	15. T: Point to "Mm" St: "m" T: Prompt if necessary.
16. Listen and repeat some words beginning with /m/: man, morning, money, map, mop market. Also, (my, Mr., Mrs., Miss, much, and any words students provide)	16. T: Model each word separately. Show visuals. St: Listen and repeat.

17. Let's make a card.

17. St: Take a pink 3 x 5 card. Write "Mm" on one side. Staple or tape a magazine picture with the initial sound /m/ or a copy of the man on p. 372 of this guide to the back the card.
   T: Assist if necessary. Make a 5 x 8 flash card.

18. Hold up the "Mm" card when you hear a word that begins with the sound /m/.

18. T: Demonstrate activity.

19. sister, man, hello, mop, hats much, hospital, teacher, mailman, mechanic

19. T: Model each word.
    St: Hold up the "Mm" card when words beginning with /m/ are modeled.

20. What's the name of this letter?

20. T: Point to or write "Mm".
    St: "m"

21. What's the sound of "m"?

21. St: /m/

22. These are the letters "h", "t", "s", and "a".

22. T: Write "h", "t", "s", and "a" on board.

23. What's the sound of "h", of "t", of "s" and of "a"?

23. St: /h/, /t/, /s/, /ă/

24. Let's read some words. This is is "Sam". Capital "S" is for names. Sam is a man's name.

24. T: Show visual 23. Print "Sam" on board.

25. Read this word.

25. St: Read "Sam" in chorus and individually.

26. This is "mat".

26. T: Print "mat" on the board. Demonstrate what a mat is. Draw a house with a mat at the front door or a table with a mat.

27. Read this word.

27. St: Read "mat" in chorus and individually.

28. This is a "mast".

28. T: Print "mast" on the board. Draw a boat and a mast.

29. Read this word.

29. St: Read "mast" in chorus and individually.

30. This is "ham". "Ham" is meat from a pig.

30. T: Print "ham" on the board. Provide a picture if possible.

31. Read this word.

31. St: Read "ham" in chorus and individually.

32. Read these words.

32. St: "at", "hat", "hats", "sat", "mat", "mast", "ham"

33. Let's write these words.

33. St: Write a row of "mat", "mast" and "ham" on lined paper. A master for lined paper is provided on p. 396 of this book.

34. Let's make cards.

34. St: Make yellow 3 x 5 flash cards of the sight words.*
    T: Assist if necessary. Make 5 x 8 cards of the sight words. Whenever possible, have students staple or tape a visual of the sight word to the back of the card.

See p. 8 for the suggested uses of the sight word flash cards and p. 10 for suggested uses of the Language Master.

Student Workbook   p. 31
Sound Symbol Association, Nn/n/

SIGHT WORDS
an, man, Nan, tan, Ann

VISUALS*
29 nickel   31 nurse
30 night   32 notebook
*or any visuals providing practice in the /n/ sound

INSTRUCTIONAL AIDS
old magazine or a copy of
  the nickel on p. 372 of this guide
a pink flash card
yellow flash cards

INSTRUCTION

1. This is a letter "Nn".

2. What's the name of this letter?

3. This is a capital "N".

4. We use capital "N" for names.

5. What's the name of this letter?

6. This is a small "n".

7. What's the name of this letter?

8. The sound of the letter "n" is /n/ as in the word "nickel". This is a nickel.

9. Listen and repeat.
   /n/ nickel /n/ night (nurse, notebook)
   Also, (no, not, nine, number, name)

10. What's the sound of "n"?

11. Let's write.

ACTIVITY/RESPONSE

1. T: Print "Nn" on the board.

2. St: "n"

3. T: Print capital "N" on the board.

4. T: Say and write a student's name beginning with "N" or provide "Nan".

5. St: "N" or "capital N"

6. T: Print "n" on the board.

7. St: "n"

8. T: Show visual 29.
   St: Listen and repeat "/n/nickel" three times.

9. T: Show visuals. Teach students to make the sound /n/. Model each word separately.
   St: Listen and repeat.
   T: Elicit words students know beginning with /n/.

10. St: /n/
    T: If learners have difficulty, repeat steps 8-10.

11. T: Draw writing lines on the board:
    ═══════════════
    ═══════════════ Demonstrate how to write "Nn".
    St: Practice on the board.

12.	Turn to p. 31 in the student workbook.	12. St:	Open book to p. 31.
13.	Capital "N" is for names. Let's write a capital "N".	13. T: St:	Demonstrate on the writing lines. Write a row of capital "N" in the workbook.
14.	Let's write the small "n".	14. T: St:	Demonstrate on the writing lines. Write a row of "n" in the workbook.
15.	What's the name of this letter?	15. St: T:	"n" Prompt if necessary.
16.	Listen and repeat some words beginning with /n/: nickel, night, nurse, notebook. Also, (no, not, nine, number, name and any other words students provide).	16. T: St:	Model each word separately. Listen and repeat.
17.	Let's make a card.	17. St: T:	Take a pink 3 x 5 card. Write "Nn" on one side. Staple or tape a magazine picture with the initial sound /n/ or a copy of the nickel on p. 372 of this guide to the back of the card. Assist if necessary. Make a corresponding 5 x 8 flash card.
18.	Hold up the "Nn" card when you hear a word that begins with the sound /n/.	18. T:	Demonstrate activity.
19.	no, man, nickel, mailman, nurse, mop, not, map, nine, my, number, six, name, etc.	19. T: St:	Model each word. Hold up the "Nn" card when words beginning with /n/ are modeled.
20.	What's the name of this letter?	20. T: St:	Point to or write "Nn". "n"
21.	What's the sound of "n"?	21. St:	/n/
22.	What's the name of these letters?	22. T: St:	Write "h", "t", "s", "a", "m" on the board. Respond.
23.	What's the sound of "h", of "t", of "s", of "m" and name some words that begin with each.	23. St:	/h/, /t/ /s/, /m/ and name words beginning with these sounds.
24.	What's one of the sounds of "a"? Name some words that begin with it.	24. St:	/ă/ apple, Avenue, Ann, etc.

25. Let's read some words. This is "an". Example: an apple, an afternoon. "An" is one.

26. Read this word.

27. Let's write "an".

28. This is "man".
    Sam is a man.

29. Read this word.

30. Let's write "man".

31. Repeat steps 27-30 for Ann, Nan and tan. Point out capital "A" and "N" for names.

32. Let's make cards.

25. T: Print "an" on the board.

26. St: Read "an" in chorus and individually.

27. St: Write a row of "an" on the lined paper. A master for lined paper is provided on p. 396 of this book.

28. T: Print "man" on the board.

29. St: Read "man" in chorus and individually.

30. St: Write a row of "man" on the lined paper.

31. St: Read and write.

32. St: Make yellow 3 x 5 flash cards of the sight words.*
    T: Assist if necessary. Make a 5 x 8 card for each sight word.
    St: Whenever possible staple a visual of the sight word to the back of the card.

*See p. 8 for the suggested uses of the sight word flash cards and p. 10 for the suggested uses of the Language Master.

Student Workbook p. 32
Hh, Tt, Ss, Aa, Mm, Nn
Visual discrimination/writing words

INSTRUCTION	ACTIVITY/RESPONSE
1. Circle the word that is the same.	1. T: Write the following on the board. mast	stam msat mast mas | St: Circle the word that is the same. T: Demonstrate with as many examples as necessary.
2. Open your books to p. 32.	2. St: Open books.
3. Let's read these words.	3. T: Point to the words in items 1-6 at the top. Model. St: Read in chorus and individually.
4. Look at the sample box.	4. T: Point to the sample box. Demonstrate that the circled word is the same as as that outside the box.
5. Circle the word that is the same.	5. St: Complete exercise. T: Check student work.
6. Let's read these words.	6. T: Point to items 1-6 at the bottom. St: Read in chorus and individually.
7. Listen and point to the word I say.	7. T: Write "hats", "hat", and "has" on the board. (Number them 1, 2, 3). Cover your mouth with a piece of paper and say "hats", "hat" and "has" randomly. St: Point to the word being said or identify it by number 1, 2 or 3.
8. Write the words.	8. T: Point to the sample box. St: Write each word at the bottom of p. 32 four times. T: Check student work. Be certain the social security number has been filled in accurately at the upper right hand corner.

65

Student Workbook p. 33
Hh, Tt, Ss, Aa, Mm, Nn
Reading/Writing Sentences

INSTRUCTION

1. Open your books to p. 33 and look at picture #1.

2. This is Sam. What's his name?

3. Sam's a man.

4. Look at #2. This is a hat. What is this?

5. Sam has a hat.

6. Look at #3. This is Ann. Who is she?

7. Ann has 2 hats.

8. Write each of the sentences 2 times.

9. Optional: Let's read.

10. Let's write.

ACTIVITY/RESPONSE

1. St: Open books.
   T: Point to picture #1.

2. T: Model response.
   St: (His name's) Sam.

3. St: Listen and read in chorus and individually.

4. T: Point to the hat in #2. Model response.
   St: (It's) a hat.

5. St: Listen and read in chorus and individually.

6. T: Point to Ann in #3. Model. response.
   St: (She's) Ann.

7. St: Listen and read in chorus and individually.

8. St: Write.
   T: Check student work.

9. T: Write the 3 sentences on sentence strips.
   St: Read and complete optional activities suggested on p. 14 of this guide.

10. T: Dictate the sentences.
    St: Write on board or lined paper.

REMINDER: Review all flash cards and sentence strips frequently.

Student Workbook p. 34
Review, Hh, Tt, Ss, Aa, Mm, Nn

INSTRUCTION

1. Open your books to p. 34.

2. Listen: /h/. Circle the letter that makes the /h/ sound as in "ham".

3. Listen and circle the letter I say:
   1. /m/ - man
   2. /s/ - Sam
   3. /a/ - apple
   4. /n/ - nickel
   5. /h/ - hello
   6. /t/ - table

4. Listen and repeat: Sam has a hat.

5. Write #1: Sam has a hat.

6. Listen and repeat:
   Ann has 2 hats.

7. Write #2: Ann has 2 hats.

8. Listen and repeat:
   Sam's a man.

9. Write #3: Sam's a man.

ACTIVITY/RESPONSE

1. St: Open books.
   T: Duplicate the sample box on p. 34 of the workbook on the board.

2. St: Circle the "h" on the board and in the sample box.
   T: Repeat until students understand. Provide as many examples as necessary.

3. St: Listen and circle correct letters.
   T: Repeat each item only two times. This will force students to listen. Check student work and provide immediate feedback.

4. St: Listen and repeat in chorus and individually.

5. St: Write.
   T: Allow students to look at p. 33 if necessary.

6. St: Listen and repeat.

7. St: Write.
   T: Allow students to look at p. 33 if necessary.

8. St: Listen and repeat.

9. St: Write.
   T: Allow students to look at p. 33 if necessary. Check student work. Make sure that "last name" has been filled in at the upper right hand corner.

Student Workbook p.35
    Sound Symbol Association
    Bb, Pp, Ll, Ff, Ee, Dd

SIGHT WORDS
For Bb: bat(s)
For Pp: pan(s)
For Ll: last, lamp, small, ball
For Ff: fat, fast
For Ee: ten, men, Ben, pen(s),
          pet(s), he, Lee
For Dd: Dad, sad, mad, and, hand

*VISUALS for Bb:
    33 bed   35 book   37 bananas
    34 boy, bat   36 barber   38 busboy

VISUALS for Pp:
    39 pen   41 penny   43 purse
    40 pencil   42 pepper   44 pan

VISUALS for Ll:
    45 lamp   47 laundromat   49 lawyer
    46 lemon   48 locker

VISUAL for Ff:
    50 flag   52 five dollars   54 father
    51 fries   53 family

VISUALS for Ee:
    54 envelope   55 exit

VISUALS for Dd:
    57 door   59 doctor   61 dime
    58 desk   60 dentist   62 dollar

*or any visuals providing practice in the respective sounds

INSTRUCTIONAL AIDS
an alphabet wall chart or alphabet flash cards
old magazines or a copy of the boy and bat, pan, lamp, father, exit, doctor on p. 373 of this guide
pink and yellow flash cards

**INSTRUCTION

1. This is the letter "____".

2. What's the name of this letter?

3. This is a capital "____".

ACTIVITY/RESPONSE

1. T: Print "____" on the board.

2. St: "____"

3. T: Print capital "____" on the board.

**Provide instruction for each letter separately.

4. We use capital "___" for names.

5. What's the name of this letter?

6. This is a small "___".

7. What's the name of this letter?

8. The sound of the letter "___" is
   /b/ as in bed, 33
   /p/ as in pen, 39
   /l/ as in lamp, 45
   /f/ as in flag, 50
   /e/ as in exit, 55
   /d/ as in door, 57

9. Listen and repeat:
   /b/ bed, boy, bat, book, barber, bananas, busboy
   /p/ pen, pencil, penny, pepper, purse, pan
   /l/ lamp, lemon, laundromat, locker, lawyer
   /f/ flag, fries, five dollars family, father. Also, (four fourteen, fifteen, fifty)
   /ĕ/ envelope, exit
   /d/ door, desk, doctor, dentist, dime, dollar

10. What's the sound of "___"?

11. Let's write.

12. Open your books to p. 35. This says "number" and "street". Write your address.

13. Capital "___" is for names and for the first word of a sentence. Let's write capital "___".

---

4. T: Say and write on the board a student's name beginning with "___" or provide a name.

5. St: "___" or "capital ___"

6. T: Print "___" on the board.

7. St: "___"

8. T: Show the respective visuals.
   St: Listen and repeat the words three times.

9. T: Show visuals. Teach students to make the respective sounds. Model each word separately.
   St: Listen and repeat.
   T: Elicit words students may know beginning with the respective sounds.

10. St: "/ /"
    T: Repeat steps 8-10 if students have difficulty.

11. T: Draw writing lines on the board: ─────────── Demonstrate how to write the letter "_".
    St: Practice on the board.

12. St: Open books to p. 35. Fill in their address at the upper right hand corner.

13. T: Demonstrate on the writing lines.
    St: Write a row of capital "___" in the workbook.

14. Let's write a small "___".

15. What's the name of this letter?

16. Listen and repeat: "/ /" ___ , ___ .

17. Let's make a card.

18. Hold up the "___" card when you hear a word that begins with the sound "/ /".

19. For /b/:
    name, pen, Ben, den, flag,
    barber, bank, sink, busboy,
    last, pin, etc.
    For /p/:
    babý, pencil, Ben, pen,
    last, purse, nurse, penny,
    first, man, pepper, etc.
    For /l/:
    ramp, lamp, light, right,
    letter, better, lemon, lawyer, run
    laundromat, fat, etc.
    For /f/:
    five, thank you, pin, fine,
    four, hello, first, purse,
    fifteen, sixteen, father, etc.
    For /ẽ/:
    at, elbow, an, envelope, lamp,
    exit, boy, elephant, etc.
    For /d/:
    table, doctor, desk, ten,
    bank, teacher, dime, different,
    dentist, tan, bed, door, etc.

14. T: Demonstrate on the writing lines.
    St: Write a row of "___" in the workbook.

15. St: "___"
    T: Prompt, if necessary.

16. T: Repeat vocabulary listed in item #9 in this lesson and other words students provide. Model each word separately.
    St: Listen and repeat.

17. St: Take a pink 3 x 5 card. Write the capital and small letter on one side. Staple or tape a magazine picture with the appropriate initial sound or a copy of the boy, pan, lamp, father, exit or doctor on p. 373 of this guide to the back of the card.
    T: Assist if necessary. Make a corresponding 5 x 8 flash card.

18. T: Demonstrate activity.

19. T: Model each word,
    St: Hold up "___" card when words beginning with "/ /" are modeled.

20. What's the name of this letter?

21. What's the sound of "___"?

22. (After presenting instructions for Bb) These are the letters "h", "t", "s", "a", "m", "n", and "b".

23. What's the sound of "h", of "t", etc?

24. Let's make some words. What's this?

25. What's this?

26. This is a bat.

27. These are bats.

28. Read these words.

29. Repeat instructions 22-28.
    For Pp: pan, pans
    For Ll: last, lamp
    (another sound for "a" is /ă/ as in all, hall, tall, small, ball)
    For Ff: fat, fast, (fall)
    ten, men, Ben, pen(s), pet(s). Another sound for "e" is /ē/ as in Lee, he
    For Dd: Dad, sad, mad, and hand.

30. Let's write these words.

---

20. T: Point to or write "___".
    St: "___"

21. St: "/ /"

22. T: Write the letters on the board or show the respective flash cards.

23. St: /h/, /t/, etc.
    T: Review previous sight words.

24. T: Write "at" on the board.
    St: "at"

25. T: Place "h" in front of "at", also "s" and "b".
    St: hat, sat, bat

26. T: Point to the bat in visual 34 or draw a simple picture of a bat, demonstrate a swing.

27. T: Draw several bats.

28. T: Write "bat, bats" on board or 5 x 8 flash cards.
    St: Read in chorus and individually.

29. T: Provide appropriate instructions.
    St: Respond.

30. St: Write a row of each sight word on lined paper. A master for lined paper is provided on p. 396 of this book.

31. Let's make flash cards.

31. St: Make yellow 3 x 5 flash cards of the sight words.*
Staple or tape a visual of the sight word to the back of the flash card whenever possible.
T: Assist if necessary. Make corresponding 5 x 8 cards.

Upon completion of instruction for all the letters in this lesson, you may wish to add other words to the student's reading repertoire to insure that the concept of decoding is solidifying.

Do remember that in ESL literacy training, it is essential to provide visuals for new vocabulary whenever possible to insure comprehension. For example:

fan   on one side of the card and   on the other. Refer to p. 7 for a further discussion.

When adding words such as the ones listed below to the reading list, do so knowing that students may only be manipulating sounds and not necessarily comprehending.

Bb	**Pp**	**Ll**	**Ff**	**Ee**			**Dd**
ban	Pat	lab	fan	Ben	bell	bad	bed
ball	pass	lap	fat	den	dell	Dad	fed
tab	Pam	slam	flat	hen	fell	fad	led
	past	slap	fall	men	sell	had	dam
		land		pen	tell	lad	Dan
				ten	spell	mad	
				bet		pad	
				let		sad	
				met			
				net			
				set			

*See p. 8 for the suggested uses of the sight word flash cards and p. 10 for the suggested uses of the Language Master.

Student Workbook   p. 36
Bb, Pp, Ll, Ff, Ee, Dd
Visual Discrimination

INSTRUCTION	ACTIVITY/RESPONSE
1. What's this word?	1. T: Write "telephone" on the board. St: "telephone"
2. What's this word?	2. T: Cover up "tele". St: phone T: Prompt, if necessary.
3. "Telephone" and "phone" are the same.	3. St: Listen.
4. Open your books to p. 36 What's this word?	4. T: Point to "phone" at the upper right hand corner. St: Open book and respond "phone". Fill in the number, write a dash or "none".
5. Let's read these words.	5. St: Read words 1-12 in chorus and individually.
6. Circle the word that is the same.	6. T: Review example. St: Complete items #1-12. T: Check student work.
7. Review all flash cards and sentence strips as necessary.	7. St: Respond.
8. Optional: Say (write) words that start with "/ /".	8. T: Have students categorize words according to initial sound. St: Work individually or in pairs.

Student Workbook p. 37
Bb, Pp, Ll, Ff, Ee, Dd
Reading/writing words

INSTRUCTIONAL AIDS
yellow flash cards

INSTRUCTION

1. Open your books to p. 37.

2. Let's read the words.

3. Let's write the words.

4. Let's make cards.

5. Optional: To insure vocabulary comprehension has been achieved, a match worksheet can be devised with stick figures and vocabulary. For example:

ACTIVITY/RESPONSE

1. St: Open books.

2. St: Read words 1-10 in chorus and individually.
   T: New vocabulary:
   Ben Lee
   dad
   fat
   pet
   mad
   fast
   sad
   Demonstrate through visuals on workbook p. 38 or role play new vocabulary.

3. St: Write the words.
   T: Check student work. Make sure city, state and zip have been filled in properly at the upper right hand corner.

4. St: Make yellow 3 x 5 flash cards of the new vocabulary listed above.
   T: Make corresponding 5 x 8 cards.

5. St: Write words in the blank.

Words:
pet, pen, sad, fast, mad, fat

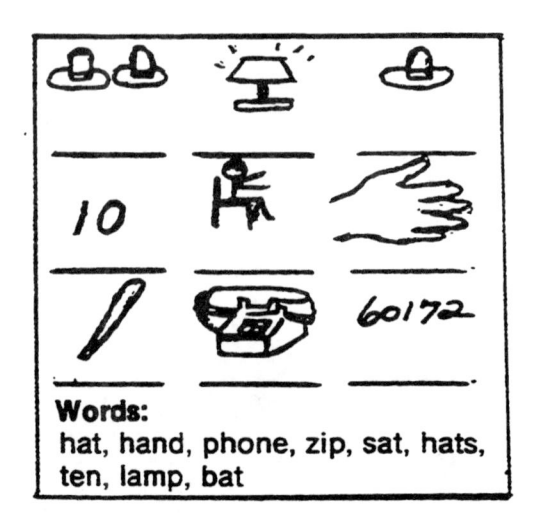

Words:
hat, hand, phone, zip, sat, hats, ten, lamp, bat

74

Student Workbook   p. 38
Bb, Pp, Ll, Ff, Ee, Dd
Reading/Writing Sentences

INSTRUCTIONAL AIDS
yellow flash cards

INSTRUCTION

1. Open your books to p. 38.

2. Look at the picture.
   What's his name?
   What's his first name?
   What's his last name?

3. What's this?

4. Let's read.

5. What's Ben?
   What does he have?
   What's Ben's last name?

6. Let's practice writing the sentences.
   Use capitals at the beginning of a
   a sentence and periods at the end.

7. Write the sentences in the book.

8. Look at the picture.

9. This is Sam. He's a dad.
   He has two children. He
   has a fat bat. He has a
   fast pet.

ACTIVITY/RESPONSE

1. St: Open books.
   T: Point to picture at the upper left hand corner.

2. T: Model responses if necessary.
   St: (His name's) Ben Lee.
   (His first name's) Ben.
   (His last name's) Lee.

3. T: Point to the pen and desk in the picture.
   St: (It's) a pen, a desk.

4. T: Model the sentences for pronunciation, stress and intonation.
   St: Repeat in chorus. Read individually.

5. St: Ben's a man.
   He has a pen.
   Ben's last name's Lee.

6. T: Draw writing lines on the board. Demonstrate how to make an apostrophe. Have student volunteers write the sentences on the board. Write the sentences on sentence strips. See p. 14 of this guide for suggested uses of the sentence strips.

7. St: Write sentences in the workbook.
   T: Check student work. Be certain that the social security number has been filled in properly at the upper right hand corner.

8. T: Point to the picture in the center of the page.

9. T: Point to each item to insure comprehension.

10. What's his name?
    What is he?
    What does he have?
    What does he have?

11. Optional, adjective placement: cover the word "fat" (fast) and uncover it to emphasize the placement of the adjective between the article and the noun.

12. Look at him.
    He's mad.

13. Look at him.
    He's sad.

14. How are you?

15. How is he?

16. How is he?

17. Let's read.

18. Let's practice writing the sentences. Use capital letters at the beginning of a sentence and periods at the end.

19. Write the sentences in the book.

20. Optional: Write the sentences again.

21. Optional, decoding:
    (a) Manipulate the letters "t, N, b, p, f, D" in front of the ending "an" in "man"

---

10. T: Point to the specific visual. being referred to. Model responses if necessary.
    St: (His name's) Sam.
        He's a dad.
        He has a fat bat.
        He has a fast pet.

11. T: Write these on the board:
        "a fat bat"
        "a fast pet"
    St: Listen.
    T: Substitute adjectives like "big", "good".

12. T: Point to the child at the left.
    St: Repeat, "He's mad".

13. T: Point to the child at the right.
    St: Repeat, "He's sad".

14. St: Fine (thank you.)

15. T: Point to the child at the left.
    St: He's mad.

16. T: Point to the child at the right.
    St: He's sad.

17. T: Model for pronunciation, stress and intonation.
    St: Repeat in chorus and read individually.

18. T: Draw writing lines on the board. Demonstrate how to make apostrophes. Have student volunteers write sentences on the board. Write the sentences on sentence strips. See p. 14 of this guide for suggested uses of the sentence strips.

19. St: Write the sentences in the workbook.
    T: Check student work.

20. St: Practice writing sentences. A master for lined paper is provided on p. 396 of this book.

21.
(a) St: Read "tan, Nan, ban, pan, fan, Dan" in chorus and individually.
    T: See p. 7 for a discussion on this concept.

- (b) Manipulate the letters "m, p, f" in front of the ending "ast" in "last".
- (c) Manipulate the letters "H, t, m, B" in front of the ending "en" in "pen".
- (d) Manipulate the letters "h, s, m, b, p, l, f" in front of the ending "ad" in "dad".
- (e) Manipulate the letters "h, s, m, b" in front of the ending "at" in "fat".
- (f) Manipulate the letters "s, m, n, b, l" in front of the ending "et" in "pet".

22. Optional, opposites:
    man - woman
    last - first
    dad - mom
    fat - thin
    fast - slow
    sad - glad, happy

23. What's the opposite of _____ ?

24. Optional: Write the sentences as on p. 38 in opposites.
    Ex: "He's glad."

25. Study the sentences on p. 38 for dictation.

- (b) St: Read "mast, past, fast" in chorus and individually.
- (c) St: Read "hen, ten, men, Ben" in chorus and individually.
- (d) St: Read "had, sad, mad, bad, pad, lad, fad" in chorus and individually.
- (e) St: Read "hat, sat, mat, bat" in chorus and individually.
- (f) Read "set, met, net, bet, let" in chorus and individually.

22. T: Demonstrate "opposite". Teach the vocabulary orally.
    St: Repeat.

23. St: Respond. Make yellow 3 x 5 flash cards:

    | man / woman |

    T: Make 5 x 8 flash cards of opposites.

24. St: Write the sentences again on lined paper. A master for lined paper is provided on p. 396 of this guide.

25. T: Explain that in dictation, the teacher talks and students write. Dictate the sentences on p. 38.
    St: Write on paper or board.

REMINDER: Review all flash cards and sentence strips frequently.

Student Workbook p.39
   Review, Bb, Pp, Ll, Ff, Ee, Dd

INSTRUCTION	ACTIVITY/RESPONSE
1. Open your books to p. 39.	1. St: Open books. T: Duplicate the sample box on p. 39 on the board.
2. Look at the sample box. Circle the capital and small letter that say /m/ as in "man".	2. St: Circle capital "M" and small "m" on the board and in the workbook sample box. T: Provide several examples if necessary.
3. Listen and circle the capital and small of the letters that make these sounds. 　1. /b/ - bat 　2. /d/ - doctor 　3. /l/ - last 　4. /e/ - envelope 　5. /p/ - pencil 　6. /m/ - man 　7. /f/ - five 　8. /n/ - name	3. St: Listen and circle the correct capital and small letters.
4. Listen and repeat: 　He has a fat bat.	4. St: Listen and repeat in chorus and individually.
5. Write: 　1. He has a fat bat.	5. St: Write. T: Dictate the sentence twice. Allow students to check workbook p. 38 if absolutely necessary.
6. Listen, repeat and write. 　2. Sam's a dad. 　3. He's sad. 　4. He has a pen. 　5. He's mad. 　6. He has a fast pet.	6. St: Listen and repeat in chorus individually. Write. T: Dictate the sentences twice. Allow students to check workbook p. 38 if absolutely necessary. Check student work. Be certain that the address has been filled in appropriately at the upper right hand corner.
7. Let's read.	7. T: Review all flash cards and sentence strips. Be certain students have a good grasp of learnings up to this point before moving forward. St: Respond.

Student Workbook p. 40
   Sound Symbol Association
   Jj, Gg, Zz, Cc, Kk, Ii

SIGHT WORDS
For Jj: jet, jam
For Gg: get, gas, flag
For Zz: zip
For Cc: cat, cap
For Kk: Ken, kiss
For Ii: ill, it, in

*VISUALS for Jj
   63 jet   23 jacket (on Sam)

VISUALS for Gg:
   64 gas   66 glasses   68 gardener
   65 glass   67 garage   69 girl

VISUALS for Zz:
   70 zip code

VISUALS for Cc:
   71 cat   73 cook   75 cup of coffee
   72 credit card   74 calendar   76 cap

VISUALS for Kk:
   77 kitchen   78 kiss

VISUALS for Ii:
   79 in   80 Indian

*or any visuals providing practice in the respective sounds.

INSTRUCTIONAL AIDS

an alphabet wall chart or alphabet flash cards
old magazines or a copy of the jet, gas, zip code, cat, kitchen, Indian on p. 374 of this guide
pink and yellow flash cards

----

*INSTRUCTION   ACTIVITY RESPONSE

1. This is the letter "___".   1. T: Print "___" on the board.

2. What's the name of this letter?   2. St: "___"

3. This is a capital "___".   3. T: Print capital "___" on the board.

4. We use capital "___" for   4. T: Say or write on the board a
   names and for the first word   student's name beginning with
   of a sentence.   "___" or provide a name.

*Provide instruction for each letter separately.

5. What's the name of this letter?

6. This is a small "___".

7. What's the name of this letter?

8. The sound of the letter "___" is
   /j/ as in jet, 63
   /g/ as in gas, 64
   /z/ as in zip code, 76
   /c/ as in cat, 71
   /k/ as in kitchen, 77
   /ĭ/ as in Indian, 80

9. Listen and repeat:
   /j/ jet, jacket. Also,
   (June, July)
   /g/ gas, glass, glasses,
   garage, gardener, girl
   /z/ zip code
   /c/ cat, credit card, cook,
   calendar, cup of coffee, cap
   /k/ kitchen, kiss
   /ĭ/ ill, Indian

10. What's the sound of "___"?

11. Let's write.

12. Open your book to p. 40.
    Your "home phone" is the same
    as your telephone number.

13. Capital "___" is for names and
    for the first word of a sentence.
    Let's write capital "___".

14. Let's write a small "___".

15. What's the name of this letter?

---

5. St: "___" or "capital ___".

6. T: Print "___" on the board.

7. St: "___"

8. T: Show the respective visuals.
   St: Listen and repeat the words
       three times.

9. T: Show visuals. Teach students
      to make the respective sounds.
      Model each word separately.
   St: Listen and repeat.
   T: Elicit words students may know
      beginning with the respective
      sounds.

10. St: "/ /"
    T: Repeat steps 8-10 if students
       have difficulty.

11. T: Draw writing lines on the board.
       ─────────────── Demonstrate
       how to write "___".
    St: Practice on the board.

12. St: Open books to p. 40. Fill
        in number, a dash or "none"
        above "home phone".

13. T: Demonstrate on the writing lines.
    St: Write a row of capital "___".
        in the workbook.

14. T: Demonstrate on the writing lines.
    St: Write a row of "___" in the workbook.

15. St: "___"
    T: Prompt if necessary.

16. Listen and repeat: "/ /" ____ , ____

17. Let's make a card.

18. Hold up the "____" card when you hear a word that begins with the sound "/ /".

19. For /j/:
June, sister, family, jacket,
July, nickel, elbow, juice,
hot dog, state, January, yes, etc.
For /g/:
you, girls, comb, name,
gardener, great, fine, grapefruit,
ham, June, jacket, go, etc.
For /z/:
sat, foot, zip code, lemon
secretary, zoo, teacher, zipper
Ann, zebra, Sam, city, etc.
For /c/:
penny, calendar, desk, doctor
coffee, cream, student, no,
map, cake, bed, cabbage, etc.
For /k/:
kiss, ham, dime, keys, man,
house, kitchen, Kentucky,
ankle, Kansas, bank, ketchup, etc.
For /ĭ/:
elbow, ankle, Illinois, how,
Indian, pin, ill, in, doughnut,
letter, Indiana, Italy, etc.

20. What's the name of this letter?

21. What's the sound of "____"?

16. T: Repeat vocabulary listed in item #9 and other words students provide. Model each word separately.
    St: Listen and repeat.

17. St: Take a pink 3 x 5 card. Write the capital and small letter on one side Staple or tape a magazine picture with the appropriate initial sound or a copy of the jet, gas, zip code, cat, kitchen or Indian on p. 374 of this guide to the back of the card.
    T: Assist if necessary. Make a 5 x 8 flash card.

18. T: Demonstrate activity.

19. T: Model each word.
    St: Hold up the "____" card when words beginning with "/ /" are modeled.

20. T: Point to or write "____".
    St: "____"

21. St: "/ /"

22. Review previously learned letters and sight words.	22. St: Respond.
23. What's this word?	23. T: Write "pet" on board. St: pet
24. Read this.	24. T: Erase the "p". St: et
25. Let's make a new word.	25. T: Write a "j" in front of "et". St: jet
26. This is a jet.	26. T: Sketch a simple picture of a jet.
27. Read this.	27. T: Write "am" on the board. St: am
28. Let's make a new word.	28. T: Write a "j" in front of "am".
29. I put jam on my bread.	29. St: Read "jam" in chorus and individually. T: Optional, bring jam to class.
30. Let's read these words.	30. T: Write "jet" and "jam" on the board or 5 x 8 flash cards. St: Read in chorus and individually.
31. Repeat concept in steps 22-30. Sight words for Gg: get(s), gas, flag, ("g" in final position) for Zz: zip (code) for Cc: cat, cap for Kk: Ken, kiss for Ii: ill, it, in	31. T: Write the words on the board. St: Listen and repeat.
32. Let's write.	32. St: Write a row of each sight word on lined paper. A master for lined paper is provided on p. 396 of this guide.
33. Let's make flash cards.	33. St: Make yellow 3 x 5 flash cards of the sight words.*

*See p. 8 of this guide for the suggested uses of the sight word flash cards and p. 10 for the suggested uses of the Language Master.

34. Optional, decoding:*
   Let's read.

34. T: Write these words on the board.
   St: Read.

an	**and**	**J**	**C**	**ick**	**ip**	**ill**	**in**
ban	band	jell	cab	Dick	dip	Bill	bin
can	hand		call	kick	hip	dill	fin
fan	land		cap	lick	lip	fill	kin
pan	sand			Nick	nip	gill	pin
tan				pick	sip	hill	sin
				sick	tip	Jill	tin
				tick		kill	
						mill	
						pill	
						sill	
						till	

ag	**iss**	**ab**	**en**	**end**	**it**
bag	kiss	cab	Ben	bend	bit
gag	miss	dab	den	lend	fit
lag		gab	hen	send	hit
nag		jab	Ken		kit
sag		lab	men		mit
tag		nab	pen		pit
flag		tab	ten		sit

*See p. 7 of this guide for discussion and suggestions regarding decoding.

Student Workbook p.41
Jj, Gg, Zz, Cc, Kk, Ii
Reading/Writing Sentences

SIGHT WORDS
age, pen, flag, lamp,
bed, cat, jet, hand

VISUALS

69 girl	33 bed
39 pen	71 cat
50 flag	63 jet
45 lamp	5 hand

STRUCTURE
It's a _____ .

INSTRUCTIONAL AIDS
yellow flash cards

INSTRUCTION

1. Today is _____ 's birthday. She's 10 years old.

2. How old is she?

3. "What's your age?" is the same as "How old are you?"

4. What's her age?

5. What's this word?

6. Optional: My age is ___ . I'm ___ years old. What's your age?

7. Open your books to p. 41.

8. Write your age.

9. Optional: Let's sing "Happy Birthday".

10. It's a pen.

11. What is it?

12. What is it?

ACTIVITY/RESPONSE

1. T: Show visual 69, draw a cake and candles. Write today's date and the date for ten years ago.

2. St: (She's) 10.

3. T: Write the word "age" on the board.
   St: Listen.

4. T: Point to "age". Prompt if necessary.
   St: 10

5. St: age

6. St: Respond.

7. T: Point to the word "age" and model.
   St: Repeat "age".

8. St: Fill in their age and close books.

9. St: Sing.

10. T: Show visual 39 and model the sentence.
    St: Listen and repeat in chorus and individually.

11. St: It's a pen.

12. T: Repeat instruction 10 and 11 for all vocabulary items on p. 41. Show respective visuals and model responses.
    St: Listen, repeat and respond.

13. Read the words.	13. T: Write the six vocabulary items on 5 x 8 cards. St: Read the words in chorus and individually.
14. Let's read the sentences.	14. T: Model the example: It's a pen. St: Complete all sentences orally.
15. Let's write.	15. St: Complete the sentences on p. 41. T: Check student work for accuracy and legibility.
16. Let's make some cards.	16. St: Make yellow 3 x 5 flash cards of "bed" only if cards have already been for the other sight words. Staple or tape a copy of the corresponding picture of each word, some of which are on p. 374 of this guide, to the back of each card.* Make a yellow 3 x 5 card of "It's" with "It is" on the back. and of "age" with the student's age on the back.
17. Optional: Write the word for the picture.	17. T: Devise a "match" worksheet as demonstrated on p. 74 of this guide. St: Match.
18. Optional: Let's read the words.	18. T: Have students read the sight words for this lesson. St: Read.
19. Optional, decoding: What's the first (last) letter in (bed) ?	19. St: Respond.

*See p. 8 for suggested uses of the flash cards and p. 10 for suggested uses of the Language Master.

Student Workbook   p. 42

SIGHT WORD
it, isn't

VISUALS
39 pen	33 bed
50 flag	71 cat
45 lamp	63 jet
	5 hand

STRUCTURE
It isn't a _____ .

INSTRUCTIONAL AIDS
yellow flash cards

INSTRUCTION

1. What is it?

2. What's the first letter in the word "pen"?

3. What's the last letter in the word "pen"?

4. What letter says /ĕ/?

5. Spell "pen".

6. Repeat steps 1-4 for flag, lamp, bed cat, jet and hand.

7. Is this a hat?

8. It isn't a hat. It's a pen.

9. Repeat steps 7-8 for flag, lamp bed, cat and jet until students can express the sentences with confidence, good pronunciation, stress and intonation.

ACTIVITY/RESPONSE

1. T: Hold up visual 39 or a real pen.
   St: It's a pen.

2. St: "p"
   T: Write "p" on the board.

3. St: "n"
   T: Write "n", for example "p n"

4. St: "e"

5. St: "p-e-n" in chorus and individually.

6. T: Show respective visuals.
   St: Respond.

7. T: Hold up visual 39 or point to a pen.
   St: Shake heads or say "no".

8. St: Listen and repeat in chorus and individually.
   T: If necessary, pound out the rhythm of the sentences on the table with your hand.
   Listen for correct stress and intonation.

9. T: Show respective visuals.
   St: Respond.

10. Repeat steps 7-8 for classroom items or the visuals on the back of the alphabet flash cards for further practice if necessary.

10. St: Respond.

11. Let's read.

11. T: Write "It isn't a hat. It's a pen." on the board. Optional: make Language Master Cards as suggested in item 12 on p. 10 of this guide. Model.
    St: Read in chorus and individually.

12. Read these words.

12. T: Point to individual words in the sentence. Contrast "It, It's."
    St: Read.

13. Read these sentences.

13. T: Write on the board as many of the sentences on p. 42 as necessary. Model.
    St: Read in chorus and individually.

14. Open your books to p. 42.

14. St: Open books.

15. What is it?

15. T: Point to the pen in the sample box.
    St: It's a pen.

16. Read the sentences.

16. T: Point to the sentences in the sample box.
    St: Read.

17. Let's read.

17. T: Call out items #1-6.
    St: Read aloud filling in the missing words orally.

18. Let's write.

18. St: Complete the sentences.
    T: Check for accuracy and legibility. Make sure "phone" has been completed at the upper right hand corner.

19. Let's make cards.

19. St: Make a yellow 3 x 5 card of "It" and another of "isn't" with "is not" on the back.*

---

*Reminder: The flash cards and sentence strips must be reviewed frequently. When possible, put sight words on Language Master Cards. See p. 10 of this guide for uses of the Language Master.

Student Workbook p.43
Reading

SIGHT WORDS
Hi, Jan, OK, She's, not, well, sick, He's, tall, sing

INSTRUCTIONAL AIDS
Yellow flash cards

INSTRUCTION

1. Open your books to p. 43.

2. Please write.

3. This is Sam and this is Ken.

4. Who is he?

5. Optional:
   What are they doing?

6. Listen.
   Hi, Ken.
   Hi, Sam.
   Is Jan OK?
   She's not well.

7. Listen and repeat.

8. Read.

9. Optional: Read the sentences.

10. Optional: Fix the sentences.

ACTIVITY/RESPONSE

1. St: Open books.
   T: Point to "zip code".

2. St: Write their zip code.

3. T: Point to the respective characters.
   St: Listen.

4. St: Respond.

5. T: Model: (They're) shaking hands.
   St: Repeat in chorus and individually.

6. T: Write "Sam" on the board and write "Ken" about 2 feet apart. When modeling Ken's words stand under the word "Ken". This gives the students the idea that the written words are a dialogue spoken by Sam and Ken and that they are not to read "Sam" and "Ken".
   St: Listen.
   T: Model again.

7. T: Model dialogues line by line.
   St: Repeat in chorus and individually.

8. St: One student (group) takes the part of Sam. Another student (group) takes the part of Ken and role play.

9. T: Make sentence strips. See p. 14 for the suggested uses of sentence strips.

10. T: Cut up sentence strips into separate components.
    St: Reorganize dialogue in a pocket chart or on the table.

11. Look at the pictures in #2-8 on p. 43 and repeat instructions 1-10.
    a) Identify and discuss visuals.
    b) Add optional vocabulary and structures. (She's asleep. She has a fever.)
    c) Model sentence(s) for the students.
    d) Optional: point out the /sh/ in "she" and "she's"; the unit sound of /k/ in "ck" in "sick"; and the /sm/ in "small".
    e) Optional: make sentence strips

12. Optional: Let's write.

13. Decoding:
    a) Point out that the letter "Ii" sometimes sounds like its own name as in the word "Hi".
    b) Substitute "b", "f", "s", "t" for the "w" in well.
    c) Substitute "D", "k", "l", "N", "p", "R", "t" and "w" for "s" in sick.
    d) Substitute "k", "r", and "w" for the "s" in sing.

14. Mechanics: Point out the question mark after the question in item #1.

15. Grammar: Remind students that "'s" is the same as "is" in "She's" and "He's". Point out that "is not" is the same as "isn't" as in the sentence "She's not well."

16. Optional, opposites:
    sick/well
    ill/well

11. St:
    a) Repeat in chorus and individually.
    b) Practice.
    c) Repeat.
    d) Listen.

    e) Read and unscramble.

12. St: Write the sentences on p. 43 on lined paper. A master for lined paper is provided on p. 396 of this guide.

13. St:
    a) Listen.

    b) Decode bell, fell, sell, tell.
    c) Decode Dick, kick, lick, Nick, pick, Rick, tick, wick.
    d) Decode king, ring, wing.

14. St: Listen.

15. St: Listen.

    St: Listen.

89

17. Optional, snyonyms:
    sick/ill
    fine/OK
    well/fine

18. Let's make cards.

19. Optional: Study these words (sentences).

17. St: Listen and substitute synonyms in rereading sentences in item #1.

18. St: Make yellow 3 x 5 cards of the sight words. Opposites and synonym cards should look like this:

    $\boxed{\text{sick}/\text{well}}$

    T: Make corresponding 5 x 8 cards.

19. T: Assign some sight words for spelling or sentences for dictation.

Student Workbook p. 44
Reading/Writing

SIGHT WORDS
the, mall, takes, pill

VISUALS
81 Ben Lee at the mall
82 Jan is sick.

INSTRUCTIONAL AIDS
yellow flash cards

INSTRUCTION

1. Look at the picture. This is Ben Lee.

2. Who is he?

3. Ben is at the mall.

4. Where is he?

5. Optional: Ben is shopping.

6. Optional: What's he doing?

7. Look at Ben's arms. He has many things.

8. What does he have?

9. He has a small lamp.

10. What does he have?

11. He has tennis balls.

12. What does he have?

ACTIVITY/RESPONSE

1. T: Point to visual 81.
   St: Listen.

2. St: (He's) Ben (Lee).

3. T: Name a familiar mall for comprehension.
   St: Listen and repeat.

4. St: He's at the mall.
   T: Prompt, if necessary.

5. St: Listen and repeat.

6. T: Model.
   St: (He's) shopping.

7. T: Role play.
   St: Listen.

8. T: Point to visual. Wait to see if any students can provide a response.
   St: a lamp, balls
   T: Prompt, if necessary.

9. T: Point to the lamp.
   St: Repeat in chorus and individually.

10. T: Point to the lamp.
    St: He has a small lamp.
    T: Prompt, if necessary.

11. T: Point to the balls and draw a tennis racquet if necessary.
    St: Repeat in chorus and individually.

12. T: Point to the tennis balls.
    St: He has tennis balls.
    T: Prompt, if necessary.

13. Look at Ben's face. Ben's glad. I'm glad.

14. Ben's glad.

15. Optional: Let's read.

16. This is the same.

17. Is this the same?

18. Is this the same?

19. Decoding:
    a) Point out the similarities in the words "mall" and "small". Demonstrate how the word "ten" is imbedded in the word "tennis".
    b) Optional: Point out the /ē/ sound in "ee" of Lee. It sounds like the name of the letter "e". Replace the "L" in Lee with b, f, g, s, t.
    (c) Optional: Point out the /sm/ in small, /gl/ in glad, and /sh/ in she.

13. T: Point to Ben's happy face. Point to your own smiling face.
    St: Listen and repeat.

14. T: Repeat and review as necessary.
    St: Respond.

15. T: Write the story on the board, overhead projector or sentence strips prior to reading from the book. Model.
    St: Read in chorus and individually.
    T: Observe for pronunciation, stress and intonation.

16. T: Review "same" and "different" if necessary. Point to "is" and "'s".
    St: Listen.

17. T: Write on the board: "Ben Lee's at the mall. Ben Lee is at the mall."
    St: Yes.

18. T: Write on the board: "Ben's glad. Ben is glad."
    St: Yes.
    T: Repeat instruction if necessary. Ideas:
    a) Write "'s" and "is" in a different color from the rest of the sentences for emphasis.
    b) Write a sentence with one form of "is" in it and have students change it to the other form.

19. St:
    a) Listen.

    b) Listen and decode.

    c) Listen.

20. Mechanics: Point to the capitals in the name "Ben Lee". Point out the capital "H" in the word "He" because it's the first word of a sentence. Point to the periods at the end of sentences.

20. St: Listen.

21. Adjective placement: Cover the word "small" and uncover it to emphasize the placement of the adjective between the article and the noun. Have students say and write original sentences. For example, "She has a small cat." or "Dad has a small hat."

21. T: Write "a small lamp" on the board.
    St: Listen, say and write.

22. Optional, opposites:
    a small lamp
    a large lamp
    What's this?

22. T: Draw pictures on the board to demonstrate or simply act out small and big. Have students substitute "man", "ball", "hat", and "house" for "lamp".
    St: Respond "small man", "a large man".
    T: Prompt, if necessary.

23. Optional, vocabulary development:
    small - little
    large - big

23. St: Repeat the phrases in instruction 22, substituting vocabulary items.

24. Read the sentence.

24. T: Write each sentence of the story on a separate sentence strip.
    St: Read the sentences in chorus and individually.

25. Optional: Fix the sentences (words).

25. T: Scramble the individual sentences (words) from the sentence strips.
    St: Unscramble.
    T: See p. 14 for suggested uses of the sentence strips and p.10 for suggested uses of the Language Master.

26. Open your books to p. 44.
    Read and write.

27. Optional: Write.

28. Look at the pictures.

    a) Point to "is" and "'s".
    b) Decoding: "pill and ill" replace "p" with b, d, f, h, J, k, m, n, s, t, w
    c) Mechanics: point out all capitals, periods, apostrophes.
    d) Opposites: sick/fine
       Synonyms: sick/ill; fine/OK
    e) Vocabulary development: substitute "medicine" and "aspirin" for "pill".
    f) Optional: make sentence strips, cut and scramble the words.

29. Open your books to p. 44.
    Read and write

30. Optional: Write.

31. Optional: Assign vocabulary in the stories for a spelling quiz or the sentence to be learned for dictation.

32. Let's make cards.

---

26. St: Fill out the blank after the word "age" and complete the reading and writing activities for the story in item #1.
    T: Check student work for accuracy and legibility.

27. St: Write the story on writing paper. A master for lined paper is provided on p. 396 of this guide.

28. T: Point to visual 82. Repeat the strategies listed in story #1 for story #2.
    St: a) Note they are the same.
        b) Listen and decode.
        c) Listen.
        d) Listen and repeat.
        e) Listen and repeat sentence substituting new vocabulary.
        f) Unscramble.

29. St: Read and complete the writing activities for the story in item #2.
    T: Check student work for accuracy and legibility.

30. St: Write the story on writing paper. A master for lined paper is provided on p. 396 of this guide.

31. St: Study.

32. St: Make yellow 3 x 5 cards of the optional sight words. Cards for opposites and and synonyns should look like this:

    | sick / fine |

Student Workbook p. 45
Review

VISUALS
81 Ben at the mall
82 Jan is sick.

INSTRUCTION	ACTIVITY/RESPONSE
1. Let's review.	1. T: Review learnings of p. 45 from visuals 81 and 82. St: Respond.
2. Unscramble the sentences.	2. T: Scramble sentence strips from p. 44. St: Unscramble.
3. Listen and write.	3. T: Write the sentences on the board in cloze style. Dictate sentence from student workbook p. 44. St: Fill in the blanks.
4. Open your books to p. 45 and write.	4. St: Open books and fill in information at the upper right hand corner. T: Duplicate sample box on p. 45 on the board.
5. I'm going to say the sound of a letter.	5. T: Read the directions. St: Listen.
6. Listen: /n/ nurse	6. St: Listen and observe that capital and small "n" have been circled. T: Repeat instructions and do as many examples as necessary.
7. # 1 /t/ telephone # 2 /j/ jet # 3 /z/ zip code # 4 /e/ elbow # 5 /k/ kitchen # 6 /g/ girl # 7 /l/ lamp # 8 /i/ Indian # 9 /b/ ball #10 /k/ cat	7. St: Listen and circle the capital and small of the letter which the teacher has sounded out.
8. Look at box #1 at the bottom.	8. T: Point to the item. Read the directions.

9. Ben Lee is <u>at</u> the mall. He <u>has</u> a small <u>lamp</u> and tennis <u>balls</u>. Ben's <u>glad</u>.

10. Look at box #2 at the bottom.

11. Jan is <u>sick</u> in bed. She takes <u>a</u> pill. She's fine.

9. T: Repeat each sentence twice.
   St: Listen and fill in the blanks.

10. T: Point to the item.
    Re-read the directions.

11. T: Repeat each sentence twice.
    St: Listen and fill in the blanks.
    T: Check student work for accuracy and legibility. Be certain that the city, state, and zip code have been filled in appropriately at the upper right hand corner.

Student Workbook p.46
Blends and Digraphs I
sh, sm, gl, fl, sp, sk, ch

SIGHT WORDS
Mr., Mrs., Miss, Ms., ship,
small lamp, glass, flag
spoon, desk, watch, chair

VISUALS for "sh":
83 ship   84 shoe

VISUALS for "sm":
45 small lamp   85 No smoking

VISUALS for "gl":
65 glass   66 glasses

VISUALS for "fl":
50 flag   86 flowers

VISUALS for "sp":
87 spoon   88 speed limit

VISUALS for "sk":
58 desk   89 skate

VISUALS for "ch":
90 chair   92 chalkboard   94 watch
91 checkout   93 China

*or any visuals providing practice in the respective sounds.

INSTRUCTIONAL AIDS
any form (application or identification) or a copy of the form on p. 399 or 400 of this guide
old magazines or a copy of ship, no smoking sign, glass, flag, spoon, skate, chair and desk on
   p. 375 of this guide
yellow and green flash cards

INSTRUCTION	ACTIVITY/RESPONSE
1. Sometimes on forms, we see these words.	1. T: Write "Mr., Mrs., Miss, Ms." on the board. Point them out on any type of a form.
2. What's this word?	2. T: Point to "Mr.". Model, if necessary. St: Mister
3. "Mr." is used for all men.	3. St: Listen. T: Name each man in the class as "Mr._____." If there aren't any men, refer to Ben Lee on p. 38 of the student workbook as "Mr. Lee" or "Mr. Ben Lee".

4. Who's "Mister"?

5. What's this word?

6. "Mrs." is for married women.

7. Who's "Mrs."?

8. What's this word?

9. "Miss" is for single women.

10. Who's "Miss"?

11. This word is "Ms."

12. We can use "Ms." for all women, married or not.

13. Who's "Ms."?

14. Read these words.

15. Let's make some cards.

16. Optional: Let's write.

4. St: "All men" or name Mr. _____ in the class.

5. T: Point to "Mrs.".
　　 Model, if necessary.
　St: Mrs.

6. T: Identify married women in the group and refer to them as "Mrs. _____".

7. St: "Married women" or name Mrs. _____ in the class.

8. T: Point to "Miss".
　　 Model, if necessary.
　St: Miss

9. T: Identify single women in the group and refer to them as "Miss _____".

10. St: "Single women" or name Miss _____ in the class.

11. St: Listen and repeat.

12. St: Listen and identify all women as "Ms. _____".

13. St: all women

14. T: Write "Mr., Mrs., Miss, Ms." on 5 x 8 cards. Scramble.
　St: Read.

15. St: Write the four words on yellow 3 x 5 cards.
　 T: Check for correct use of capitals and periods.

16. St: Practice saying/writing:
　　 a) their names using "Mr., Mrs., Miss or Ms." on lined paper. A master for lined paper is provided on p. 396 of this guide.
　　 b) the names of other students using "Mr., Mrs., Miss or Ms."
　　 c) the forms for themselves and their spouse: "Mr. and Mrs. _____".

17. Open your books to p. 46.

18. Circle the correct word.

19. Close your books.

20. This is a ship (shoe).
    This is a shirt.

21. "Ship", "shoe" and "shirt" start with /sh/.

22. "s" and "h" together say /sh/ as in the word "ship".

23. Repeat, "/sh/ ship".

24. Repeat instruction:
    for /sm/ small lamp, no smoking
    for /gl/ glass, glasses (glad)
    for /fl/ flag, flower
    for /sp/ spoon, speed limit
        (spell, Spring, Spanish)
    for /sk/ desk, skate (skirt)
    for /ch/ chair, check out,
        chalkboard, China, watch

25. Let's make some cards.

17. St: Open books.

18. T: Point to the upper right hand corner.
    St: Circle "Mr., Mrs., Miss, or Ms." and complete writing their names.

19. St: Close books.

20. T: Show respective visuals and point to someone's shirt.
    St: Repeat.
    T: Continue practice until vocabulary is learned.

21. St: Listen.

22. T: Hold up visual 83 of the ship. Write "ship" on the board.

23. St: Listen and repeat.
    T: Underline the "sh" and elicit any words students may know beginning with /sh/ such as "she".

24. T: Show the respective visuals. Write the sight words on the board. Underline the blends and digraphs.
    St: Listen and repeat.
    T: Elicit any words students may know beginning with the respective blend or digraph.

25. St: Write each of the 7 blends and digraphs on one side of a green 3 x 5 card. Staple or tape a magazine picture of the respective sounds or a copy of the ship, no smoking sign, glass, flag, spoon, skate and chair on p. 375 of this guide to the back of each corresponding card.

Student Work   p. 47
  Blends and Digraphs I
  Review

VISUALS

83 ship	87 spoon
45 small lamp	90 chair
65 glass	58 desk
50 flag	94 watch

INSTRUCTION

REVIEW

1. What is it?

2. What two letters say /sh/?

3. Repeat #1 and 2 for the <u>sm</u>all lamp, <u>gl</u>ass, <u>fl</u>ag, <u>sp</u>oon, <u>ch</u>air, de<u>sk</u>, and wa<u>tch</u>.

4. Is it a ship?

5. Can you spell/write "ship"?

6. Repeat #4 and 5 for the <u>sm</u>all lamp, <u>gl</u>ass, <u>fl</u>ag, <u>sp</u>oon, <u>ch</u>air, de<u>sk</u>, and wa<u>tch</u>.

7. Review previous letter sounds, sight words, visuals and sentence strips as necessary.

NEW LESSON

1. Open your books to p. 47.

2. Listen and write.

ACTIVITY/RESPONSE

1. T: Hold up visual 83 of the ship or the visual side of the "sh" flash card.
   St: (It's a) ship.

2. St: s-h
   T: Assist if necessary.

3. T: Hold up the visuals or the visual side of the respective flash cards.
   St: Respond.
   T: Assist if necessary.

4. T: Hold up any visual other than that of the ship.
   St: It isn't a ship. It's a _____.

5. St: Spell s-h-i-p or write it on the board or paper, if possible.
   T: Allow students to look to p.46 if necessary.

6. T: Hold up appropriate visuals.
   St: Respond.

7. St: Respond.

1. St: Open books.

2. T: Write "wat __ __" on the board. Say "watch".
   St: Fill in the "c-h".
   T: Demonstrate activity as frequently as necessary.

101

Student Work p. 47
   Blends and Digraphs I
   Review

VISUALS
83 ship   87 spoon
45 small lamp   90 chair
65 glass   58 desk
50 flag   94 watch

INSTRUCTION

ACTIVITY/RESPONSE

REVIEW

1. What is it?

   1. T: Hold up visual 83 of the ship
         or the visual side of the
         "sh" flash card.
      St: (It's a) ship.

2. What two letters say /sh/?

   2. St: s-h
      T: Assist if necessary.

3. Repeat #1 and 2 for the small lamp, glass, flag, spoon, chair, desk, and watch.

   3. T: Hold up the visuals or the
         visual side of the respective
         flash cards.
      St: Respond.
      T: Assist if necessary.

4. Is it a ship?

   4. T: Hold up any visual other than
         that of the ship.
      St: It isn't a ship. It's a _____

5. Can you spell/write "ship"?

   5. St: Spell s-h-i-p or write it
          on the board or paper,
          if possible.
      T: Allow students to look to p.46
         if necessary.

6. Repeat #4 and 5 for the small lamp, glass, flag, spoon, chair, desk, and watch.

   6. T: Hold up appropriate visuals.
      St: Respond.

7. Review previous letter sounds, sight words, visuals and sentence strips as necessary.

   7. St: Respond.

NEW LESSON

1. Open your books to p. 47.

   1. St: Open books.

2. Listen and write.

   2. T: Write "wat __ __" on the board.
         Say "watch".
      St: Fill in the "c-h".
      T: Demonstrate activity as
         frequently as necessary.

3. Listen and write.

   #1 ship
   #2 small
   #3 chair
   #4 desk
   #5 flag
   #6 glass
   #7 spoon
   #8 watch

4. Close your books.
   Let's make a sentence.

5. Repeat Step #4 for each scrambled sentences if necessary.

6. Open your books to p. 47.
   Let's write.

3. St: Write the appropriate blend or digraph.
   T: Check student work.

4. T: Write the scrambled sentence in the sample box on a sentence strip. Cut it into the components.
   St: Unscramble the sentence.
   T: Demonstrate if necessary.

5. St: Unscramble the sentences.

6. St: Write the sentences:
   #1 Jan is not sick.
   #2 Ben and Sam sing.
   #3 It's a small glass.
   #4 Ben Lee has tennis balls.
   #5 His zip code is 31579.
   T: Check for accuracy and legibility. Make sure "State" and "Zip" have been filled in at the upper right hand corner.

Student Workbook p. 48
Sound Symbol Association
Rr, Oo, Vv, Ww, Xx, Yy, Uu, Qq

SIGHT WORDS
For Rr: red
For Oo: on open
For Vv: very
For Ww: walk, what('s)
For Xx: exit
For Yy: yes, you
For Uu: up, us
For Qu, qu: quiet

*VISUALS for Rr:
   95 restrooms   96 restaurant   97 refrigerator

VISUALS for Oo:
   98 operator   100 onion   101 orange
   99 on   116 Open

VISUALS for Vv:
   102 vacuum   103 vegetables

VISUALS for Ww:
   94 watch   105 woman   107 waiter
   104 walk   106 window   108 wallet

VISUALS for Xx:
   109 x-ray

VISUALS for Yy:
   110 yo-yo

VISUALS for Uu:
   111 umbrella

VISUALS for Qu, qu:
   112 quiet   113 quarter

*or any visuals providing practice in the respective sounds.

INSTRUCTIONAL AIDS
an alphabet wall chart or alphabet flash cards
old magazines or a copy of the restrooms, operator, vacuum, woman, x-ray, yo-yo, umbrella,
   quarter on p. 376 of this guide
pink and yellow flash cards
a red crayon

INSTRUCTION

1. This is the letter "__".

ACTIVITY/RESPONSE

1. T: Print "__" on the board.

**Provide instruction for each letter separately.

2. What's the name of this letter?

3. This is a capital "__".

4. We use capital "__" for names and for the first word of a sentence.

5. What's the name of this letter?

6. This is a small "__".

7. What's the name of this letter?

8. The sound of the letter "__" is
   /r/ as in restrooms
   /o/ as in operator, on, onion, orange
   /v/ as in vacuum
   /w/ as in watch
   /x/ as in x-ray
   /y/ as in yo-yo
   /u/ as in umbrella
   /qu/ ("q" is never alone. It is always together with "u") as in quarter

9. Listen and repeat:
   /r/ restrooms, restaurant, refrigerator
   /ŏ/ operator, on, onion, orange
   /v/ vacuum
   /w/ watch, walk, woman, window, waiter, wallet
   /x/ x-ray (also Mexico)
   /y/ yo-yo (also yes, you)
   /ŭ/ umbrella (also up, us, under)
   /qu/ quiet, quarter (also question)

10. What's the sound "__"?

11. Let's write.

2. St: "__"

3. T: Print capital "__" on the board.

4. T: Say or write on the board a student's name beginning with the letter or provide a name.

5. St: "__" or "capital __".

6. T: Print "__" on the board.

7. St: "__"

8. T: Show the respective visuals.
   St: Listen and repeat the words three times.

9. T: Show respective visuals. Teach students to make the respective sounds. Model each word separately.
   St: Listen and respond.
   T: Elicit words students may know beginning with the same sounds.

10. St: "/ /"
    T: Repeat steps 8-10 if students have difficulty.

11. T: Draw writing lines on the board.
    ────────────
    ──────────── Demonstrate how to write "__".
    St: Practice on the board.

12. Turn to p. 48 in your workbook. Fill in the blank.

13. Capital "__" is for names and for the first word of a sentence. Let's write "__"

14. Let's write a small "__".

15. What's the name of this letter?

16. Listen and repeat: "/ /" ___, ___

17. Let's make a card.

18. Hold up the "__" card when you hear a word that begins with the sound "/ /".

---

12. T: Point to upper right hand corner.
    St: Open books to p. 48 and complete personal information.

13. T: Demonstrate on writing lines.
    St: Write a row of capital "__" in the workbook.

14. T: Demonstrate on the writing lines.
    St: Write a row of "__" in the workbook.

15. St: "__"
    T: Prompt, if necessary.

16. T: Repeat vocabulary listed in item #9 and other words students provide. Model each word separately.
    St: Listen and repeat.

17. St: Take a pink 3 x 5 card. Write the capital and small letter on one side. Staple or tape a magazine picture with the appropriate initial sound or a copy of the restrooms, operator, vacuum, woman, x-ray, yo-yo, umbrella, quarter on p. 376 of this guide to the back of the card.
    T: Assist if necessary. Make a 5 x 8 flash card.

18. T: Demonstrate activity.

19. For /r/: watch, no, June, restaurant, red, yes, road, pen, run, bat, rat
For /ŏ/: apple, operator, pen ship, onion, fine, orange, dad, on
For /v/: vest, rest, dad, in, very, mom, best, vacuum, window, refrigerator, vase, stop
For /w/: vest, watch, red, yes, window, what, fat, gas, west, hello, nurse, we
For /x/: (Usually words do not begin in "x" in English. For listening comprehension, words beginning with 'ex" may be used.) x-ray, boy, ill, exit, coffee, extra, girl, woman
For /y/: yes, no, cat, elbow, July, yo-yo, you, Hello, ill, chair, pet, yellow
For /ŭ/: us, yes, umbrella, red, slow, under, on, in, first, code up, snow
For /qu/: cake, what, it, quarter, glass, quiet, mister, question, number, street, quit, bed

19. T: Model each word.
St: Hold up the "___" card when words beginning with "/ /" are modeled.

20. What's the name of this letter?

20. T: Point to or write "___".

21. What's the sound of "___"?

21. St: "/ /"

22. Review previously learned letters, blends, digraphs, sight words and sentence strips as deemed appropriate.

22. St: Respond.

23. When instruction for "Rr" is completed, ask: What's this word?

23. T: Write "bed" on board.
St: bed

24. Read this.

24. T: Replace "b" with "r".
St: red

25. This is red and this is red.

25. T: Point to objects that are red.
St: Listen.

26. Is this red?

26. T: Point to objects of various colors.
    St: "Yes, it is." or "No, it isn't."
    T: Model response if necessary.

27. Let's write.

27. St: Write a row of "red" on the writing lines on p. 49.

28. Let's make a card.

28. St: Make a yellow 3 x 5 card for "red" and draw a swatch of red on the back with a red crayon or marker.
    T: Make a 5 x 8 flash card.

29. When instruction for "Oo" is completed, say: This word is "on".

29. St: Listen and repeat.

30. The pen is "on" the desk and the _____ is "on" the _____ .

30. T: Write "on" on the board.
    St: Listen and repeat.
    T: Demonstrate as frequently as necessary.

31. Where's the _____?

31. St: (It's) on the (_____).

32. Read this word.

32. T: Write "pen" on the board.
    St: "pen"

33. This is "open". The name of the letter is "o" and the sound is sometimes /ō/.

33. St: Listen and repeat.

34. This store is open.

34. T: Show visual 116.
    St: Listen and repeat.

35. Let's write.

35. St: Write a row of "on" and "open" on the writing lines on p. 49.

36. Let's make cards.

36. St: Make a yellow 3 x 5 card for "on" and "open".
    T: Make a 5 x 8 flash card.

37. Repeat concept of ESL vocabulary development and sight word recognition
    for Vv: very
    for Ww: walk, what('s)
    for Xx: exit
    for Yy: yes, you
    for Uu: up, us
    for Qu: quiet

37. T: Write the words on the board.
    St: Listen and repeat.

38. Let's write.

38. St: Practice writing the sight words on the writing lines on p. 49.

39. Let's make cards.

39. St: Make yellow 3 x 5 flash cards of the sight words.*

40. Optional, vocabulary review: Look and hold up the card.

40. St: Gather all the sight word flash cards from this lesson in their hands and hold up the correct card when the teacher demonstrates the word.

41. a) T: Open the door and say "The door is ____".
    b) T: Point up and say "This is ____"
    c) T: Nod yes and say "This is ____"
    d) T: Point to a red object and say "This is ____"
    e) T: Hold up right forefinger to the lips and say "/sh/".
    f) T: Walk around the room.
    g) T: Point to a student.
    h) T: Put a pen on a book and say "The pen is ___ the book."
    i) T: "Out" is the same as ____

41. St: Hold up
    a) open
    b) up
    c) yes
    d) red
    e) quiet
    f) walk
    g) you
       on
    i) exit

42. Upon completion of sound symbol association for all the letters of the alphabet, play the games in Appendix D, p. 406-407.

42. St: Play.

*See p. 8 of this guide for the suggested uses of the sight word flash cards and p. 10 for the suggested uses of the Language Master.

43. Optional, decoding:
    Let's read.

43. T: See p. 7 for further discussion and suggestions.
    St: Decode.

an	**ag**	**all**	**ell**	**ick**	**at**	**in**
ran	rag	wall	bell	Rick	rat	win
van	wag		cell	wick		
			dell	quick		
			fell			
			jell			
			sell			
			tell			
			well			

od	**op**	**ot**	**ub**	**un**	**up**
cod	bop	cot	cub	bun	cup
nod	cop	dot	hub	fun	
pod	hop	got	pub	gun	**ut**
rod	mop	hot	rub	hun	but
sod	pop	jot	tub	pun	cut
plod	chop	lot		run	gut
	shop	not	**ud**	sun	hut
	flop	pot	dud		nut
		rot	mud		rut
		spot			shut

Student Workbook   p. 50
Rr, Ii, Vv, Ww, Xx, Yy, Uu, Qq
Visual Discrimination/Writing

SIGHT WORDS
Hello, thank, your, are, sex, how

INSTRUCTIONAL AIDS
yellow flash cards

INSTRUCTION	ACTIVITY/RESPONSE
1. Circle the word that is the same.	1. T: Copy the sample box on p. 50 onto the board. St: Circle the word that is the same. T: Demonstrate with as many examples as necessary.
2. Open your books to p. 50.	2. St: Open books.
3. Let's read these words.	3. T: Point to the words in items 1-10 at the top. Model. St: Read in chorus and individually. T: Establish meaning for the vocabulary.
4. Look at the box.	4. T: Point to sample box. Demonstrate that the circled word is the same as that outside the box.
5. Circle the word that is the same.	5. St: Complete exercise and personal information at the upper right hand corner. T: Check student work.
6. Let's read.	6. T: Point to items 1-3 at the bottom. Model. St: Read in chorus and individually.
7. Let's write.	7. St: Copy the sentences. T: Check for capitals and punctuation.
8. Optional: Let's make cards.	8. St: Make 3 x 5 yellow cards of any word in 1-10 at the top of p. 50 for which flash cards have not been made. See p. 8 of this guide for suggested uses of sight words.
9. Optional: Read.	9. T: Make sentence strips of items 1-3 at the bottom if you have not already done so.
10. Synonyms: "Hi" and "Hello" are same.	10. St: Listen. T: Demonstrate.
11. Decoding, h<u>ow</u>: bow, cow, now, vow	11. St: Decode.

Student Workbook   p. 51   VISUAL
Reading   1 Hello. How are you?

INSTRUCTION   ACTIVITY/RESPONSE

1. Listen.   1. T: Tape visual 1 above your head
                                               on the board and model dialogue
                                               #1 from p. 51.
                                           St: Listen. Do not open books until
                                               instructions have been completed.

2. Hi.   2. T: Stand under "A" facing "B".
                                               Gesture an extended hand for a
                                               hand shake.

3. Hello.   3. T: Stand under "B" facing "A".
                                               Shake hands with imaginary "A".
                                           St: Listen.

4. How are you?   4. T: Stand under "A" facing "B".
                                           St: Listen.

5. Fine, thank you.   5. T: Stand under "B" facing "A".
                                           St: Listen.

6. Repeat.   6. T: Divide half the class into "A"
                                               and other half into "B". Model.
                                           St: Repeat.
                                           T: Watch for proper stress, intonation
                                               and pronunciation.

7. You are "A" and you are "B".   7. T: Model.
                                           St: Groups and individuals assume roles
                                               and reverse upon completion.

8. Let's read.   8. T: Write the dialogue on the board
                                               or sentence strips.
                                           St: Read in chorus and individually.
                                           T: Model, if necessary.

9. Capital letters are for the first   9. T: Point to capital H and F.
   word of a sentence.   St: Listen.

10. This is a period. I write a period 10. T: Point to the periods.
    when I am finished.   St: Listen.

11. This is a question mark. I write   11. T: Point to the question mark.
    this after a question.   St: Listen.

111

12. This is a comma. I write it after "Fine" when I say "Fine, thank you."

13. Optional: Let's write.

14. Optional: Fix this.

15. Optional: Spell "_____".

16. Listen.

17. " 's" is the same as "is".

18. Optional: Let's write.

19. Let's read again. Put in your name.

20. Open your books to p. 51.

21. Let's read #1 and 2.

22. Read and write #3 and 4.

12. T: Point to the comma.
    St: Listen.

13. T: Erase the capitals in the dialogue on the board.
    St: Fill in the capital letters.
    T: Erase the punctuation.
    St: Fill in the punctuation.

14. T: Cut the sentence strips into the component parts and scramble them.
    St: Unscramble them in a pocket chart on the table or floor.

15. St: Spell "_____" aloud.

16. T: Repeat instructions 1-13 for dialogue #2 on p. 51.
    St: Listen, repeat, read, etc. Do not open books until instruction has been completed.

17. T: Write "What is" on the board. Cross out the "i" and replace it with an apostrophe: "What is" is "What's". Do the same for "name's".
    St: Listen and observe.

18. T: Repeat steps 13-15 for dialogue #2.

19. T: Model dialogue #2.
    St: Repeat and work in pairs.

20. St: Open books and fill in their address at the upper right hand corner.

21. St: Read in chorus and individually and assume roles.
    T: Students should have little or no difficulty reading these dialogues if all pre-reading activities have been completed.

22. St: Read silently and fill in the blanks.
    T: Check for accuracy of personal information and for items #3 and 4.

Student Workbook   p. 52
Writing Sentences

INSTRUCTION	ACTIVITY/RESPONSE
1. Open your books to p. 52.	1. St: Open books.
2. Let's read.	2. St: Read the six sentences individually filling in their own names when they read items #2, 4, 6. T: Model if necessary.
3. Let's write.	3. St: Copy and complete the sentences. T: Check for legibility, capitals and punctuation.
4. Optional: Let's write.	4. St: Practice writing the sentences again on any of the free writing pages in the workbook or on writing paper. A master for writing paper is provided on p. 396 of this guide.
5. Optional: Study the sentences for dictation.	5. St: Study. T: Dictate the sentences as a review at the beginning of the next class. St: Write sentences on the board or paper.

Student Workbook   p. 53, 54
Reading signs

SIGHT WORDS
watch your step, store, closed
No U Turn, stop, check out

VISUALS

112 Quiet	117 Closed
56 Exit	118 No U Turn
114 Watch Your Step	104 Walk
	16 Stop
115 Telephone	91 Check out
116 Open	

INSTRUCTIONAL AIDS
yellow flash cards

INSTRUCTION

1. These are signs.

2. What are these words?

3. Look at this picture.
   They're in the library.
   (There are many books in the library).

4. Optional: Where are they?
   How many people (men, women) are there in the library?

5. "sh" - Quite. "Q" and "u" are always together.

6. What's this?

7. This door is to go out.
   "EXIT" is a door to go out.

8. Read this.

9. He's running. He isn't looking.
   Be careful!

ACTIVITY/RESPONSE

1. T: Point to the words in each visual.
   St: Listen and repeat "signs".

2. St: (They're) signs.

3. T: Hold up visual #112.
   Listen.

4. St: (They're in the) library.
   (There are) 3 (2, 1) (in the library).

5. T: Hold up forefinger to the mouth.
   Write "Quiet" on the board.
   St: Repeat "quiet" in chorus and individually.

6. T: Point to the door in visual 56.
   St: (It's a) door.
   T: Prompt, if necessary.

7. St: Listen.
   T: Write "EXIT" on the board.
   St: Repeat in chorus and individually.

8. T: Point to "QUIET" and "EXIT".
   St: Read in chorus and individually.

9. T: Hold up visual 114 and role play the visual.

10.	WATCH YOUR STEP!	10. T: St:	Write the words on the board. Read in chorus and individually.
11.	What's the sound of these letters?	11. T: St:	Point to the "c - h" in "WATCH" and "s - t" as in "step". /ch/, /st/
12.	What words start with /ch/?	12. St: T:	Repond. Provide "chair" (chicken, cheeseburger)
13.	What is this?	13. T: St: T:	Hold up visual 115. (It's a) telephone. Write "telephone" on the board.
14.	Let's read.	14. St:	QUIET, EXIT, WATCH YOUR STEP and TELEPHONE from the board or the respective visuals.
15.	This is a store. It's open.	15. T:	Hold up visual 116. Write "STORE" and "OPEN" on the board.
16.	Let's read.	16. St:	Read "STORE" and "OPEN" in chorus and individually.
17.	What's the sound of these letters?	17. T: St:	Point to the "S-T" in "STORE". /st/
18.	What other words start with /st/?	18. St: T:	Respond if possible. Provide "step, street, state".
19.	Optional: It's a pot, broom, etc.	19. T:	Teach the vocabulary provided in the visuals.
20.	This store is closed.	20. T: St:	Show visual 117 and write "CLOSED" on the board. Listen and repeat.
21.	Read.	21. St:	Read "CLOSED" in chorus and individually.
22.	These two letters say /cl/.	22. T:	Point to the "C-L" in "CLOSED".
23.	What other words start with /cl/?	23. St: T:	Respond if possible. Provide "class".
24.	I see this sign on the street. It says "NO U TURN".	24. T: St: T:	Hold up visual 118 and write "NO U TURN" on the board. Listen and repeat. Draw a simple visual of a 2 lane street and demonstrate a "U" turn.

25. Read this sign.	25. St:	Read "NO U TURN" in chorus and individually.
26. This sign says "WALK". This is "walk".	26. T:	Hold up visual 104 and act it out. Listen and repeat.
27. Read this word.	27. T: St:	Write "WALK" on the board. Read in chorus and individually.
28. Let's read the signs.	28. T:	Re-read the signs.
29. Read this sign.	29. T: St:	Hold up visual 16. "STOP"
30. Stop means don't go.	30. St:	Listen.
31. What's the sound of these letters?	31. T: St:	Point to the "S-T" in "STOP". /st/
32. I see this sign in a food store.	32. T: St:	Hold up visual 91. Name some local food stores. Listen.
33. This says "CHECK OUT"	33. T: St:	Write "CHECK OUT" on the board. Listen and repeat.
34. Read this sign.	34. St:	Read "CHECK OUT".
35. What sound do these letters make?	35. T: St:	Point to the "C-H" in the sign. /ch/
36. What other words start with /ch/?	36. St: T:	Respond. Provide "chair".
37. Remember "c-k" sounds like /k/ as in "sick" and "check".	37. St:	Listen.
38. Open your books to p. 53 and 54.	38. St:	Read signs 1-10.
39. Let's make cards.	39. St: T:	Make yellow 3 x 5 cards of any of the signs for which cards were not previously made. Make 5 x 8 cards of the signs.
40. These are signs.	40. T:	Hold up the 10 5 x 8 flash cards of the signs.
41. What are they?	41. St:	(They're) signs.

42. Optional: Let's find more signs.

43. Optional: Vocabulary development from the visual on p. 53-4:
    #1 library
    #3 steps, stairs, shirt, pants
    #4 booth, pay phone
    #5 & 6 coffee pot, mirror, knives, brooms, etc.
    #8 traffic light
    #10 cash register

44. Look at #1-4 at the bottom on p. 54.
    Unscramble the sentences.

42. T: If possible, take students around the school building or grounds finding, reading and copying some significant signs. Use these for additional vocabulary development and sight words. Encourage students to bring in signs they've copied from around the community.
    St: Listen, read, copy, make cards, etc.

43. St: Listen and repeat.

44. T: Write the words on sentence strips and have students unscramble, if necessary.
    St: Unscramble the sentences.
    T: Check for accuracy and proper placement of the punctuation. Be certain that the personal information has been properly filled in at the upper right hand corner of each page.

Student Workbook p. 55
Blends and Digraphs II
wh, th, st, cl, ph, qu

SIGHT WORDS
Male, Female, whale, three
stop, quarter, telephone, clock

*VISUALS for "wh":
119 whale

VISUALS for "th":
120 three   121 3:30

VISUALS for "st":
15 students   17 stove   117 store
16 stop   55 stamp

VISUALS for "cl":
117 closed   121 clock (3:30)

VISUALS for "ph":
1 phone

VISUALS for "qu":
113 quarter   112 Quiet

*or any visuals providing practice in the respective sounds

INSTRUCTIONAL AIDS

any form (application or identification) or a copy of the form on p. 399-400 of this guide
old magazines or a copy of the whale, three, stop (sign), clock, (tele)phone and quarter on
   p. 377 of this guide
yellow and green flash cards

INSTRUCTION

1. Sometimes on forms we see these words.

2. This word says "Male".

3. "Male" means man. ____, you are a male. Put an X on or circle this word when you see it.

4. This word says "Female".

5. "Female" means woman. ____, you are a female. Put an X on or circle this word when you see it.

ACTIVITY/RESPONSE

1. T: Write "Male" and "Female" on the board. Point to these words on the form.

2. T: Point to "Male".
   St: Listen and repeat.

3. T: Name a male student and demonstrate.
   St: Listen.

4. T: Point to "Female".
   St: Listen and repeat.

5. T: Name a female student and demonstrate.
   St: Listen.

6. Who is a male, a female?

7. Read these words.

8. Let's make some cards.

9. This is a whale.

10. This word is "what".

11. "Whale" and "what" start with /wh/.

12. "w" and "h" together say /wh/ as in whale.

13. /wh/ whale, /wh/ what (also, what's, where, when, why, etc.)

14. Repeat instruction:
    for /th/ three, three-thirty (thanks, thank you, Thursday, thirteen, etc.)
    for /st/ students, stop, stove, stamp, store
    for /qu/ quarter, Quiet, (also, question)
    for /ph/ phone
    for /cl/ closed, clock

15. Let's make cards.

6. St: Name men and women in the class respectively.
   T: If students have difficulty distinguishing the meaning of "male" and "female", point out that both "man" and "male" start with "m".

7. St: Read.

8. St: Write "male" and "female" on yellow 3 x 5 cards. Students may write "man" and "woman" respectively on the backs of the cards.

9. T: Show visual 119 and write "whale" on the board.
   St: Listen and repeat in chorus and individually.

10. T: Write "what" on the board.
    St: Listen and repeat.

11. T: Circle the "w-h" in each word.

12. T: Hold up visual 119.
    St: Listen.

13. St: Listen and repeat.
    T: Elicit any words the students may know beginning with /wh/.

14. T: Show the respective visuals. Write the sight words on the board. Underline the blends and digraphs.
    St: Listen and repeat.
    T: Elicit any words the students may know beginning with the respective blend or digraph.

15. St: Write each of the 6 blends and digraphs on one side of a green 3 x 5 card. Staple or tape a magazine picture of the respective sounds or a copy of the whale, three, stop sign, clock, (tele)phone and quarter on p. 377 of this guide to the back of each corresponding card.
    T: Make corresponding green 5 x 8 cards.

16. Let's talk: Is it a ___?

17. What are the first two letters in this word?

18. Open your books to p. 55. Put an X in the correct box.

19. Look at the sample box.

20. "Closed" begins with "c-l".

21. Let's read.

22. Let's write.

23. Optional: Let's write.

24. Optional: Make Language Master cards with visuals corresponding to the blends and digraphs in lesson clipped onto the card. Students can be requested to:
    a. name the object
    b. pronounce the blend or digraph
    c. spell the blend or digraph

25. Let's make some cards.

16. T: Practice with all the visuals or 5 x 8 flash cards for this lesson.
    St: "Yes, it is" or "No, it isn't."

17. T: Show the visuals and then write the blend or digraph on the board for reinforcement.
    St: Respond for all the blends and digraphs.

18. St: Mark "Male" or "Female".

19. T: Model the question and response.
    St: Listen and repeat.

20. St: Observe that "c-l" has been filled in the blanks.

21. St: Read #1-6.
    T: Point out the punctuation and and capitals in the sentences.
    St: Observe.

22. St: Complete items #1-6.
    T: Check student work and be certain they have correctly marked "Male" or "Female".

23. St: Practice writing the sight words or sentences. A master for lined paper is provided on p. 396 of this guide.

24. T: See p. 10 of this guide for more suggestions for the use of this Language Master.
    St: Respond.

25. St: Make yellow 3 x 5 cards of the sight words and staple or tape a corresponding visual to the back of the card if necessary from p. 377 of this guide.

26. Let's read.

26. St: Read the sight words from the flash cards.
    T: See p. 8 of this guide for additional suggestions for the use of the sight word flash cards.

Reminder: Review flash cards and sentence strips frequently.

Student Workbook   p.56
   Blends and Digraphs II
   wh, th, st, cl, ph, qu

VISUALS

119 whale	113 quarter
120 three	3 telephone
16 stop	121 clock

INSTRUCTION

1. What is it?

2. What two letters say /wh/?

3. What other words start with /wh/?

4. Repeat steps #1-3 for three, stop, quarter, telephone and clock.

5. What's the word? Write the letters.

6. Open your books to p. 56. What's the word?

7. Write the letters.

8. Look at the words at the bottom. Let's read.

9. Look at this word. Put a line under /st/.

ACTIVITY/RESPONSE

1. T: Hold up visual 119 of the whale or the visual side of the "wh" flash card.
   St: (It's a) whale.

2. St: "w-h"
   T: Assist if necessary.

3. St: Respond.

4. T: Hold up the respective visuals or the visual side of the respective flash cards.
   St: Respond.
   T: Assist if necessary.

5. T: Write several words on the board with the blend or digraph in blanks. For example:
   __ __ ale, __ __ osed, de __ __ ,
   __ __ ore, etc.
   St: Respond and write.
   T: Assist if necessary.

6. St: Say the words for #1-6.

7. St: Fill in the blend or digraph.

8. St: Read words #1-12.

9. T: Write "first" on the board.
   St: Underline "s-t".
   T: Provide as many examples as necessary.

10. Listen and put a line under
the letters I say:

#1 /th/	#7 /wh/
#2 /st/	#8 /th/
#3 /wh/	#9 /st/
#4 /cl/	#10 /st/
#5 /ph/	#11 /cl/
#6 /st/	#12 /th/

10. St: Underline the letters.
    T: Check for accuracy and be certain that the social security number has been properly filled in.

Student Workbook   p. 57
  Rr, Oo, Vv, Ww, Xx, Yy, Uu, Qq
  Blends and Digraphs I, II
  Review

VISUALS	VISUALS	VISUALS
Blends and Digraphs I	Sound Symbol Association	Blends and Digraphs II
83 ship	95 restrooms	119 whale
45 small lamp	98 operator	120 three
65 glass	102 vacuum	16 stop
50 flag	94 watch	113 quarter
87 spoon	109 x-ray	3 phone
89 skate	110 yo-yo	117 closed
90 chair	111 umbrella	
	112 quiet	

INSTRUCTION

1. What is it?

2. What letter(s) does (flag) start with?

3. What letter(s) say(s) "/ /"? Write it.

4. Listen and circle the letter.

5. Open your books to p. 57. Listen and write:
   #1 /ŭ/ as in umbrella
   #2 /r/ as in red
   #3 /y/ as in yes
   #4 /x/ as in x-ray
   #5 /ŏ/ as in operator
   #6 /w/ as in watch
   #7 /v/ as in vacuum
   #8 /y/ as in yo-yo

6. Listen and write the 2 letters: /fl/.

ACTIVITY/RESPONSE

1. T: Hold up visuals for review.
   St: It's a _____ .

2. St: Respond.

3. St: Respond and write on the board.
   T: Review all sounds and repeat instruction as necessary.

4. T: Copy the sample box from p. 57 onto the board. Say "/v/ vacuum".
   St: Circle the "v".

5. St: Open books and circle the correct letter.

6. St: Write "f-l" on the board.
   T: Repeat as often as necessary.

7. Listen and write the 2 letters at the bottom of p. 57:

   #1 /gl/ as in glass
   #2 /st/ as in stop
   #3 /wh/ as in whale
   #4 /sk/ as in desk
   #5 /sm/ as in small
   #6 /ph/ as in phone
   #7 /cl/ as in clock
   #8 /qu/ as in quarter
   #9 /th/ as in three
   #10 /ch/ as in chair
   #11 /sp/ as in spoon
   #12 /sh/ as in shoe

7. St: Write the blends and digraphs.
   T: Check student work and personal information for accuracy.
   Review and repeat instruction.
   as necessary.

Student Workbook   p. 58
Extension, Reading signs

SIGHT WORDS
Speed limit 45 MPH
Hill, Push, Pull
Cashier, No Smoking,
Restrooms, women

VISUALS
112 Quiet	117 Closed
56 Exit	118 No U Turn
114 Watch Your Step	104 Walk
	16 Stop
115 Telephone	91 Check out
116 Open	

INSTRUCTION

1. What are these words?

2. Let's read the signs.

3. Let's read the signs.

4. Open your books to p. 58. Write your phone number and let's read more signs.

5. Where do you see sign #1?

6. Speed limit 45 M.P.H.

7. What do "s" and "p" say?

8. Limit means no more than 45. "M.P.H." means Miles Per Hour.

9. What does this say?

10. Read the sign.

11. "Hill" means the street is going up or down.

ACTIVITY/RESPONSE

1. T: Show group of visuals listed above.
   St: (They're) signs.

2. T: Show each visual individually.
   St: Read.
   T: Assist if necessary. Make sure students comprehend the meaning of each sign.

3. T: Review any signs students copied from the school building, school grounds or community.

4. St: Open books, fill in their phone numbers and read.
   T: Allow students to attempt decoding. They should be familiar with #6 and 7.

5. St: (It's on the) street.

6. T: Model and write it on the board.
   St: Read #1 individually and in chorus.

7. St: /sp/

8. T: Write Miles Per Hour on the board underlining the "M", "P" and "H". Explain and translate as necessary.

9. T: Write "ill" on the board.
   St: "ill"

10. St: Read "Hill" in chorus and individually.

11. T: Demonstrate.

12. Look at #3. What's this?

13. This says "Push".

14. Where is the sign "Push"?

15. What do "s" and "h" say?

16. Look at #4.

17. Look at #5. Where is this sign?

18. Read this.

19. Sometimes "i" and "e" together say /ē/. Read this.

20. Read #6.

21. What do "s" and "m" say?

22. Read #7.

23. Optional decoding: Let's read.
    for #1: (sp)eed
             deed
             need
             seed
             weed
    for #2: (h)ill
             bill
             dill
             fill
             kill
             mill
             nill
             pill
             sill
             till
             will
    for #3: (p)ush
             bush
    for #4: (p)ull
             bull
             full

12. St: It's a door.

13. T: Model and demonstrate "Push".
    St: "Push" in chorus and individually.

14. St: (At a) store, restaurant, etc.

15. St: /sh/

16. T: Model and demonstrate "Pull".
    St: "Pull" in chorus and individually.

17. St: (At a) store, restaurant, etc.

18. T: Write "sh" then "ash" then "cash"
    St: Decode progressively.

19. St: Listen and decode "cashier".
    T: Assist if necessary.

20. St: Read in chorus and individually.

21. St: /sm/

22. St: Read in chorus and individually.

23. St: Decode and read in chorus and individually.

127

24. Optional, opposites:
    for #3: push/pull
    for #6: no/yes
    for #8: men/women

25. Optional, vocabulary development: Other words for "restroom" are "bathroom", "washroom", "ladies' (men's) room" and "john".

26. Let's make cards.

27. These are signs.

28. What are they?

29. Optional: Let's find more signs.

24. St: Read and make 3 x 5 cards like this:

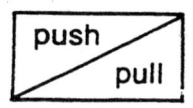

    ```
    push
        pull
    ```

25. St: Listen, repeat and make flash cards.
    T: Teach students to ask where the restroom is.

26. St: Make yellow 3 x 5 cards of the signs.
    T: Make 5 x 8 cards of the signs.

27. T: Hold up the 7 5 x 8 flash cards.

28. St: (They're) signs.

29. T: If possible, take students around the school building or grounds finding, reading and copying some significant signs. Use these for additional vocabulary development and sight words. Encourage students to bring in signs they've copied from around the community.

Student Workbook p. 59-62
Sound Symbol Association
Test

OBJECTIVES

Listening Comprehension: To determine if students can
1. Follow simple oral directions.
2. Associate at least one sound of each of the consonants with its written symbol.
3. Associate some short vowel sounds with the written symbols.
4. Associate the names of the letters with the written symbols.
5. Identify the numbers between 31-76.

Reading and Writing   To determine if students can
1. Complete the personal information requested at the upper right hand corner correctly without being reminded.
2. Understand and follow the directions as exemplified in the sample box.
3. Associate lower case letters with their respective capitals.
4. Write basic sight words and sentences when dictated.
5. Use commas, apostrophes, periods and question marks correctly.
6. Complete a simple identification form correctly.
7. Write numbers between 31-76 when dictated.

NOTES TO INSTRUCTOR:

1. There are too many test pages to administer in one sitting. Student fatigue may affect results. It is suggested that p. 59-60 and 61-62 be completed at different sittings. Allow students as much time as necessary to complete work.

2. Each letter is tested twice, once for the association of one of the sounds of the letter with its written symbol, and once for the association of the name of the letter with its corresponding symbol.

3. A large number of errors may indicate a full review of concepts taught up to this point, vision testing or a learning disability. Refer to p. 3 in the Introduction for further discussion.

4. For p. 59 and 60, read the directions and work out the example together.

p. 59 sample	/t/ as in table	7.	/ĭ/ as in Indian
1.	/n/ as in nickel	8.	/f/ as in father
2.	/s/ as in sink	9.	/ă/ as in apple
3.	/l/ as in lamp	10.	/h/ as in hot dog
4.	/b/ as in boy	11.	/m/ as in man
5.	/t/ as in teacher	12.	/qu/ as in quarter
6.	/p/ as in pan	13.	/g/ as in girl

p. 60 sample /b/ as in book
1. /ŭ/ as in umbrella
2. /ŏ/ as in operator
3. /r/ as in red
4. /y/ as in yes
5. /j/ as in jet
6. /ĕ/ as in exit
7. /z/ as in zip
8. /c/ as in coffee
9. /v/ as in vacuum
10. /d/ as in dime
11. /w/ as in woman
12. /k/ as in kitchen
13. /x/ as in x-ray

5. For p. 61, read and demonstrate the directions for the first exercise. For the second exercise, say the following letters:

	CAPITALS		SMALL
1.	I	1.	m
2.	C	2.	f
3.	K	3.	q
4.	L	4.	o
5.	E	5.	a
6.	U	6.	j
7.	H	7.	y
8.	Z	8.	d
9.	N	9.	x
10.	B	10.	v
11.	W	11.	g
12.	T	12.	s
13.	K	13.	p

6. For p. 62, dictate the following:

   1. It's a lamp.
   2. Fine, thank you.
   3. He's a man.
   4. What's your name?
   5. Hello.
   6. How are you?
   7. She's fine.
   8. 38 40 55 68 72

7. Check all student work as soon as possible. Be certain that the personal information has been correctly completed at the upper right hand corner of each test page.

Student Workbook   p. 63
   Colors

SIGHT WORDS
sex, white, black, brown,
red, green, blue, color

VISUALS
122 snowman   123 dress
 71 cat   124 plant
 57 desk   125 sweater

INSTRUCTIONAL AIDS
teacher made 5 x 8 flash cards with a different swatch of color on each including white, black,
   brown, red, green, and blue: ■   (black)

yellow flash cards
colored markers or crayons
sentence strip

STRUCTURE
What color is it?   It's _____ .

INSTRUCTION	ACTIVITY/RESPONSE
1. What do these letters say?	1. T: Write "ex" on the board. St: Respond.
2. Read this word.	2. T: Write "s" in front of "ex". St: Sex
3. "Sex" asks you "Are you a man or a woman?"	3. St: Listen.
4. If you are a man, mark male. If you are a woman, mark female.	4. T: Demonstrate. St: Listen.
5. Open your books to p. 63. Do this.	5. T: Point to the upper right hand corner. St: Open books and mark "M" or "F".
6. Let's make cards.	6. T: A card may already have been made for "Sex". If so, skip this step. St: Make a yellow 3 x 5 card with "Sex" on one side and "male" or "female" on the back. T: Make a 5 x 8 flash card.
7. Read this word.	7. St: Sex
8. Close your books and listen. These are colors.	8. T: Spread out the 6 teacher made 5 x 8 flash cards with color swatches on them. St: Listen and repeat.

9.	What are they?	9. St:	(They're) colors.
10.	What color is it?	10. T: St: T:	Hold up the white flash card. (It's) white. Model "It's white" if necessary.
11.	What color is it?	11. T: St:	Repeat instruction until students can identify white, black, brown, red, green and blue. Respond "It's _____ ."
12.	What color is it?	12. T: St:	Point to or name various objects in the classroom for practice. Respond.
13.	What color is the _____ ?	13. St:	Respond.
14.	Listen: /wh/ white. What 2 letters say /wh/?	14. St: T:	"w-h" Assist if necessary. Remind students of "whale" and "what".
15.	This is white and this is white.	15. T: St:	Show the 5 x 8 flash card of the color white and write "white" on the board. Listen and repeat.
16.	What's this?	16. T: St:	Point to the color and the word. white
17.	Let's make a card.	17. St:	Make a 3 x 5 flash card with a color swatch of white on one side and the word "white" on the other.
18.	Optional decoding: Read this: (wh)ite bite kite quite	18. T: St:	Cover the "wh" on the word "white". "ite" and decode.
19.	This is _____ and this is _____ .	19. T: St:	Repeat steps #15 - 17. Respond and make cards.

20. Optional decoding: Let's read.

   (bl)<u>ack</u>:   back   rack
                   Jack   sack
                   pack   tack
                   quack

   for (br)<u>own</u>:   down   gown

   for (r)<u>ed</u>:   bed   Ted
                     fed   wed
                     led

   for (gr)<u>ee</u>(n):   /ē/ as in Lee

   for (bl)<u>ue</u>:   due   Sue

20. St: Decode.

21. Optional reinforcement:
Hold up the color word.
What color is it?

21. T: Name or point to various classroom objects.
    St: Hold up the color word.
    T: Demonstrate as necessary.

22. Optional sound symbol association: Listen. What is the last letter?

22. T: black, brown, red, green
    St: k, n, d, n

23. Additional activities for review and reinforcement:
   a. Show me something that is this color.

23.
   a. T: Write the 5 color words on the board or place the cards in the pocket chart. Point to any color word.
      St: Point to (or name) an object that is that particular color.
      T: Demonstrate as necessary.

   b. Ask each other "What color is it?"

   b. St: Ask each other "What color is it?" holding up their 3 x 5 cards either on the color or word side and/or pointing to classroom objects.

24. This is "What color is it?"

24. T: Write the question on a sentence strip.
    St: Repeat in chorus and individually.

25. Read the words.

25. T: Cut the sentence strip into components. Hold up the individual words.
    St: Read.

26. This word says "color". Let's make a card.

26. St: Make a 3 x 5 card of the word "color".
    T: Make a corresponding 5 x 8 card.

27. What other words start with c /k/?

27. St: cat, cook, credit card, etc.

28. This is a snowman.

28. T: Hold up visual 122.
    St: Listen and repeat.

29. What is it?

30. What color is it?

31. Repeat steps 29-31 for cat, desk, dress, plant and sweater.

32. Open your books to p. 63 and read.

33. Optional:
 a. Write the colors.

 b. Learn the colors for spelling.
 c. What color is it?

29. St: (It's a) snowman.

30. St: It's white.
 T: Model, if necessary.

31. T: Hold up the respective visuals. Note: the plant is green and the pot is brown.
 St: Listen, repeat and respond.

32. St: Open books and read.
 T: Model, repeat and review as necessary.

33.
 a. St: Write the colors on writing paper. A master for lined paper is provided on p. 396 of this guide.
 b. St: Spell.
 c. T: Teach the other major colors such as yellow, orange and gray.

Student Workbook   p. 64

SIGHT WORDS
yellow, orange, gray

VISUALS
122 snowman   123 dress
 71 black cat   124 plant
 58 brown desk   125 sweater

INSTRUCTIONAL AIDS
teacher made 5 x 8 color flash cards from the previous lesson and new color cards including yellow, orange and gray.
yellow flash cards
colored markers or crayons

STRUCTURE

What color is it?	It's (color) .

INSTRUCTION	ACTIVITY/RESPONSE
1. Review all vocabulary, visuals, structures and flash cards from the previous lesson.	1. St: Respond. T: Do not proceed unless students have concepts, vocabulary, etc. down fairly well.
2. This color is yellow. It's yellow.	2. T: Hold up the 5 x 8 flash card with a swatch of yellow colored on it. St: Listen and repeat in chorus and individually.
3. What color is it?	3. T: Point to yellow classroom objects. St: It's yellow.
4. What is the first letter in /y/ yellow?	4. St: "y" T: Assist if necessary.
5. This is yellow and this is yellow.	5. T: Show the yellow swatch and write the word yellow on the board.
6. Let's make a card.	6. St: Make a 3 x 5 card with a yellow color swatch on one side and the word "yellow" on the other.
7. Repeat steps 2-6 for orange and gray.	7. St: Listen, repeat, respond and make cards.

8. Let's play.

8. T: Pair students.
   St #1: Lays all the color flash cards on a table with the color swatch up.
   St #2: Lays all the color flash cards on the table with the color word up.
   St #1,2: Match color swatches with color words. Upon completion students can check their own work.
   T: See also games in #11b on p. 8.

9. Optional:
   a. Write the words.
   b. Spell the words.

9. St:
   a. Write yellow, orange and gray. A master for lined paper is provided on p. 396 of this guide.
   b. Spell.

10. Open your books to p. 64. Let's read.

10. St: Open books and read all of the exercises supplying the correct response orally.

11. Circle the correct answer.

11. T: Point to the sample box. Demonstrate "red" has been circled. If necessary, provide further examples.
    St: Circle the correct color word.
    T: Check student work for accuracy. Make sure that the social security number has been correctly filled in at the upper right hand corner.

12. Optional: Label classroom objects by color for a few days.

12. St: Observe and digest.

Student Workbook p. 65
  Colors
  Blends and Digraphs III
  bl, gr, sw, br, pl, dr, sn

SIGHT WORDS
plant, sweater, dress, snowman

*VISUALS for "bl":
  71 black cat   125 blue sweater   126 blouse

VISUALS FOR "gr":
  12 green plant   127 grass

VISUAL for "sw":
  125 sweater

VISUALS for "br":
  58 brown desk   128 broom   129 brother

VISUAL for "pl":
  124 plant

VISUALS for "dr":
  123 dress   19 soft drink

VISUAL for "sn":
  122 snowman

*or any visuals providing practice in the respective sounds.

INSTRUCTIONAL AIDS

old magazines or a copy of the blouse, grass, sweater, broom, plant, dress and snowman on p. 378
  of this guide
yellow and green flash cards

STRUCTURE

What is it?   It's a (adjective) (noun).

INSTRUCTION	ACTIVITY/RESPONSE
1. This is a cat. It's black. It's a black cat.	1. T: Show visual 71. St: Repeat "It's a black cat" in chorus and individually.
2. What is it?	2. T: Show visual 71 and point to other black items in the classroom. St: It's a black <u>noun</u>.
3. "Black" starts with /bl/. "b" and "l" together say /bl/.	3. T: Write "black" on the board. St: Listen.

137

4. /bl/ black

5. What is this?

6. What color is it?

7. It's a blue sweater.

8. Listen: /bl/ blue. What are the first two letters in "blue"?

9. /bl/ blue, /bl/ black

10. This is a blouse and this is a blouse. What is it?

11. What are the first two letters in "blouse"?

12. What other words start with /bl/?

13. Repeat instruction:
    for /gr/ green, green plant, grass
    for /sw/ sweater
    for /br/ brown, brown desk, broom, brother
    for /pl/ plant (Please)
    for /dr/ dress, drink (drive)
    for /sn/ snowman (sneeze)

14. Let's make some cards.

15. Hold up the card with the letters when you hear a word that starts with those letters. For example: "black", hold up "b-l".

---

4. T: Underline the "b-l" in the word "black".
   St: Listen and repeat.

5. T: Hold up visual 125.
   St: It's a sweater.

6. St: It's blue.

7. St: Repeat.

8. St: b-l
   T: Assist, if necessary. Write "blue" on the board.

9. T: Underline the "b-l" in blue.
   St: Repeat.

10. T: Hold up visual 126 and point to a student's blouse.
    St: Listen and respond.

11. St: b-l
    T: Prompt if necessary.

12. St: Response will vary. (Bless you, blow, etc.)
    T: If there are no responses, do not add any vocabulary.

13. T: Show the respective visuals. Write the sight words on the board. Underline the blends and digraphs.
    St: Listen and repeat.
    T: Elicit any words students may know beginning with the respective blend or digraph.

14. St: Write each of the seven blends and digraphs on one side of a green 3 x 5 card. Staple or tape a magazine picture of the respective sounds or a copy of the blouse, grass, sweater, broom, plant, dress and snowman on p. 378 of this guide to the back of each corresponding card.

15. T: Demonstrate activity.

16.	blue, drive, snow, sweater, please, drink, brown, blouse, broom, etc.	16. St:	Hold up the respective green 3 x 5 card of the blends and digraphs.
17.	Optional: Hold up the picture when when you hear the word.	17. T:	Demonstrate activity.
18.	blouse, broom, dress, plant sweater, snowman, black cat	18. St:	Hold up the respective visuals.
19.	Spell /bl/ as in black, etc.	19. St:	Spell "b-l" and all the blends and digraphs learned up to this point.
20.	What does "b-l" say?	20. St: T:	/bl/, etc. Repeat question for all blends and digraphs learned up to this point.
21.	Open your books to p. 65.	21. St:	Open books.
22.	Look at the sample box. What is it?	22. T: St:	Point to the sample box. (It's a) black cat.
23.	"black" begins with "b-l".	23. St:	Observe that "b-l" has been filled in the blanks.
24.	Let's read.	24. St:	Read #1-6 orally.
25.	Let's write.	25. St: T:	Fill in the blanks for items #1-6. Check student work. Be certain students have correctly marked "M" or "F" at the upper right hand corner.
26.	Optional: Let's write.	26. St:	Practice writing the words (or the sentences on p. 65). A master for lined paper is provided on p. 396 of this guide.
27.	Optional: Make Language Master Cards with visuals corresponding to the blends and digraphs in this lesson clipped onto the cards. Students can be requested to: a. Name the object. b. Pronounce the blend or digraph. c. Spell the blend or digraph.	27. T: St:	See p. 10 of this guide for suggested uses of the Language Master. Respond.
28.	Let's make some cards.	28. St:	Make yellow 3 x 5 cards of the sight words and staple or tape a corresponding visual onto the back of each card from p. 378 of this guide.

29. Let's read.

30. Optional: To practice the "It's a adjective noun" structure, have teams write as many sentences as possible using the above structure with regard to classroom objects. For example: "It's a yellow pencil."

31. Optional: Study the sentences (sight words) on p.65 for dictation (spelling).

29. St: Read the sight words from the flash cards.
    T: See p. 8 of this guide for additional suggestions for the use of the sight word flash cards.

30. T: Demonstrate the activity.
    St: Write the sentences.
    T: Collect all the sentences and write them on a ditto. Do not include duplicates. Use the ditto as a reading exercise in the following class.

31. St: Study.

Reminder: Review all flash cards and sentence strips frequently.

Student Workbook   p. 66
   Colors, Blends and Digraphs II

VISUALS
122 snowman   123 dress
 71 black cat   124 plant
 58 brown desk 125 sweater

STRUCTURES

What color is the (noun) ?   The (noun) is (adjective) .

INSTRUCTION

ACTIVITY/RESPONSE

1. Review all the colors, vocabulary, structures, and blends and digraphs from the previous color lessons.

1. St: Respond.

2. What is it?

2. T: Hold up visual 122, snowman.
   St: (It's a) snowman.

3. What are the first 2 letters in snowman?

3. St: "s - n"

4. Listen: The snowman is white.

4. St: Listen and repeat in chorus and individually.

5. What color is the snowman?

5. St: The snowman is white.

6. Repeat steps 2-4 until students can respond: The (noun) is (adjective).

6. St: Respond.

7. Optional: Let's read.

7. T: Write the 6 sentences from p. 66 on sentence strips.
   St: Read.

8. Optional: Fix the sentences.

8. T: Cut the sentence strips into components and scramble them.
   St: Unscramble the sentences.

9. Open your books to p. 66 and read.

9. St: Open books and read the sentences filling in the correct response orally.

10. Let's write.

10. St: Fill in the correct vocabulary.
    T: Check for accuracy and legibility. Be certain that students complete their address correctly at the upper right hand corner.

11. Optional: Let's change the sentences.

11. T: Using the ditto suggested in item #30 on p. 140 of this guide, have the students rewrite all of the sentences. For example, change "It's a yellow pencil" to "The pencil is yellow." Write the new sentences on another ditto for a reading exercise for the following class.

12. Optional: Study the sentences on p. 66 for dictation.

12. St: Study and write.

13. Optional: What is your (personal information) ?

13. T: Review orally name, address, city, state, etc. for accuracy, pronunciation, stress and intonation.
    St: Respond.

Student Workbook   p. 67
Reading/Writing

SIGHT WORDS
my, hair, eyes

VISUALS
50 flag   16 stop
21 apple   88 Speed Limit
81 Ben Lee at   3 telephone
   the mall

INSTRUCTIONAL AIDS
yellow 3 x 5 cards

STRUCTURE
What color is the (noun) ?

The (noun) is (color) , (color) and (color).

INSTRUCTION

1. Read the words.

2. What is it?

3. It's the American flag.

4. The American flag is red, white and blue.

5. What color is the American flag?

6. Spell (color) .

7. What color is your flag?

8. This is an apple. What color is it?

9. Spell "red".

10. This is the stem. What is it?

11. What color is the stem?

12. Spell "brown".

13. This is Ben. He has yellow tennis balls.

ACTIVITY/RESPONSE

1. T: Hold up all the color word flash cards and the word "color".
   St: Read in chorus and individually.

2. T: Hold up visual 50, flag.
   St: (It's a) flag.

3. St: Repeat in chorus and individually.

4. St: Listen and repeat.

5. St: It's red, white and blue.

6. St: Spell.

7. T: If necessary, say "the (Mexican) flag" for comprehension.
   St: Respond.

8. T: Hold up visual 21.
   St: It's red.

9. St: Spell.

10. T: Point to the stem. Write stem on the board.
    St: (It's a) stem.

11. St: The stem is brown.

12. St: Spell.

13. T: Hold up visual 81, Ben Lee at the mall.

143

14.	What color are the tennis balls?	14. St:	(They're) yellow.
15.	Spell "yellow".	15. St:	Spell.
16.	What is it?	16. T: St:	Hold up visual 16, stop sign. (It's a) stop (sign).
17.	What color is it?	17. St:	It's red.
18.	Spell "red".	18. St:	Spell.
19.	What is it?	19. T: St:	Hold up visual 88, speed limit sign. (It's a) speed limit (sign).
20.	What color is it?	20. St:	It's black and white.
21.	Spell "black, white."	21. St:	Spell.
22.	What is it?	22. T:	Hold up visual 3, telephone.
23.	My home phone is (color) . What color is your telephone?	23. St:	"My home phone is (color)" or "I don't have a phone."
24.	This is "my". Sometimes "y" sounds like "i".	24. T: St:	Write "my" on the board. Listen and read "my".
25.	This is my (noun) . What's this?	25. T: St:	Point to a personal object of your own and then that of a student. This is my (noun) .
26.	Let's make a card.	26. St:	Make a yellow 3 x 5 flash card of "my".
27.	This is my hair.	27. T: St:	Hold up a piece of your hair. Repeat, touching a piece of their own hair.
28.	My hair is (color) . What color is your hair?	28. St: T:	My hair is (color) . Model, if necessary.
29.	What's the first letter in /h/ hair?	29. St:	"h"
30.	This is "hair".	30. T: St:	Write "hair" on the board. Read.
31.	Let's make a card.	31. St:	Make a yellow 3 x 5 card with "hair" on one side and a picture like on the other.
32.	These are eyes. My eyes are (color). What color are your eyes?	32. T: St:	Point to your eyes. My eyes are (color) .

33. This is "eyes".

34. Let's make a card.

35. Review all sentences and sight words from this lesson.

36. Open your books to p. 67. Let's read.

37. Write the colors.

38. Optional: Let's write.

33. T: Write "eyes" on the board.
    St: Read.

34. St: Make a yellow 3 x 5 card with "eyes" on one side and a picture like [eyes image] on the other.

35. St: Respond.

36. St: Open books and read.

37. St: Write in the colors for "hair color" at the upper right hand corner and for items #1, 5, and 6.
    T: Check for accuracy and legibility.

38. St: Write the sentences on p. 67 on writing paper.
    T: A master for lined paper is provided on p. 396 of this guide.

Student Workbook p. 68
Review
Blends and Digraphs I, II, III

VISUALS for Blends and Digraphs I
- 50 <u>fl</u>ag
- 65 <u>gl</u>ass
- 83 <u>sh</u>ip
- 85 No <u>sm</u>oking
- 87 <u>sp</u>oon
- 89 <u>sk</u>ate
- 90 <u>ch</u>air

VISUALS for Blends and Digraphs II
- 17 <u>st</u>ove
- 113 <u>qu</u>arter
- 115 <u>ph</u>one
- 119 <u>wh</u>ale
- 120 <u>th</u>ree
- 121 <u>cl</u>ock

VISUALS for Blends and Digraphs III
- 58 <u>br</u>own desk
- 71 <u>bl</u>ack cat
- 122 <u>sn</u>owman
- 123 <u>dr</u>ess
- 124 <u>gr</u>een <u>pl</u>ant
- 125 <u>sw</u>eater

INSTRUCTIONAL AIDS

all the green 3 x 5 cards of the blends and digraphs

INSTRUCTION	ACTIVITY/RESPONSE
1. What is it?	1. T: Hold up visual 50, flag. St: It's a flag.
2. What 2 letters say /fl/?	2. St: "f-l"
3. Repeat steps 1 and 2 for all the visuals.	3. St: Respond.
4. Read this.	4. T: Hold up the "fl" green 3 x 5 flash card. St: /fl/
5. Say some words that begin with /fl/.	5. St: flag, flowers, etc.
6. Repeat steps 4-5 for all of the blend and digraph flash cards.	6. St: Respond.
7. Optional: Match the cards with the visuals.	7. T: Spread all the visuals out. Distribute the 5 x 8 blend and digraph cards to the students. St: Match the cards with the visuals. T: Students can work in pairs using their 3 x 5 green flash cards.
8. Optional: Let's play.	8. T: Introduce any or all of the games suggested in 7h on p. 6 of this guide. St: Play.
9. Open your books to p. 68. Listen and and write the letters.	9. T: Demonstrate the activity on the board: W h ale St: Listen and write.

10. Listen and write the letters:
    #1 brown   #5 green
    #2 sweater #6 dress
    #3 black   #7 snow
    #4 plant   #8 blue

11. Listen. Circle the letters:
    /st/ as in stop.

12. Listen. Circle the letters.
    #1 /cl/ as in clock
    #2 /ch/ as in chair
    #3 /wh/ as in white
    #4 /gl/ as in glass
    #5 /fl/ as in flag
    #6 /th/ as in thank you
    #7 /dr/ as in dress
    #8 /sh/ as in shoe
    #9 /sm/ as in smoking
    #10 /pl/ as in plant

10. St: Write.
    #1 br   #5 gr
    #2 sw   #6 dr
    #3 bl   #7 sn
    #4 pl   #8 bl

11. T: Copy the sample box for the second exercise on p. 68 on the board.
    St: Circle the "st".

12. St: Circle the letters.
    #1 cl
    #2 ch
    #3 wh
    #4 gl
    #5 fl
    #6 th
    #7 dr
    #8 sh
    #9 sm
    #10 pl
    T: Check student work for accuracy. Be certain that "eye color" has been properly filled in.

Student Workbook   p. 69
  Blends and Digraphs IV
  sl, tr, cr, fr, pr, kn, tw

*VISUAL for "sl":
  130 slow

VISUAL for "tr":
  14 truck

VISUAL for "cr":
  72 credit card

VISUAL for "fr":
  51 fries

VISUAL for "pr":
  131 present

VISUAL for "kn":
  132 knife

VISUAL for "tw":
  133 twenty

SIGHT WORDS
slow, truck, credit card, fries, present, knife, twenty

*or any visuals providing practice in the respective sounds

INSTRUCTIONAL AIDS
old magazines or a copy of the slow sign, truck, credit card, fries, present, knife and twenty on
   p. 379 of this guide
yellow and green flash cards

INSTRUCTION

1. This is a sign. It says "slow".

2. Slow means 15-20 m.p.h., not fast.

3. What is this? What does it say?

4. "Slow" starts with /sl/. "S" and "l" together say /sl/.

5. /sl/ slow

6. What other words start with /sl/?

7. What's this?

ACTIVITY/RESPONSE

1. T: Hold up visual 130.
   St: Listen.

2. St: Listen.

3. St: (It's a) sign. (It says) slow.

4. T: Write "slow" on the board.
   St: Listen.

5. T: Underline the "s-l" in the word "slow".

6. St: Provide any words they know.

7. T: Hold up visual 14.
   St: It's a truck.

148

8. Listen: /tr/ truck. The first two letters in truck are "t - r".

9. What are the first two letters in /tr/ truck?

10. /tr/ truck

11. What other words start with /tr/?

12. What is it?

13. I use a credit card now and pay money later.

14. Listen: /cr/ credit. The first two letters in credit are "c - r".

15. What are the first two letters in /cr/ credit?

16. /cr/ credit card

17. What other words start with /cr/?

18. Repeat instructions:
    for /fr/ fries (Friday)
    for /pr/ present (pretty)
    for /kn/ knife (knee)
    for /tw/ twenty (twelve)

19. Let's make some cards.

20. Hold up the letter card when you you hear a word that starts with those letters. For example: "truck", hold up "tr".

21. sleep, twelve, Friday, tree, knee, twenty, slow, credit card, truck present, knife, pretty, etc.

---

8. St: Listen.

9. St: "t - r"
   T: Write "truck" on the board.

10. T: Underline the "t-r" in truck.
    St: Repeat.

11. St: Provide any words they know.

12. T: Hold up visual 72.
    St: It's a credit card.

13. St: Listen.

14. St: Listen.

15. St: "c - r"
    T: Write "credit card" on the board.

16. T: Underline the "c-r" in credit card.
    St: Repeat.

17. St: Provide any words they know.

18. T: Show the respective visuals. Write the sight words on the board. Underline the blends and digraphs.
    St: Listen and repeat.
    T: Elicit any words students may know beginning with the respective blend or digraph.

19. St: Write each of the 7 blends and digraphs on one side of a green 3 x 5 card. Staple or tape a magazine picture of the respective sounds or a copy of the slow sign, truck, credit card, fries, present, knife and twenty on p. 379 of this guide to the back of each corresponding card.

20. T: Demonstrate activity.

21. St: Hold up the respective green 3 x 5 card of the blends and digraphs.

22. Optional: Hold up the picture when you hear the word: fries, knife, slow, truck, present, twenty, credit card.	22. T: Demonstrate activity. St: Hold up the respective visuals.
23. Spell /sl/ as in slow, etc.	23. St: Spell "s - l" and all the other blends and digraphs learned up to this point.
24. What does "s-l" say?	24. St: /sl/, etc. T: Repeat question for all the blends and digraphs learned up to this point.
25. Open your books to p. 69.	25. St: Open books.
26. Look at the sample box. It's a "slow" sign.	26. T: Point to the sample box. St: Listen.
27. What is it?	27. St: Repeat "It's a slow sign" and observe that "s - l" has been filled in the blanks.
28. Let's read.	28. St: Read #1 - 6 orally. T: Model when necessary.
29. Let's write.	29. St: Fill in the blanks for items #1 - 6. T: Check student work. Be certain "zip" has been filled in at the upper right hand corner of the page.
30. Optional: Let's write.	30. St: Practice writing the sight words (or sentences) on p.69. T: A master for lined paper is provided on p. 396 of this guide.
31. Optional: Make Language Master cards with the visuals corresponding to the blends and digraphs in this lesson clipped onto the cards. Students can be requested to: a. Name the object. b. Pronounce the blend or digraph. c. Spell the blend or digraph.	31. T: See p. 10 of this guide for suggested use of the Language Master. St: Respond.
32. Let's make some cards.	32. St: Make yellow 3 x 5 ards of the sight words and staple or tape a corresponding visual onto the back of each card from p. 379 of this guide.
33. Let's read.	33. St: Read the sight words from the flash cards. T: See p. 8 of this guide for additional suggestions for the use of the sight word flash cards.

35. Optional: Study the sentences (sight words) on p. 69 for dictation (spelling).

35. St: Study.

36. Optional, opposites:
    slow/fast
    up/down

36. St: Make cards.

Reminder: Review all fash cards and sentence strips frequently.

Student Workbook p. 70
Blends and Digraphs IV

VISUALS
130 Slow (sign)   131 present
 14 truck   132 knife
 72 credit card   133 twenty
 51 fries

the yellow 3 x 5 sight word flash cards
 of the visuals above
the green 3 x 5 flash cards of
 Blends and Digraphs IV

INSTRUCTION

1. What is it?

2. What are the first two letters in the word "slow"?

3. Name some other words that start with /sl/.

4. Continue review as in steps #1 - 3. for the remaining visuals.

5. Optional: Match the cards with the visuals.

6. Optional: Let's play.

7. Listen. Spell the sound.
   /sl/ as in slow
   /tr/ as in truck
   /cr/ as in credit card
   /fr/ as in fries
   /pr/ as in present
   /kn/ as in knife
   /tw/ as in twenty

8. Open your books to p. 70. Let's read.

9. Circle the letters and write them in the blanks.

ACTIVITY/RESPONSE

1. T: Hold up visual 130, Slow sign.
   St: (It's a) slow (sign).

2. St: "s - l"

3. St: Respond, if possible.

4. St: Respond.

5. T: Spread out the visuals. Distribute the 5 x 8 blend and digraph cards to the students.
   St: Match the blend and digraph and sight word flash cards with the visuals.

6. T: Introduce any or all of the games suggested in 7h on p. 6 of this guide.
   St: Play.

7. St: Spell.
   s - l
   t - r
   c - r
   f - r
   p - r
   k - n
   t - w

8. St: Open books and read the sentences.

9. T: Duplicate the sample box on the board.
   St: Circle the "t-w" and write "t-w" in the blanks.

10. Do #1 - 6.

10. St: Write.
T: Check for accuracy. Be certain that the home phone has been filled in at the upper right hand corner.

Student Workbook   p. 71
Test
Blends and Digraphs I, II, III, IV

VISUALS for Blends and Digraphs I
   50 flag   83 ship   87 spoon
   65 glass   85 No smoking   89 skate
                                                    90 chair

VISUALS for Blends and Digraphs II
   17 stove   115 phone   120 three
   113 quarter   119 whale   121 clock

VISUALS for Blends and Digraphs III
   58 brown desk   122 snowman   124 green plant
   71 black cat   123 dress   125 sweater

VISUALS for Blends and Digraphs IV
   14 truck   72 credit card   131 present
   51 fries   130 slow   132 knife
                                                    133 twenty

INSTRUCTIONAL AIDS
all the green 3 x 5 flash cards of the blends and digraphs
all the flash cards of the vocabulary for the visuals listed above

---

INSTRUCTION	ACTIVITY/RESPONSE
1. What is it?	1. T: Hold up and review all the visuals. St: It's a _____ .
2. For each visual, ask: What are the first two letters in _____?	2. St: Respond.
3. Read the sounds and say a word that starts with the sound.	3. T: Hold up all the green 5 x 8 flash cards cards of the blends and digraphs. Provide the example /fl/ flag. St: Respond.
4. Spell the sounds. For example, spell /fl/ as in flag.	4. T: Review all the green 3 x 5 flash cards of the blends and digraphs. St: f - l
5. Let's read.	5. T: Show all the sight word flash cards of the blend and digraph visuals. St: Read.
6. Match the visual with the word (blend or digraph).	6. T: Spread out the visuals. St: Match the visuals with their 3 x 5 word (blend or digraph) cards.

7. Optional: Let's play.

8. Open your books to p. 71. Listen. Write the letters in the blanks.

9. Listen and write.
   #1 <u>kn</u>ife   #5 <u>cr</u>edit card
   #2 <u>fr</u>ies   #6 <u>sl</u>ow
   #3 <u>tw</u>enty   #7 <u>p</u>resent
   #4 <u>tr</u>uck   #8 <u>st</u>op

10. Look at the pictures and write the the letters in the blanks.

7. T: Introduce any or all of the games suggested in 7h of p. 6 of this guide.
   St: Play.

8. St: Open books and listen.
   T: Provide as many examples as necessary.

9. St: Write.
   #1 <u>k n</u>   #5 <u>c r</u>
   #2 <u>f r</u>   #6 <u>s l</u>
   #3 <u>t w</u>   #7 <u>p r</u>
   #4 <u>t r</u>   #8 <u>s t</u>

10. T: Point to the second exercise on p. 71. Demonstrate #1, the sample box.
    St: Write the blends and digraphs in the blanks:
    #1 <u>t h</u>   # 7 <u>d r</u>
    #2 <u>p h</u>   # 8 <u>k n</u>
    #3 <u>w h</u>   # 9 <u>g r</u>
    #4 <u>p l</u>   #10 <u>c h</u>
    #5 <u>s h</u>   #11 <u>f r</u>
    #6 <u>t r</u>   #12 <u>f l</u>

    T: Allow as much time as necessary. Check student work for accuracy. Be certain that students have completed the personal information at upper right hand corner. A large number of errors may indicate a full review, that you are progressing too quickly, or that the student is visually or learning disabled. See p. 3 of this guide for further discussion.

Student Workbook   p. 72
Test, Blends and Digraphs I - IV*

INSTRUCTION	ACTIVITY/RESPONSE
1. Open your books to p. 72.	1. T: Demonstrate #1, the sample box.
2. Look at the pictures and write the letters in the blanks.	2. St: Write the blends and digraphs in the sample box.

2. St (continued):

#1 gl	# 7 cr
#2 tw	# 8 sm
#3 sk	# 9 cl
#4 qu	#10 pr
#5 bl	#11 cl
#6 sp	#12 sw

T: Allow as much time as necessary.

3. Listen and write.
   #1 The dress is red.
   #2 The plant is green.
   #3 It's a white snowman.
   #4 It's a brown desk.

3. St: Listen and write.
   T: Dictate sentences only two times if possible. Check student work for accuracy. Be certain students have filled in city and state at the upper right hand corner. A large number of errors may indicate a full review, that you are progressing too quickly, or that the student is visually or learning disabled. See p. 3 of this guide for further discussion.

*When the students have successfully accomplished the objectives for sound symbol association of the letters and blends and digraphs, any of the games in Appendix D, Games for Duplication, may be played.

Student Workbook p.73
Letter sequence

SIGHT WORD
alphabet

INSTRUCTIONAL AIDS
an alphabet wall chart or the alphabet flash cards
a dictionary, a phone book
a yellow 3 x 5 card

INSTRUCTION

1. This is the alphabet.

2. What is it?

3. Each of these is a letter.

4. What are these?

5. How many letters are there?

6. Each letter has a name and a sound. What's the name and the sound of this letter?

7. It is important to know the alphabet: "a-b-c-d". Why?

8. This is a dictionary. It is a book of words. It tells me what words mean.

9. This is a telephone book. It has names, addresses and phone numbers for people in (city).

10. Open your books to p. 73.

11. Let's say the alphabet together.

ACTIVITY/RESPONSE

1. T: Point to the alphabet wall chart or the alphabet flash cards.

2. St: (It's the) alphabet.

3. St: Listen.

4. St: (They're) letters.

5. St: 26
   T: If students do not remember, recount the letters together.

6. St: Listen and respond.
   T: Review all the letters and their respective sounds.

7. St: For the telephone book and the dictionary.
   T: Assist if necessary.

8. T: Hold up the dictionary. Demonstrate how it goes according to alphabetical order.
   St: Listen.

9. T: Hold up the telephone book. Demonstrate how it goes according to alphabetical order.
   St: Listen.

10. St: Open books.

11. Cl:
    Gr: } Say the alphabet.

12. Say the "a, b, c, d, e, f, g" without looking.

12. T: Have students look at the first line of letters on p. 73, look away, and say the letters. Continue this activity until the first 7 letters are learned. At the next class period have students say first 7 letters and memorize the next seven. Repeat this activity for several days until the letters are learned in order.

13. Optional: Let's sing.

13. T: Teach students the alphabet via the alphabet song.

14. Optional: Once the alphabet has been memorized, have contest in which all students are timed to see who can say the alphabet correctly in the shortest period of time.

14. St: Say the alphabet.

15. Let's write.

15. St: Once the alphabet is memorized, try to write the alphabet without looking at the letters above on p. 73.
    T: Check for accuracy. Be certain that the personal information has been correctly filled in at the upper right hand corner of the page.

16. This word says "alphabet".

16. T: Write "alphabet" on the board. Point out the word "bet". Note that the "ph" says /f/ as in "phone".
    St: Listen and repeat "alphabet".

17. Let's make a card.

17. St: Make a yellow 3 x 5 card with "alphabet" on one side and perhaps the "a-b-c" on the back or the entire alphabet.
    T: Assist if necessary. Make a corresponding 5 x 8 flash card.

Student Workbook   p. 74
Letter sequence
Capitals

SIGHT WORDS
before, after

INSTRUCTIONAL AIDS
an alphabet wall chart or
alphabet flash cards
yellow 3 x 5 cards

INSTRUCTION

1. Let's say the alphabet.

2. Take out your alphabet cards. Mix them up. Fix them according to the alphabet.

3. The letter "a" is before "b", "m" is before "n", etc. (Also, "1" is before "2", "5" is before "6", etc.)

4. What letter is before "s"?

5. What letter is before?

6. Repeat instructions #3-5, teaching the concept of "after".

7. Let's make cards.

8. Open your books to p. 74. Write the capital letter that is before or after the letters.

ACTIVITY RESPONSE

1. St: Say the alphabet in chorus, groups and individually.

2. St: Work in pairs or individually. Shuffle the set of pink 3 x 5 alphabet cards and place them in alphabetical order in a pocket chart, on a table or on the floor.
   T: Check for accuracy.

3. St: Listen and digest the concept of "before".

4. St: "r"
   T: Continue activity until several examples have been given.

5. T: Write several letters on the board with a blank in front of them.
   St: Write the letters that come "before". For example: (n) o.

6. St: Listen, digest, respond, and write.

7. St: Make a yellow 3 x 5 card with "before" on one side and "a is before b" on the other and of "after" on one side with "b is after a" on the other.
   T: Assist if necessary and check for accuracy. Make corresponding 5 x 8 cards.

8. St: Open books and listen.
   T: Demonstrate the samples. Note that all the letters are capitals.

9. When you finish, write the alphabet at the bottom.

9. St: Write.
   T: Check student work and personal information at the upper right hand corner.

Student Workbook p. 75
   Letter sequence
   Small letters

INSTRUCTION	ACTIVITY/RESPONSE
1. What's this word?	1. T: Write "alphabet" on the board or hold up the 5 x 8 flash card. St: alphabet
2. What are these words?	2. T: Review "before" and "after" as indicated by the previous lesson. St: Respond.
3. Let's say the alphabet.	3. St: Respond in chorus and individually.
4. Let's say the alphabet.	4. St: Say the alphabet "round robin" fashion: Student #1 says "a", #2 says "b", etc.
5. Open your books to p. 75. Write the letters that are before and after.	5. St: Open books. T: Demonstrate examples. Note that all the letters in this exercise are small. St: Write the letters.
6. Write the alphabet.	6. St: Write the alphabet at the bottom of p. 75. T: Check student work. Be certain that "address" has been completed at the upper right hand corner.
7. Optional: Fold p. 76 in half, lengthwise. Number 1-13 on one side and 14-26 on the other. Write the alphabet, capitals and smalls. Write a word (any word, sight word, name, street, city, etc.) for each letter.	7. T: Demonstrate activity. St: Write. For example: 1. Aa address 2. Bb bed, etc.
8. Optional: Use p. 76 or a writing page to have students write the alphabet as a final test.	8. St: Write. T: A master for lined paper is provided on p. 396 of this guide.
9. Optional, game: Make two teams. Each person must say what they want in alphabetical order.	9. T: Demonstrate activity. For example: Team #1: I want an apple. Team #2: I want a bat. Team #1: I want a cat. St: Play.
10. Optional, alphabetizing: Teach students to alphabetize by first letter (then second and third if possible). Use a few sight word flash cards for this task.	10. St: Alphabetize. T: An alphabetizing worksheet is provided as an additional exercise in Appendix C, Exercises for Duplication on p. 398 of this guide.

Part 3 - Reading and Writing

**Correlated to Lessons 1-10 of
Delta's Effective ESL for the 21st Century
Personal Information, continued**

Part 3: Reading and Writing
Student Workbook   p. 77-194

OBJECTIVES

<u>Listening Comprehension:</u> The students will be able to:
1. Identify the numbers 77-100 and 200-1,000.
2. Recognize the sounds of English that correspond to the vocabulary introduced.
3. Comprehend the following personal information vocabulary when spoken: area code, height, weight, birthplace, country, place of birth, middle name, marital status, married, single, divorced, widowed, separated and name of spouse.
4. Identify common classroom and household items.
5. Identify the hours, half, quarter and three quarter hours and set a clock.
6. Identify common occupations such as doctor, nurse, waiter, etc.
7. Demonstrate an understanding of singular and plural.
8. Identify the days of the week.
9. Identify all American coins and calculate some monetary amounts.
10. Identify some fruits and vegetables.
11. Distinguish between "this" and "that", "these" and "those".
12. Differentiate between the articles "a" and "an".
13. Identify common locations: at the bank, beauty shop, laundromat, etc.
14. Distinguish between the expressions "here" and "there".
15. Use the following prepositions: in, on, at, under.
16. Identify family relationships within immediate family.

<u>Listening and Speaking:</u> The students will be able to:
1. Say the numbers between 77-100 and 200-1,000.
2. Recognize, enunciate and spell additional basic sight words.
3. Provide correct responses when asked their area code, height, weight, place of birth, middle name, marital status and name of spouse.
4. Describe actions and objects from pictures after readiness activities.
5. Ask and respond to simple questions such as <u>"Who/What/Where</u> <u>is/are</u> <u>he/she/it/they?"</u> and "What time is it?"
6. Use and respond to greetings such as "Good morning/afternoon/evening/night."
7. Use and respond to amenities such as "Please, thank you, Excuse me, I'm sorry."
8. Ask about a third person in the present tense and answer with the short "yes" or "no" response.

9. Ask "what" and "yes-no" questions with "this" and "that", "these" and "those".
10. Give answers using "it" with the present tense.
11. Ask/give the money value of coins and the price of lesson items.
12. Purchase produce items at a market.
13. Use "a" and "an" with lesson vocabulary.
14. Give an appropriate response when asked to identify lesson locations.
15. Use locative phrases with "in, on, at" and "under".
16. Comprehend and use the following homophones: they're/there, I/eye and to/two.
17. Give family relationships using the noun possessive ('s).
18. Read passages orally from controlled beginning materials and/or student/teacher prepared language experience stories with good pronunciation, intonation and expression.
19. Perform the above with acceptable pronunciation.

Reading and Writing:

The students will be able to:
1. Write the numbers 77-100, 200-1,000.
2. Fill in a basic form asking for personal information including: area code, height (ht.), weight (wt.), birthplace, country, place of birth, middle (name), married, single, divorced, widowed, separated, marital status, signature, sign here, and name of spouse.
3. Read and write basic sight words and lesson sentences.
4. Demonstrate comprehension of specific vocabulary by matching pictures with words, using synonyms and antonyms, filling in blanks, classifying words and composing sentences from sentence parts.
5. Recognize some compound words such as notebook, afternoon, airplane, salesman, etc.
6. Recognize word forms and endings such as plural -s and verbal -s.
7. Recognize the following homophones: they're/there, I/eye, and to/two.
8. Recognize some generalizations about some word structures such as the c-v-c in the "pen".
9. Recognize some generalizations about some sound patterns such as the /oo/ sound in noon and shoe; the /ē/ sound in street and each; or the /ō/ sound in Joe and doughnut.
10. Recognize, comprehend and use the following contractions: ___'m, ___'s, ___'re, ___n't and o'clock.
11. Convert sentences into questions.
12. Complete written activities in the workbook and teacher prepared exercises.

13. Capitalize the names of people, I, the first letter of a sentence, the days of the week (and the months).
14. Punctuate with a period at the end of a sentence, a comma in a short answer, a question mark after questions. and an apostrophe for contractions and possessives.
15. Sign their name and write letters, words and sentences in legible cursive.
16. Accurately copy a story/dialogue from the board/book.
17. Read dialogues after they have been practiced orally.
18. Demonstrate comprehension of reading selections by answering the following types of questions: what, who, what color, where, when, and how many.

Student Workbook p. 79-80
Lesson One, Section II
What is it?

SIGHT WORDS
pencil, book, notebook, door, window, chalkboard, table

VISUALS

10 table	58 desk
32 notebook	90 chair
35 book	92 chalkboard
39 pen	94 watch
40 pencil	106 window
50 flag	121 clock
57 door	

INSTRUCTIONAL AIDS
yellow flash cards

STRUCTURE
What is it?   It's a (pen).

INSTRUCTION

1. A pen. It's a pen.

2. A _____ . It's a _____ .

3. Show me a (book).

4. What is it?

5. Let's read these words.

6. This word is "pencil". "Pen" is in "pencil".

7. How do you spell "pencil"?

ACTIVITY/RESPONSE

1. T: Hold up the object or visual 39.
   St: Listen and repeat.

2. T: Repeat instruction for all of the vocabulary in this lesson.
   St: Listen and repeat.

3. Cl:
   St: Hold up or point to a (book).

4. T: Hold up a visual from this lesson.
   St: It's a _____ .
   T: Repeat for all of the visuals in this lesson until students can identify the objects with acceptable pronunciation.

5. T: Write "pen, flag, chair, watch, clock, desk" on the board or hold up the 5 x 8 cards of these words. Students who have studied Part 2 of this book should recall them fairly easily.
   St: Read the words in chorus and individually.

6. T: Write "pencil" on the board or a yellow 5 x 8 card. Cover up the "cil".
   St: Listen and repeat "pencil".

7. St: Respond.

167

8. Show me a pencil.	8. St: Hold up or point to a pencil.
9. Let's make a card.	9. St: Make a yellow 3 x 5 card with "pencil" written on one side. Staple or tape a magazine picture of a pencil on the other side if possible.
	T: Make a corresponding yellow 5 x 8 card. Repeat steps 6-9 for book, notebook, door, window, chalkboard and table.
10. What two letters say /fl/?	10. St: f - l
11. What word starts with /fl/?	11. T: Hold up the lesson visuals.
	St: Point to or say "flag".
	T: Repeat steps 10-11 for /sk/ desk, /ch/ chair, chalkboard and watch, /cl/ clock.
12. Optional, syllabication: A syllable is a sound a word makes. For example, "pen", one sound.	12. T: Pound out "pen" on a table to demonstrate "pen" makes only one sound. Repeat the process, saying student names and pounding out the syllables until students achieve the concept of syllable.
	St: Listen.
13. How many syllables are there in "pencil"?	13. St: two
	T: Repeat question for all the vocabulary words in the lesson.
14. Optional, compound words: Sometimes, I can make one word by putting 2 words together. For example "Rest" and "rooms" together say "Restrooms". "Snow" and "man" together say "snowman".	14. T: Write "Rest" and "rooms", "snow" and "man" on the board.
	St: Listen.
15. What are the two words in notebook (and chalkboard)?	15. St: Respond.
16. Optional, alphabetizing: Let's put these words in order according to the alphabet.	16. St: Alphabetize the 3 x 5 cards for this lesson or alphabetize words on a worksheet devised by the instructor.
	T: Check for accuracy.
17. Open your books to p. 79 and write.	17. T: Point to the upper right hand corner.
	St: Open books and write their first name.

18. Let's read.

19. Let's read again.

20. Let's write.

21. Optional: Assign the words to be studied for a spelling quiz for the following class.

18. T: Model all of the questions and responses on p. 79 and 80 supplying the missing words on p. 80.
    St: Listen and repeat in chorus and individually.

19. St: Read each item on p. 79-80 and/or work in pairs taking turns asking "What is it?" and responding.

20. St: Fill in the blanks on p. 80 and the color of their eyes.
    T: Check for accuracy including capitals, periods and question marks.

21. St: Study.

Student Workbook   p. 81-82   **VISUALS**
                                                (from previous lesson)

INSTRUCTION   ACTIVITY/RESPONSE

1. What is it?   1. T: Review structure with the visuals
                                                       from the previous lesson.
                                                   St: It's a _____ .

2. Let's read these words.   2. St: Read all the flash cards from the
                                                       previous lessons.

3. Match the word with the picture.   3. St: Match the 3 x 5 sight words with
                                                       the teacher's visuals.

4. Let's write.   4. T: Quiz students for spelling if sight
                                                       words have been assigned for spelling, or
                                                   St: Practice writing the words on a writing
                                                       page.
                                                   T: A master for lined paper is provided on
                                                       p. 396 of this guide.

5. Open your books to p. 81.   5. St: Open books and fill in their phone
                                                       number, a dash or "none" at the upper
                                                       right hand corner.

6. Let's read.   6. St: Read each exercise and respond in
                                                       chorus and individually.

7. Circle the correct answer.   7. T: Point to the sample box in item #1.
                                                   St: Listen and circle the correct answer
                                                       for 2-18.
                                                   T: Check student work for accuracy and
                                                       review as necessary. Be certain students
                                                       have filled in their zip code at the upper
                                                       right hand corner of p. 82.

Student Workbook   p. 83-84

INSTRUCTION	ACTIVITY/RESPONSE
1. What is it?	1. T: Review visuals and sight words from student workbook p. 79-80 as necessary.
2. Let's write. What is it?	2. T: Show visuals. St: Write "It's a _____ " on the board or writing paper for practice.
3. Open your books to p. 83.	3. St: Open books and check "M" or "F" at the upper right hand corner.
4. What is it?	4. St: Respond. "It's a _____ ." for 1-13 orally.
5. Let's write.	5. St: Write "It's a _____ ." T: Allow students to check their own work on p. 79-80 in the student workbook. Be certain capitals, apostrophes and periods have been used correctly.

Student Workbook p. 85
   Lesson Two, Section I
   What's your address?

SIGHT WORDS
your, street, Avenue

VISUALS
16 stop (sign on a street)
55 envelope

INSTRUCTIONAL AIDS
yellow flash cards

STRUCTURE
What's your address (city, state zip code)?

My address is (city's, state's, zip code's) _____ .

INSTRUCTION

1. My address is _____ .

2. What's your address?

3. My city's (state's, zip code's) ____ .

4. What's your city (state, zip code)?

5. Let's read.

6. Mila is a woman, Bill is a man. They are talking to each other.

7. I am Mila. You are Bill.

8. You are Mila and you are Bill.

ACTIVITY/RESPONSE

1. T: Say your address and write it on the board.
   St: Listen.

2. T: Model the student's address if necessary.
   St: Respond individually.

3. T: Say your city (state, zip code) and write it on the board.
   St: Listen.

4. T: Model the student's city (state, zip code) if necessary.
   St: My city's (state's, zip code's) _____ .

5. T: Write the dialogue from p. 85 on the board or on sentence strips.

6. T: Model the entire dialogue.
   St: Listen.
   T: Model the dialogue again, sentence by sentence.
   Cl:
   Gr: } Repeat
   St:

7. T: Assume role.
   Cl: Assume role and reverse upon completion.

8. Gr: Assume roles and reverse roles upon completion.

172

9. Who wants to be Mila (Bill)?

9. T: Encourage students to volunteer or assign roles.

10. Optional: Let's fix the words.

10. T: Cut up the sentence strips into the individual words. Hand out individual components to the students.
St: Rearrange the dialogue.

11. This word is "your". This is your (pen) and your (book).

11. T: Point to items belonging to the students.

12. What is it?

12. T: Hold up an item of your own.
St: It's your _____ .
T: Continue practice until students comprehend the possessive use of "your". Distinguish between "my" and "your" as necessary.

13. Look at the " 's" in "what's", "city's" and "zip code's". What is it?

13. T: Point to the " 's".
St: is
T: Review as necessary.

14. Let's change " 's" to "is".

14. St: Erase " 's" on the board and replace replace it with "is" or replace " 's" with an "is" component in the sentence strips.

15. Open your books to p. 85. When there are 2 lines like this, write your address on one line and city, state and zip code on the second.

15. T: Point to the upper right hand corner.
St: Open books and fill in their address.
T: Check for accuracy and legibility.

16. Look at the picture. Who is Mila (Bill)?

16. St: Point to the woman (man).

17. What is it?

17. T: Point to the telephone, lamp, pen and/or letter in picture.
St: Respond.

18. Let's read.

18. St: Assume roles and read.

19. Close your books. This is a street.

19. T: Hold up visual 16 and point to the street.
St: Listen and repeat.

20. What are the first two letters in /st/ street?

20. St: "s - t"
T: Write "st" on the board.

21. What is the last letter in street?

21. St: "t"
T: Write a "t" (st   t).

22.	What letters say /ē/?	22. St:	"e" or "ee"
		T:	Remind students of the /ē/ in Lee. Fill in the "ee" on street.
		St:	Read.
23.	Another word for "Street" is "Avenue"; /ă/ apple, Avenue.	23. T:	Write "Avenue" on the board.
		St:	Listen and repeat.
24.	Optional, abbreviations: I can write "Street" and "Avenue" in a short way.	24. T:	Write "St." and "Ave." on the board.
		St:	Listen.
25.	What is it?	25. T:	Hold up visual 55.
		St:	(It's an) envelope.
26.	What is it?	26. T:	Point to the 2 names and addresses.
		St:	(It's) a (first, last) name (address, city, state, zip code).
27.	Is Mila married?	27. St:	No, (she's "Miss").
28.	Let's read.	28. T:	Model the address.
		Cl:	Repeat.
		T:	Watch for stress and intonation.
29.	Open your books to p. 85. Listen and repeat.	29. T:	Model the addresses.
		Cl: Gr: St:	} Repeat.
30.	This is a comma. I write a comma between the city and state.	30. St:	Listen.
31.	What is it?	31. T:	Point to the stamp.
		St:	(It's a) stamp.
		T:	Model, review and repeat learnings as necessary.
32.	Let's make some cards.	32. St:	Make a yellow 3 x 5 card of "your, Street, Avenue". Optional: Write the abbreviations for "Street" and "Avenue" on the back of the respective cards.
		T:	Make corresponding 5 x 8 cards. See p. 8 for suggested uses of the sight word flash cards.

Student Workbook   p. 86   VISUAL
                                              55 envelope

INSTRUCTION   ACTIVITY/RESPONSE

1. Let's read.   1. T: Review dialogue, sight words
                                           (abbreviations) and addresses from
                                           student workbook p. 85.
                                       St: Respond.

2. What's Bill's address?   2. T: Hold up visual 55.
                                       St: It's 105 Fay Avenue.

3. What is another word for "Avenue"?   3. St: Street.

4. What's Bill's city (state, zip code)? 4. St: Respond.

5. Let's read.   5. T: Write "What's Bill's address?" on
                                           the board.

6. What is Bill's address?   6. T: Point to the " 's" in "What's".
   This " 's" means "is".   St: Listen.

7. This " 's" means "his". What's   7. T: Point to the " 's" in "Bill's".
   his address?   St: Listen.

8. (Ann) 's pen, (Mila) 's book,   8. T: Point to objects belonging to the
   (Ben) 's pencil, etc.   the students.
                                       St: Listen.

9. Is this " 's" the same as this " 's"? 9. T: Point to the " 's" in "What's" and
                                           " 's" in "Bill's".
                                       St: No.

10. Open your books to p. 86.   10. St: Open books and read items #1-4 in
    Let's read.   chorus and individually.
                                       T: Model if necessary.

11. Let's read.   11. T: Point to the exercise at the bottom.
                                       St: Read filling in their own personal
                                           information.

12. All of the " 's" say "is".   12. T: Point to the " 's" in all the words
                                           in the bottom exercises.
                                       St: Listen.

13. Let's write.   13. St: Fill in their personal information
                                           in the exercises at the bottom and
                                           "hair color" at the upper right
                                           hand corner.
                                       T: Check for accuracy and legibility.

175

Student Workbook   p. 87-88

SIGHT WORDS
area code, height

INSTRUCTIONAL AIDS
a state map or map of the United States
yellow 3 x 5 cards
a measure for measuring height

INSTRUCTION

1. What's your phone number?

2. Your area code is _____ .

3. We use area code when we call far away. Look at this map. We are here. If we call here, we need to use an area code.

4. What's your area code?

5. This is "area code".

6. Let's make a card.

7. What's your name (address, city, state, zip code, phone number, area code)?

8. Open your books to p. 87.

9. Let's read.

10. Let's write.

ACTIVITY/RESPONSE

1. St: "It's _____ " or "I don't have one."

2. St: Listen and repeat, "My area code is _____ ."

3. T: Point to your city and another far away.
   St: Listen.

4. St: (My area code's) _____ .

5. T: Write "area code" on the board.
   St: Read.

6. St: Write "area code" on one side and the area code on the back.
   T: Make a corresponding card.

7. St: My name's (address is, city's, state's, zip code's, phone number is, area code is) _____ .
   T: Students may use " 's" and "is" interchangeably.

8. St: Open books and fill in the area code and phone number at the upper right hand corner or a dash or "none".

9. St: Read the sentences on p. 87-88, filling in their personal information.

10. T: Explain that the questions are to be copied on the following lines and that responses are to be completed on the first line and duplicated on the following line.
    St: Write, filling in their personal information.
    T: Check for accuracy and legibility.

11. This word is "height". Height means how tall you are.	11. T: Write "height" on the board. Demonstrate height with your hand. St: Listen.
12. My height is (5) ' (6) ".	12. T: Write your height on the board. Explain the symbols for "feet" and "inches".
13. What's your height?	13. T: Measure the students and write their height on one side of a yellow 3 x 5 card. Teach them to say their height. St: I'm ___ ' ___ ".
14. Let's make a card.	14. St: Write the word "height" on the opposite side of the card on which their height has been written. T: Make a corresponding card.
15. Open your books to p. 88. Write your height.	15. St: Open books and fill in their height. T: Check for accuracy and legibility.

Student Workbook   p. 89

VISUAL
55 envelope

INSTRUCTIONAL AIDS
an envelope for each student (optional)

INSTRUCTION

1. When you write a letter, you write your address here.

2. You write the address of your friend, mother, brother, etc. here.

3. Open your books to p. 89.

4. Look at #1. Ask another student to write his address for you on paper. Then you write the address on the envelope.

5. Look at #2. Write an envelope to me.

6. Optional: Let's write.

ACTIVITY/RESPONSE

1. T: Hold up visual 55 and point to the the return address.
   St: Listen.

2. T: Point to address.
   St: Listen.

3. St: Open books and fill in the area code and phone number or write a dash or "none".

4. St: Fill in the envelope.
   T: Check for accuracy and legibility.

5. T: Write your address on the board.
   St: Address the envelope.
   T: Check for accuracy and legibility.

6. T: Hand out a blank envelope to each student.
   St: Address an envelope to whomever they please.
   T: Check for accuracy and legibility.

Student Workbook p. 90-91
Lesson Two Section II
What time is it?

SIGHT WORDS
Good morning, Good afternoon
Good evening, time, Hello,
thanks, o'clock

VISUALS
24 Good morning   30 Good evening
22 Good afternoon

INSTRUCTIONAL AIDS
a cardboard clock with movable
   hands
yellow 3 x 5 cards

STRUCTURE

What time is it?   It's ___: 00 (o'clock).

INSTRUCTION

1. This is a clock.

2. What is it?

3. A clock says the time.

4. What does a clock say?

5. A clock has 2 hands: a short hand and a long hand.

6. What are these?

7. What is this (and this)?

8. The short hand is for the hour. What is it for?

9. Optional: There are 24 hours in a day. Today is (Mon) day. There are 24 hours in (Mon) day. How many hours are there in a day?

ACTIVITY/RESPONSE

1. T: Hold up a cardboard clock, point to a clock or draw one on the board.
   St: Listen and repeat.

2. St: (It's a) clock.

3. St: Listen.

4. St: (It says the) time.
   T: Assist and repeat as necessary.

5. T: Point to the hands.
   St: Listen.

6. St: (They're) hands.

7. St: (It's the) short (long) hand.

8. T: Demonstrate.
   St: (It's for the) hour.

9. St: Listen and respond "24".

179

10. What time is it? It's one (two, three, etc.) o'clock.

11. What time is it?

12. You ask, "What time is it?"

13. You fix the clock. It's _____ o'clock.

14. Look at this picture. To say "Hi" or "Hello", I can say "Good morning".

15. Look at this picture. To say "Hi" or "Hello" at 12:00 or after, I say "Good afternoon".

16. Look at the picture. To say "Hi" or or "Hello" at 6:00 I say "Good evening".

17. This is "Good morning" ("time" and "thanks").

18. "Thanks" is the same as "Thank you".

19. Let's read.

10. T: Set (or draw) the minute hand on the 12 and the hour hand at various numbers. Call out the times.
    Cl:
    Gr: Repeat, "It's _____ o'clock."
    St:

11. T: Change the hour hand until all hours have been reviewed.
    St: It's _____ o'clock.

12. T: Hand the clock to a student.
    St: Sets the clock and asks the next student "What time is it?" That student responds, sets a new time and asks the next student "What time is it?" and so on.

13. T: Hand the clock to a student and call out a time.
    St: Listens and sets the clock.
    T: Continue practice until students can ask "What time is it?" and answer with good pronunciation and set a clock on the hour with accuracy.

14. T: Hold up visual 24.
    St: Listen and repeat "Good morning".

15. T: Hold up visual 22.
    St: Listen and repeat.

16. T: Hold up visual 30.
    St: Listen and repeat.
    T: Repeat and review instruction as necessary.

17. T: Write dialogue #1 from student workbook p. 90 on the board or on sentence strips. Point out the new words. Model the entire dialogue.
    St: Listen.

18. St: Listen and read "Thanks".

19. T: Model the entire dialogue line by line.
    Cl:
    Gr: Repeat.
    St:

20. I'm "A" and you are "B".

21. Let's read.

22. This is "Good afternoon".

23. This is "Good evening".
    (o'clock)

24. Optional: Fix the sentences.

25. Optional, punctuation:
    This is a comma. I use a comma before saying somebody's name. For example, "Hello, Ben."

26. Optional, compound words:
    There are 2 words in "afternoon" "after" and "noon". Noon means 12:00. What other words have 2 words in them?

27. Open your books to p. 90.

28. Let's read.

---

20. T: Assume role.
    Cl:
    Gr: } Assume role.
    St:
    T: Reverse roles upon completion.

21. T: Pair students up.
    St: Read and then reverse roles.

22. T: Repeat steps 17-21 for dialogue #2 on student workbook p. 90.

23. T: Repeat steps 17-21 for dialogue #3 on student workbook p. 90.

24. T: Cut up the sentence strips for each dialogue into the components. Deal the components out to the students.
    St: Rearrange the dialogue.

25. T: Point to the commas in the dialogues. Give instructions for periods, question marks, apostrophes, capitals and the colon for the hour.
    Game: Rewrite the dialogue leaving out all the punctuation and capitals. See how many the students can fill in.

26. T: Write "afternoon" on the board.
    St: Listen and respond, "chalkboard, notebook, snowman, restrooms."

27. St: Open books and write their home number, a dash or "none" at the upper right hand corner.

28. T: Ask for volunteers or assign roles.
    St: Read, roleplay and reverse roles.
    T: Continue reading 90-91. Be certain students have accurately filled in area code and zip code at the upper right hand corner.

29. Optional, vocabulary development: They are jogging.

29. T: Point to the first visual on p. 90.
    St: Listen and repeat.
    T: Continue to develop vocabulary, depending on the time available and the ability of the students. For the second visual: They're walking/talking (in the park). It's a bench. For the third visual: She's walking the dog. He's reading.

30. Let's make cards.

30. St: Make yellow 3 x 5 cards of the sight words.
    T: Make corresponding 5 x 8 cards. See p. 8 of this guide for suggested uses of the sight word flash cards.

31. Optional: Let's write.

31. St: Copy the dialogues or practice writing the sight words on p. 98 of the student workbook.
    T: A master for lined paper is provided on p. 396 of this guide.

32. Optional: Listen to the time. Draw the hands on the clock (and write the time). It's 3:00. Variation: Teacher draws the hands and students write the time.

32. T: Duplicate the blank clocks on p. 397 of this guide in Appendix C. Provide several examples on the board. Call out the times.
    St: Draw the hands (and write the times if the teacher has requested them to do so).
    T: Check for accuracy.

33. Optional: What time do you get up (eat breakfast, go to work, etc.)?

33. T: Instruct students on how to respond and provide a time on the cardboard clock if necessary.
    St: I get up at 6:00.

Student Workbook   p. 92-93

SIGHT WORDS
I'm, early, on time, late, sorry

VISUALS
134 early   136 late
135 on time

INSTRUCTIONAL AIDS
cardboard clock with movable hands
yellow flash cards

STRUCTURE
What time is it?   It's ___ :30.

INSTRUCTION	ACTIVITY/RESPONSE
1. What is it?	1. T: Hold up or point to a clock. St: It's a clock.
2. What does it say?	2. St: (It says) the time.
3. What are they?	3. T: Point to the hands. St: (They're) hands.
4. What is it?	4. T: Point to the short (long) hand. St: (It's the) short (long) hand.
5. What is this hand for?	5. T: Point to the short hand. St: (It's for) the hour.
6. Optional: How many hours are there in a day?	6. St: (There are) 24.
7. What time is it?	7. T: Set and reset the hour hand until all the hours have been reviewed. St: It's ___ :00.
8. How do I say "Hi" or "Hello"?	8. T: Hold up visuals 24, 22 and 30. St: Good morning (afternoon, evening).
9. Let's read.	9. T: Review the sentence strips or dialogues from the student workbook p. 90. Review the sight words, optional vocabulary and punctuation from the previous lesson.
10. This is the long hand, it tells me the minutes.	10. T: Point to the long hand and show the minute lines. St: Listen.
11. There are 60 minutes in one hour.	11. St: Count them together if necessary.

183

12. How many minutes in an hour?

13. What time is it?
    It's 1:30, (2:30, 3:30, etc.)

14. What time is it?

15. You ask, "What time is it?"

16. You fix the clock. It's ___ : 30.

17. Look at this picture. The class starts at 8:00. It is 7:30. He's early.

18. Look at this picture. The class starts at 8:00. It is 8:00. He's on time.

19. Look at this picture. The class starts at 8:00. It's 8:30. He's late.

20. This is "I'm early."

21. Let's read.

12. St: (There are) 60 (minutes in an hour).

13. T: Set the hour and minute hands and call out the times.
    Cl:
    Gr: Repeat: "It's ___ : 30."
    St:

14. T: Change the hands until all half hours have been reviewed.
    St: It's ___ : 30.

15. T: Hand the clock to a student.
    St: Sets the clock and asks the next student "What time is it?". That student responds and repeats the activity for the next student and so on.

16. T: Hand the clock to the student and call out a time.
    St: Listen and set the clock.
    T: Continue practice until students can ask for the time and respond "It's ___:30." with good pronunciation and set a clock on the half hour with accuracy.

17. T: Hold up visual 134.
    St: Listen and repeat "He's early."

18. T: Hold up visual 135.
    St: Listen and repeat "He's on time."

19. T: Hold up visual 136.
    St: Listen and repeat "He's late."
    T: Continue to review until students have the concept and can say the vocabulary.

20. T: Write dialogue #1 of student workbook p. 92 on the board or on sentence strips. Point to the new words "I'm early" and point to yourself. Model the entire dialogue.
    St: Listen.

21. T: Model the entire dialogue line by line.
    Cl:
    Gr: Repeat.
    St:

22. I'm "A" and you are "B".

22. T: Assume role.
    Cl:
    Gr: } Assume role.
    St:
    T: Reverse roles upon completion.

23. Let's read.

23. T: Pair students up.
    St: Read and reverse roles.

24. This is "I'm on time".

24. T: Repeat steps 20-23 for dialogue #2 on student workbook p. 92.

25. This is "I'm late. Sorry."
    I say "Sorry" when I do something wrong.

25. T: Roleplay accidently stepping on someone's toe, bumping into someone, knocking someone's book down, etc. Each time say "Sorry" to demonstrate the concept of the word. Repeat steps 20-23 for dialogue #3 on student workbook p. 92.

26. Optional: Fix the sentences.

26. T: Cut up the sentence strips for each dialogue into the components. Deal the components out to the students.
    St: Rearrange the dialogue.

27. Optional, punctuation:
    This is a comma. I use a comma before saying someone's name. For example, "Hi, Ann."

27. T: Point to the commas in the dialogues. Give instruction for periods, question marks, apostrophes, capitals and the colon for the time.
    Game: Rewrite the dialogue leaving out all the punctuation and capitals (or cut them off of the strips). See how many the students can fill in.
    St: Listen and play.

28. Open your book to p. 92.

28. St: Open books and fill in "height".
    T: Review "height" if necessary.

29. Let's read.

29. T: Ask for volunteers or assign roles.
    St: Read, roleplay and reverse roles.
    T: Continue reading 92-93. Be certain students have accurately filled in the time at the upper right hand corner of p. 93.

30. Optional, vocabulary development:
They're sitting on a bench.
They're reading newspapers.
They're waiting for the bus at the bus stop.

31. Let's make cards.

32. Optional: Let's write.

33. Optional: Listen to the time.
Draw the hands on the clock.
(and write the time). It's 3:30.
Variation: Teacher draws the hands and students write the time.

34. Optional: What time do you eat lunch (go to school, go to sleep, etc.)?

30. T: Point to the first visual on p. 92.
    St: Listen and repeat.
    T: Continue to develop vocabulary depending on the time available and the ability of the students.
    For the second visual:
    They're eating in a restaurant, salt, pepper, ketchup, mustard, etc.
    For the third visual:
    (He has) flowers, (They're) single/married, etc.

31. St: Make yellow 3 x 5 cards of the sight words.
    T: Make corresponding 5 x 8 cards. See p. 8 of this guide for the suggested uses of the sight word flash cards.

32. St: Copy the dialogues or practice writing the sight words on p. 98.
    T: A master for lined paper is provided on p. 396 of this guide.

33. T: Duplicate the blank clocks on p. 397 of this guide in Appendix C. Provide several examples on the board. Call out the times. Mix ___:00 and ___:30 if desired.
    St: Draw the hands (and write the times if the teacher has requested them to do so).
    T: Check for accuracy.

34. T: Instruct students on how to respond and provide a time on the cardboard clock if necessary.
    St: I eat lunch at 12:30.

Student Workbook   p. 94-95

INSTRUCTIONAL AID
cardboard clock with movable hands

INSTRUCTION

1. What time is it?

2. You set the clock: It's ___ : 00 / ___ : 30.

3. Read the words.

4. Open your books to p. 94.

5. Let's read.

6. Circle the correct answer.

ACTIVITY/RESPONSE

1. T: Review all the hours and half hours.
   St: Respond.

2. T: Call out all the hours and half hours.
   St: Set the clock.

3. T: Review all the sight words and expressions from p. 90 on.
   St: Read.

4. St: Open books and put a check or an "X" on "M" or "F".

5. St: Read all the exercises on p. 94-95, giving the correct answers orally.

6. T: Point to the sample box in item #1. Demonstrate that the correct answer has been circled.
   St: Circle the answers.
   T: Check student work for accuracy. Be certain that "area code" and "home phone" or a dash or "none" have been filled in at the upper right hand corner of p. 95.

Student Workbook   p. 96

INSTRUCTION

1. What time is it?

2. Open your books to p. 96 and write.

3. Let's look at #1. What time is it?

4. Look at #2. What time is it?

5. Let's write.

6. Optional: Let's write.

ACTIVITY/RESPONSE

1. T: Review all times at the hour and and half hour. Review sight words and sentence strips as necessary.
   St: Respond.

   St: Open books and fill in their height. Students can use the back of their "height" flash card for assistance if necessary.

3. St: It's 12:30.

4. St: It's 2:30.
   T: Continue until all times have been read orally.

5. St: Write the question "What time is it?" and answer "It's __:__" for items 2-9.
   T: Check for accuracy.

6. T: If students need further practice, p. 397 in Appendix C of this guide provides a master for blank clocks. On a copy, fill in the hands and the lines for writing before duplicating the exercise for the students.
   St: Write "What time is it?" and "It's __:__."
   T: Check for accuracy.

Student Workbook   p. 97-98

INSTRUCTIONAL AID
a cardboard clock with movable hands

INSTRUCTION

1. Show me 4:30.

2. Open your books to p. 97 and write.

3. Draw the hands.

4. Optional: Draw the hands.

5. Optional: Open your books to p. 98.

6. Listen and write.

ACTIVITY/RESPONSE

1. T: Hand the clock with movable hands to a student.
   St: Set the clock at 4:30.
   T: Continue until all times at the hour and half hour have been reviewed. Review sight words and sentence strips as necessary.

2. St: Open books and fill in their hair and eye color.

3. T: Provide several examples on the board. Be certain there is a clear distinction between the short and long hand.
   St: Draw the hands.
   T: Check for accuracy.

4. T: If students need further practice, p. 397 in Appendix C of this guide provides a master for blank clocks. You may call out the times or fill in the times on a copy before duplicating the exercises.
   St: Draw the hands.
   T: Check for accuracy.

5. T: If p. 98 has been used already, p. 396 of Appendix C is a master for lined paper.
   St: Open books and circle their appropriate title.

6. T: Show the students how to number the lines. Dictate times (It's 6:30), sight words or sentences the students have been practicing.
   St: Write.

Student Workbook   p. 99
   Lesson Three, Section I
   What is he/she?

SIGHT WORDS
doctor, nurse, busboy, waiter, cook, housewife, gardener, secretary, salesman, saleslady

VISUALS

9 housewife	68 gardener
20 secretary	73 cook
31 nurse	107 waiter
38 busboy	137 salesman
59 doctor	138 saleslady

INSTRUCTIONAL AIDS
yellow flash cards
old magazines or a copy of the visuals corresponding to the sight words on p. 380-1 of this guide

STRUCTURE

What is (s)he?   (S)He's a _____ .

INSTRUCTION

ACTIVITY/RESPONSE

Do not begin instruction until a thorough review has been provided and students have successfully achieved concepts, responses, reading and writing skills to this point.

1. All of these people are workers. They work.

2. He's a doctor.

3. She's a nurse.

1. T: Fan out the lesson visuals.
   St: Listen.

2. T: Show visual 59.
   St: Listen and repeat in chorus and individually.

3. T: Show visual 31.
   St: Listen and repeat in chorus and individually.

   T: Continue instruction until students can name the occupation, distinguish between "He's" and "She's", point to the correct visual when asked to identify a particular occupation and respond with good pronunciation, stress and intonation.

190

4. Ask, "What is (s)he?"

5. Let's read.

6. Let's read: doctor, nurse, busboy, etc.

7. Let's make some cards.

8. Let's read the cards.

9. What is (s)he?

10. Open your books to p. 99 and write.

11. Listen.

12. Listen and repeat.

13. I am "A" and you are "B".

---

4. T: Deal out the visuals to the students.
   St: Asks "What is (s)he?" pointing to his own visual. The next student responds and asks the following student "What is (s)he?"

5. T: Write "What is he?" and "What is she?" on the board or on sentence strips.
   St: Read in chorus and individually.

6. T: Write the sight words on the board or on yellow 5 x 8 flash cards. Model.
   St: Listen and repeat in chorus and individually.

7. St: Make yellow 3 x 5 cards of the sight words. Staple or tape a picture from a magazine or a copy of the visuals corresponding to the sight words on p. 380-1 of this guide to the back of the cards.
   T: Make corresponding 5 x 8 cards if you have not yet done so.

8. T: Model.
   Cl:
   Gr: } Repeat, read.
   St:

9. T: Hold up a sight word flash card.
   St: (S)He's a _____ .
   T: Continue practice until students can successfully read the sight word flash cards and answer "What is (s)he?"

10. St: Open books and fill in the city, state and zip.
    T: Check for accuracy.

11. T: Model the entire dialogue.
    St: Listen.

12. T: Model each line separately.
    St: Listen and repeat.

13. T:
    St: } Assume roles and then reverse roles.

14. Let's read again.

15. Read #1 (#2, and so on).

16. Optional: Let's write.

17. Optional: Let's match.

18. Optional, alphabetizing:
Place your cards according to the alphabet.

19. Optional, opposites:
   doctor/nurse
   salesman/saleslady

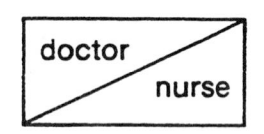

20. Optional, compound words:
Some words in English are made of two words together such as:
   busboy
   housewife
   salesman
   saleslady

21. Optional, syllables:
How many syllables are there in doctor?

14. Gr:
      } Assume roles.
    Gr:
    St:
      } Assume roles.
    St:

15. St: Read.
    T: Repeat as necessary.

16. St: Practice writing the dialogue and/or sentences on p. 99.
    T: A master for lined paper is provided on p. 396 of this guide.

17. St #1: Places his flash cards onto a table, visual side up.
    St #2: Matches the visual with the 3 x 5 sight word.
    St #1,2: Check for accuracy upon completion.

18. St: Alphabetize the sight word cards from this lesson.
    T: An alphabetizing worksheet is provided as an additional exercise in Appendix C on p. 398 of this guide.

19. T: Review previous opposites such as man/woman, last/first, white/black
    St: Make yellow 3 x 5 flash cards:

    | doctor |
    | nurse |

20. T: See if students can provide the compound words. If not, give the answers.
    St: Respond/Listen.

21. T: Name all the sight words. Pound out the sounds on the table.
    St: Respond.

22. Optional:
    a) a, e, i, o, u are special letters. They are the vowels. What are the vowels?
    b) Every word in English has a vowel. Each syllable has a a vowel.
    c) All the other letters in English are consonants. There
       are   5 vowels
       and   21 consonants
       and   26 letters

23. Optional: Sometimes a person who does something is spelled with "er". For example a person who sings is a "singer". A person who works is a worker (dances, dancer; writes, writer, etc.) What are the two words in this lesson that show "er", a person who does something?

24. Optional, decoding:
    (n)urse   (w)ife
    purse   knife
                    life

    (c)ook
    book
    brook   (h)ouse
    crook   blouse
    hook   louse
    look   mouse
    nook   spouse
    took
    shook

25. Optional, new structure: "What are you?" and "I'm a (occupation)."

22.
    a) T: Write a, e, i, o, u on the board.
       St: Listen and respond.
    b) T: Demonstrate, using the sight words from this lesson.
       St: Listen.
    c) St: Listen.
       T: Review and practice as necessary.
       St: Respond.

23. St: waiter, gardener
    T: Review and repeat instruction as necessary.

24. T: See p. 7 for further discussion and suggestions.

25. T: Teach students to give a personal response.
    St: Practice. "I'm a (occupation)."

Student Workbook   p. 100

VISUALS
all visuals listed for Student Workbook p. 99 on p. 380-1 of this guide

STRUCTURE
Is (s)he a (occupation) ?

Yes, (s)he is.
No, (s)he isn't.

INSTRUCTION

1. What is (s)he?

2. Is she a nurse?

3. Is he a doctor?

4. Is (s)he a _____ ?

5. Is she a nurse?

6. Is he a doctor?

7. Is (s)he a _____ ?

ACTIVITY/RESPONSE

1. T: Review all vocabulary and sight words from the previous lesson.
   St: Respond.

2. T: Show visual 31. Elicit affirmative answer. Model "Yes, she is."
   St: Repeat answer.

3. T: Show visual 59. Elicit affirmative answer. Model "Yes, he is."
   St: Repeat answer.
   T: Continue asking until all vocabulary has been practiced.

4. T: Elicit affirmative answers only.
   Cl:
   Gr: Answer "Yes, (s)he is."
   St:

5. T: Show visual 20, secretary. Elicit negative answer. Model "No, she isn't."
   St: Repeat answer.

6. T: Show visual 68, gardener. Elicit negative answer. Model, "No, he isn't."
   St: Repeat answer.
   T: Continue asking until all vocabulary has been practiced.

7. T: Elicit negative answers only.
   Cl:
   Gr: Answer "No, (s)he isn't."
   St:
   T: Repeat instruction and practice as necessary.

8. Optional: Ask your partner
"Is (s)he a _____ ?"

9. Optional, making questions:
To make a question, I move the "is" to the beginning.

10. Open your books to p. 100.

11. Let's read.

12. Let's read again.

13. Optional, new structure:
"Are you a (occupation) ?" and
"Yes, I am." or "No, I'm not."

8. St #1: Asks partner "Is (s)he a _____ " using the visual side of the sight word flash cards.
   St #2: Responds "Yes, (s)he is." or "No, (s)he isn't."

9. T: Write all the sentences on p. 99 on sentence strips. Cut the words into components or write the sentences on the board. Move "is" to the beginning, capitalize "I" and change the period to a question mark.
   St: Listen and practice changing sentences to questions orally, on the board and/or on a teacher made ditto.

10. St: Open books and fill in their age at the upper right hand corner.

11. T: Model.
    Cl:
    Gr: Repeat.
    St:

12. St: Read.
    T: Continue practice and review as necessary.

13. T: Teach students to give a personal response.
    St: Practice responses.

Student Workbook   p. 101

INSTRUCTIONAL AID
a scale (optional)
a yellow 3 x 5 flash card

INSTRUCTION

1. What is (s)he?

2. Is (s)he a _____ ?

3. Optional: "What are you?" and "Are you a (occupation)?

4. I'll show the word and you give your answer.

5. This word is "weight".

6. "Weight" means how much you weigh.

7. How much do you weigh?

8. Let's write "weight".

9. Open your books to p. 101.

10. Let's read.

ACTIVITY/RESPONSE

1. T: Show visuals and sight words from workbook p. 99.
   St: (S)He's a _____ .

2. T: Show visual and sight words from Student Workbook p. 99.
   St: "Yes, (s)he is." or "No, (s)he isn't."

3. St: "I'm a (occupation)." and "Yes, I am." or "No, I'm not."

4. T: Show several or all of the personal information sight word flash cards such as "name", "area code" and "hair color".
   St: Provide their own personal information.

5. T: Write "weight" on the board.
   St: Repeat in chorus and individually.

6. T: Show a scale. Stand on it and (optional) write your weight on the board: ___ (lbs.). Explain that "lbs." is the abbreviation for pounds.

7. T: Weigh each student privately.
   St: Write their weight on one side of a yellow 3 x 5 flash card.

8. St: Write "weight" on the other side of the 3 x 5 flash card.
   T: Make a corresponding 5 x 8 flash card. Continue practice as necessary.

9. St: Open books and write their weight at the upper right hand corner.

10. T: Model all questions if necessary.
    St: Repeat and provide the response.

11. Yes or No? Let's write.

12. Optional: Let's write.

11. T: Point out example #1. Note capital letter, the comma after "No" (or "Yes"), the apostrophe for "isn't" and the period at the end of the sentence.
    St: Listen and observe. Write the responses.
    T: Check for accuracy and legibility.

12. St: Practice writing the questions, responses and/or sight words.
    T: A master for lined paper is provided on p. 396 of this guide.

Student Workbook   p. 102

INSTRUCTION	ACTIVITY/RESPONSE
1. Is (s)he a _____ ?	1. T: Show visuals and sight word flash cards from workbook p. 99. Elicit a negative response. St: No, (s)he isn't.
2. What is (s)he?	2. St: (S)He's a _____ . T: Continue practice until all visuals and vocabulary items have been reviewed.
3. Open books to p. 102. Listen.	3. St: Open books and listen. T: Model the entire dialogue.
4. Listen and repeat.	4. T: Model the dialogue line by line. Cl: Gr: Repeat. St:
5. I am "A" and you are "B".	5. T: Cl: Assume roles and then reverse.
6. Read.	6. St: Work in pairs. Assume roles and reverse upon completion.
7. Let's read.	7. T: Assign roles for items #2-6. St: Read and supply missing questions and responses for items #5-6.
8. Let's write.	8. St: Write the questions and responses as necessary in items #5-6. T: Check for accuracy and legibility. Be certain that area code and phone number, a dash or "none" have been filled in at the upper right hand corner.

Student Workbook p. 103

INSTRUCTION	ACTIVITY/RESPONSE
1. What is (s)he?	1. T: Review visuals and sight word flash cards from workbook p. 99. St: (S)He's a _____ .
2. Is (s)he a _____ ?	2. T: Review visuals and sight word flash cards from workbook p. 99. St: "Yes, (s)he is." or "No, (s)he isn't."
3. Optional: What are you?	3. St: I'm a (occupation).
4. Optional: Are you a (occupation)?	4. St: "Yes, I am." or "No, I'm not."
5. Match the word with the picture.	5. T: Pair the students. St #1: Turns his sight word flash cards from workbook p. 99 to visual side. St #2: Matches the sight word with the visual or T: Using a copy of the visuals on p. 380-1 of this guide, make a match worksheet similar to that on p. 74 of this guide. St: Write.
6. Open your books to p. 103. Circle the correct answer.	6. T: Demonstrate directions as per sample box. St: Open books and circle the correct answer. T: Check for accuracy. Be certain that "soc. sec. number" has been filled in at the upper right hand corner.

Student Workbook   p. 104-105

INSTRUCTION

1. Open your books to p. 104.

2. Let's read.

3. Let's write.

4. Optional: Let's write again.

5. Optional: Study the sentences on p. 104-105 for dictation.

ACTIVITY/RESPONSE

1. T: Review as per steps #1-4 on p. 199 of this guide prior to instruction as necessary.
   St: Open books.

2. St: Read all questions and fill in all responses on p. 104-105 orally.

3. St: Write the responses and fill in their address at the upper right hand corner of p. 104 and their height and weight at the upper right hand corner of p. 105.
   T: Check for accuracy and legibility.

4. St: Write the questions and rewrite the responses.
   T: A master for lined paper is provided on p. 396 of this guide.

5. St: Study.
   T: Dictate the sentences at the beginning of the following class.

Student Workbook   p. 106

INSTRUCTION

1. Listen and write.

2. Is (s)he a _____ ?

3. Open your books to p. 106.

4. Let's read.

5. Circle the correct answer.

ACTIVITY/RESPONSE

1. T: Dictate sentences from workbook p. 104-105 if they were assigned for study. A master for lined paper is provided on p. 396 of this guide.

2. T: Review visuals and sight words from workbook p. 99.
   St: "Yes, (s)he is." or "No, (s)he isn't."

3. St: Open books and put an "X" or a "✓" in the correct box at the upper right hand corner.

4. St: Read questions and orally supply the correct responses for items #1-9.

5. T: Demonstrate directions in the sample box.
   St: Circle the correct response.
   T: Check student work for accuracy. Be certain that students have checked their correct title at the upper right hand corner.

Student Workbook p.107

SIGHT WORDS
his, her

VISUAL
2 What's your name?

INSTRUCTIONAL AIDS
yellow flash cards

STRUCTURE

What's his/her name?   His/Her name's _____ .

INSTRUCTION   ACTIVITY/RESPONSE

1. My name's (Kay Renshaw).   1. St: My name's _____ .
   What's your name?   T: Review first, last and full name
                                          orally with all students.

2. His name's _____ .   2. T: Point to a male student (or to Ben in
                                          visual 2).
                                      Cl:
                                      Gr: } Listen and repeat.
                                      St:
                                      T: Be certain the "s" is pronounced
                                          in "His" and "name's".

3. His name's _____ .   3. T: Point to another male student and
                                          continue until students understand
                                          that we use "his" for males.
                                      St: Listen and repeat.

4. Her name's _____ .   4. T: Point to a female student (or to Ann in
                                          visual 2).
                                      Cl:
                                      Gr: } Listen and repeat.
                                      St:
                                      T: Listen for "s" in "name's".

5. Her name's _____ .   5. T: Point to another female student and
                                          continue until students understand
                                          that we use "her" for females.

6. What's his (her) name?   6. T: Point to various students in the class.
                                          Be certain all students have an
                                          opportunity to practice "his" and "her".
                                      St: His (Her) name's _____ .

7. His name's Ben.   7. T: Point to Ben in visual 2.
                                      St: Listen and repeat.

8.	What's his name?	8.	St:	His name's Ben.
9.	Her name's Ann.	9.	T:	Point to Ann in visual 2.
			St:	Listen and repeat.
10.	What's her name?	10.	St:	Her name's Ann.
			T:	Continue to practice as necessary.
11.	How do you spell "his"?	11.	T:	See if students can at least provide the "h".
			St:	Respond if possible.
12.	This is "is" and this is "his". Sometimes the letter "Ss" sounds like a "Zz" as in "is", "his" and "Ms."	12.	T:	Write "is" on the board and then place an "h" in front of it.
			St:	Listen and then read "his" in chorus and individually.
13.	How do you spell "her"?	13.	T:	See if students can at least produce the "h" and "r".
			St:	Respond if possible.
14.	This is "her".	14.	T:	Write "her" on the board.
			St:	Listen and then read "her" in chorus and individually.
15.	Listen.	15.	T:	Write the first dialogue from p. 107 on the board or on sentence strips. Model the entire dialogue.
			St:	Listen.
16.	Let's read. I am "A" and you are "B".	16.	T:	Assume role and reverse upon completion.
			Cl: Gr: St:	Assume role.
17.	Let's read. You are "A" and you are "B".	17.	T:	Seek volunteers or assign roles.
			Cl: Gr: St:	Assume roles and reverse upon completion.
18.	What does this mean?	18.	T:	Point to the " 's" in "What's".
			St:	is
			T:	Ask the same question for other verbal " 's" in the dialogue.
19.	These are capital letters. We use capital letters for the first word of a sentence and for names.	19.	T:	Point to the capital letters at the beginning of each sentence.
			St:	Listen.

20.	Why is this capital "B" and "A"?	20. T:	Point to the capital "B" in Ben and "A" in "Ann".
		St:	(We use capital letters) for names.
		T:	Assist if necessary.
21.	This is a question mark. We use a question mark after a question.	21. T:	Point to the question marks.
		St:	Listen.
22.	This is a period. We use a period to finish a sentence.	22. T:	Point to the periods.
		St:	Listen.
23.	Listen and read.	23. T:	Write the second and third readings on p. 107 on the board or on sentence strips. Model.
		St:	Listen and read.
		T:	When students read with good pronunciation, stress and intonation, point out the " 's", capitals, periods and abbreviations.
24.	What's her name?	24. T:	Ask content questions with regard to readings on p. 107.
		St:	Respond.
25.	Optional: Is (s)he a (occupation) ? Is his/her name _____ ?	25. T:	Ask yes/no questions eliciting affirmative or negative responses for practice.
		St:	Respond.
26.	Open your books to p. 107.	26. St:	Open books.
27.	Let's read.	27. T:	Ask for volunteers or assign roles for dialogue #1.
		St:	Assume roles and read the entire page supplying answers orally.
28.	Let's write.	28. T:	Have capable students write the correct responses on the board for other students to copy if necessary.
		St:	Write the responses.
		T:	Check for accuracy and legibility. Be certain students have correctly checked "M" or "F" at the upper right hand corner.

29. Let's make cards.	29. St:	Make yellow 3 x 5 cards of the sight words and a ┌─────────┐ with "his / her" card for opposites.
	T:	Review opposites and make corresponding 5 x 8 cards.
30. Optional: Let's write.	30. St:	Practice writing the dialogue and readings on p. 107.
	T:	A master for lined paper is on p. 396 of this guide.
31. Optional, word order: Fix the sentences.	31. T:	Cut the sentence strips into the component parts and scramble them.
	St:	Rearrange dialogue and readings.
32. Optional, vocabulary development: It's a stapler (adding machine, lawn mower, etc.).	32. T:	Point out objects in the visuals on p. 107 to add vocabulary to the the student's repertoire.
	St:	Listen, repeat, learn to spell and make cards.
33. Optional: Study the sentences for dictation.	33. St:	Study the sentences on p. 107 for dictation.
	T:	Dictate the sentences at the beginning of the next class.

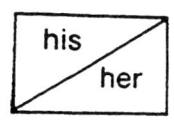

Student Workbook   p. 108
Odd Man Out

INSTRUCTION	ACTIVITY/RESPONSE
1. What's his(her) name?	1. T: Review structure from the previous lesson by asking the names of other students.
2. Let's read.	2. T: Review readings from the previous lesson via the sentence strips for p. 107.
3. Optional, dictation: Listen and write.	3. T: Dictate sentences from p. 107 if they had been assigned for study. St: Listen and write. T: Repeat sentences only 2 times, forcing students to listen.
4. Look at the words. Put an X on the word that is different.	4. T: Copy the sample box on p. 108 onto the board. Explain that all the words request personal information except "time" and therefore, it is different. St: Listen.
5. Look at the words. Put an X on the the one that is different.	5. T: The Odd Man Out game is extremely difficult. Provide several examples explaining why each answer is chosen:

57	60	53	55	59
a	b	c	d	X
Miss	Ms.	Mr.	pal	Mrs.
ship	cook	waiter	busboy	doctor
green	blue	bed	black	red
his	my	your	her	sick

6. Open your books to p. 108 and put an X on the one that is different.

6. T: Have the students work as a class, in small groups, pairs or individually.
   St: Put an X on the one that is different.
   T: Check for accuracy. The answers are:
   1. pencil
   2. man
   3. bed
   4. 6:00
   5. flag
   6. I'm early.
   7. sick
   8. gardener
   9. mall
   10. ss
   Be certain that the correct box has been checked at the upper right hand corner.

7. Optional: Put an X on the one that is different.

7. T: Devise a worksheet similar to the one on p. 108 using any of the 212 sight words learned up to this point or have the students devise some exercises.
   St: Put an X on the one that is different.
   T: Check for accuracy.

Student Workbook   p. 109
   Lesson Four, Section I
   What are they?

SIGHT WORDS

they, They're, teacher(s), barber(s), lawyer(s), student(s), baker(s), dentist(s)

VISUALS

11 teacher	140 teachers
15 student	141 students
36 barber	142 barbers
49 lawyer	143 lawyers
60 dentist	144 dentists
139 baker	145 bakers

INSTRUCTIONAL AIDS

old magazines or a copy of the visuals corresponding to the sight words on p. 381 of this guide
yellow flash cards

STRUCTURE

What are they?   They're (occupation) s.

INSTRUCTION

1. All of these are workers. They're workers.

2. She's a teacher.

3. What is she?

4. This is one teacher. With one, I use "is". Also, "a" means one.

5. They're teachers.

6. What are they?

ACTIVITY/RESPONSE

1. T: Fan out the lesson visuals.
   St: Repeat "They're workers."

2. T: Show visual 11.
   St: Repeat in chorus and individually.
   T: Write "She's a teacher." on the board.

3. T: Write "What is she?" on the board.
   Cl:
   Gr: She's a teacher.
   St:

4. T: Show visual 11.
   Point to "She's" and "a" in the sentence and "is" in the question.
   St: Listen.

5. T: Show visual 140.
   Write "They're teachers." on the board.
   St: Repeat in chorus and individually.

6. T: Write the question on the board.
   Cl:
   Gr: They're teachers.
   St:

7. If there is more than one teacher, 2, 3, 4, etc., I use "are" and an "s".

7. T: Show visual 140. Point to "They're" in the sentence. Explain the apostrophe takes the place of the "a" in "are". Point to the "are" in the question. Point to the plural "s".

8. (S)He's a (student).
They're (students).

8. T: Repeat instructions #2-7 for
   student - students
   barber - barbers
   lawyer - lawyers
   dentist - dentists
   baker - bakers
Continue practice until students make the verbal and cognitive distinction between singular "is" and plural "are" and "s".

9. Ask "What is (s)he?" or "What are they?"

9. T: Deal out the visuals to the students.
   St: Asks appropriate question of the next student who responds and asks the appropriate question regarding his visual of the following student.

10. Let's read.

10. T: Write "What are they?" on the board or on a sentence strip.
    St: Read in chorus and individually.

11. Let's read: teachers, barbers, lawyers, etc.

11. T: Write the plural occupations on the board or on yellow 5 x 8 flash cards. Model.
    St: Listen and repeat in chorus and individually.

12. This is "They" and this is "are". When I put them together, it says "They're".

12. T: Write the three words on the board or on yellow 5 x 8 cards.
    St: Listen and repeat "They're".
    T: Practice sight words until students can read them with relative ease.

13. Let's make cards.

13. St: Make yellow 3 x 5 cards of the sight words. Staple or tape a picture from a magazine or a copy of the plural occupations corresponding to the sight words on p. 381 of this guide to the back of the cards.
    T: Make corresponding 5 x 8 cards if necessary.

14. Let's read the cards.	14. T: Model. Cl: Gr: } Repeat, read. St:
15. Open your books to p. 109.	15. St: Open books.
16. Listen and repeat.	16. T: Model each question and response. St: Listen and repeat.
17. Repeat.	17. St: Read the questions and responses orally. T: Repeat oral reading if necessary.
18. Let's write.	18. St: Complete exercise 5 and 6 and fill in their social security number at the upper right hand corner. T: Check for accuracy and legibility.
19. Optional: Let's write.	19. St: Practice writing the questions and answers on p. 109. T: A master for lined paper is provided on p. 396 of this guide.
20. Optional: Let's match.	20. St #1: Places the sight word flash cards from this lesson onto the table, visual side up. St #2: Matches the visual with the sight word. St #1,2: Check for accuracy upon completion.
21. Optional, opposites: is/are	21. T: Review previous opposites. Make a yellow 3 x 5 card: is / are
22. Optional, alphabetizing: Place your cards according to the alphabet.	22. St: Alphabetize the sight word cards from this lesson. T: An alphabetizing worksheet is provided as an additional exercise in Appendix C on p. 398 of this guide.
23. Optional, syllables: How many sounds are there in "teachers"?	23. T: Name all the sight words. Pound out the sounds on the table. St: Respond.

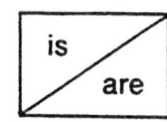

24. Optional, vowels:
   a) a, e, i, o, u are special letters. They're vowels. What are the vowels?
   b) Every word in English has a vowel. Each syllable has a vowel.
   c) All the other letters in English are consonants.
   There are   5 vowels
   　　　and 21 consonants
   　　　and 26 letters

25. Optional: Sometimes a person who does something is spelled with "er". For example, a person who teaches is a teacher (bakes, baker; cuts hair, barber).

24. T: Write a, e, i, o, u on the board.
   a) St: Listen and respond.
   b) T: Demonstrate using sight words from this lesson.
      St: Listen.
   c) St: Listen.
      T: Review and practice as necessary.

25. St: Listen.
   T: Review and repeat instruction from p. 193 of this guide as necessary.

Student Workbook   p. 110-111

VISUALS
all visuals listed for workbook p. 109
p. 208 of this guide

INSTRUCTION

1. All of these are workers. They're workers.

2. Optional: I'm a worker and you're a worker. We're workers.

3. What is (s)he?

4. This is one (teacher). With one, I use "is"; "a" means one, too.

5. What are they?

6. If there are 2, 3, 4 or more (teachers), I use "are" and "s".

7. What is (s)he?

8. What are they?

ACTIVITY/RESPONSE

1. T: Fan out all the visuals from the previous lesson.
   St: Repeat "They're workers."

2. T: Point to yourself and to the class.
   St: Repeat "We're workers".
   T: Continue practice until students understand the difference between "I'm, you're" and "we're".

3. St: (S)He's a (teacher).
   T: Review all singular visuals from the previous lesson.

4. T: Write "She's a teacher." on the board. Point to the " 's". Point to the "a".
   St: Listen.
   T: Write the sentence for each singular visual pointing out the " 's" and "a".

5. St: They're (teachers).
   T: Review all plural visuals from the previous lesson.

6. T: Write "They're teachers." on the board. Point to the " 're" and plural "s". Explain that the apostrophe takes the place of the "a" in "are" in the word "They're".

7. T: Hold up the singular sight words from the previous lesson.
   St: (S)He's a _____.
   T: Observe for pronunciation of the verbal "s". Review as necessary.

8. T: Hold up the plural sight words from the previous lesson.
   St: They're _____.
   T: Observe for the pronunciation of the plural "s". Review as necessary.

9. Hold up your word when I point to a picture.
   Variation: Hold up the picture side of your card when I point to the word.

10. Optional: What are you? What is (s)he? What are they?

11. Optional: Let's read p. 109 again.

12. Optional: What's the opposite of "is"?

13. Open your books to p. 110.

14. What is (s)he? What are they?

15. Let's read.

16. If there is "he" (she, is, they, are) in the question, I use "he" (she, is they are) in the answer.

17. With one (baker), I use "is" and "a".

18. With 2 or more (bakers), I use "are" and "s".

19. In English, I always start a sentence with a capital letter.

20. In a question, I use a question mark.

21. I always use a period to finish a sentence.

---

9. T: Spread your visuals out on a table or on the board. Point to a a particular visual.
   St: Find their corresponding sight word and hold it up.

10. T: Hand out visuals to students. For plurals, hand out one visual to be shared by 2 students.
    St: Hold up visuals and respond: "I'm a _____.", "We're _____.", "(S)He's a _____." or "They're _____."

11. St: Read.

12. T: Review opposites, syllables and vowels from the previous lesson.
    St: Respond.

13. St: Open books.

14. T: Review all the visuals on p. 110-111 orally.
    St: Respond.

15. St: Read the questions and provide the responses for p. 110-111 orally.

16. T: Point this out in the example on p. 110 or on the board.
    St: Listen.

17. T: Point this out in the example on p. 110 or on the board.
    St: Listen.

18. T: Point this out in the example on p. 110 or on the board.
    St: Listen.

19. T: Point out the capital letters in the questions and answers in the exercises.
    St: Listen.

20. T: Point out the question marks in the example on p. 110.
    St: Listen.

21. T: Point out the periods.
    St: Listen.

22. When I put 2 words together, such as "He is" and "They are", I use an apostrophe.

23. Let's practice.

24. Let's write.

25. Optional: Study the sentences for dictation.

22. T: Demonstrate how to write "He's and "They're" on the board.
    St: Listen.

23. T: Write these sentences on the board and have the students correct or complete them:
    a. what is (s)he
    b. they're students.
    c. he's a dentist.
    d. They're barbers
    e. (She is) a teacher.
    f. (They are) lawyers.
    St: Fill in the question mark, capital letters, period, and make abbreviations.
    T: Continue practice as necessary.

24. St: Write the responses on p. 110-111.
    T: If students have too much difficulty, have capable students write the responses on the board so others can copy. Check for accuracy and legibility. Be certain that zip code is filled in at the upper right hand corner on p. 110 and the time on p. 111.

25. St: Study.
    T: Dictate a few sentences at the beginning of the following class.

Student Workbook p. 112

SIGHT WORD
aren't

VISUALS
all visuals listed for workbook p. 109 on p. 208 of this guide

INSTRUCTIONAL AID
yellow 3 x 5 flash card

STRUCTURE

Are they (occupation) s?   Yes, they are.
                           No, they aren't.

INSTRUCTION

1. What is (s)he?

2. What are they?

3. Optional: Listen and write.

4. Finish the sentences.

5. How do you change this sentence into a question?

6. Optional: Let's make questions.

ACTIVITY/RESPONSE

1. T: Review all singular occupational visuals and sight words.
   St: (S)He's a _____ .

2. T: Review all plural occupational visuals and sight words.
   St: They're _____ .

3. T: Dictate a few sentences from workbook p. 110-111 if they were assigned for study.
   St: Write.

4. T: Write several sentences on the board omitting a period, question mark, apostrophe or capital for review.
   St: Correct or complete the sentences.

5. T: Write "He's a (dentist) ." on the board. See if students remember that to form a question, the "is" is brought to the beginning of the sentence and capitalized, the "H" is made small, and a question mark is added. If not, reteach the concept.
   St: Respond.

6. T: Write several singular sentences from workbook p. 110-111 on the board or on a ditto.
   St: Change the sentences to questions.

7. Is (s)he a (occupation) ?

7. St: "Yes, (s)he is." or "No, (s)he isn't."
   T: Assist if necessary.

8. "Isn't" is "is" and "not" together.

8. T: Demonstrate on the board.
   St: Listen.

9. Optional: You ask "Is (s)he a (occupation) ?

9. T: Deal out the singular occupational visuals.
   St #1: Asks St #2 "Is (s)he a _____ ?"
   St #2: Responds "yes" or "no" and asks St #3 "Is (s)he a _____ ?" and so on.

10. How do you change this sentence into a question?

10. T: Write "They're (occupation)s ." on the board. See if the students can transfer the concept of forming yes/no questions from the singular to the plural.
    St: Respond.
    T: If students cannot respond, demonstrate how the "are" is brought to the beginning of the sentence and capitalized, the "T" is made small, and a question mark is added.

11. Optional: Let's make questions.

11. T: Write several plural sentences from workbook p. 110-111 on the board or on a ditto.
    St: Change the sentences to questions.

12. Are they (occupations)s ?

12. T: Elicit an affirmative response and model "Yes, they are."
    St: Repeat.
    T: Continue until all plural visuals have been practiced and students can respond correctly.

13. Are they (occupations)s ?

13. T: Elicit a negative response and model "No, they aren't."
    St: Repeat.
    T: Continue until all plural visuals have been practiced and students can respond correctly.

14. Optional: You ask "Are they (occupation)s ?

14. T: Deal out the plural occupational visuals.
    St #1: Asks St #2 "Are they _____ ?"
    St #2: Responds "yes" or "no" and asks St #3 "Are they _____ ?" and so on.

15. "Aren't" is "are" and "not" together.

15. T: Demonstrate on the board.
    St: Listen.

16. Let's make a card.

16. St: Make a yellow 3 x 5 card with "aren't" on one side and "are not" on the other.
    T: Make a corresponding 5 x 8 card.

17. Open your books to p. 112 and write.

17. St: Open books and fill in their area code and phone number, a dash or "none".
    T: Check for accuracy.

18. Let's read.

18. T: Model questions and responses. When the responses are negative, ask "What are they?".
    St: Repeat and respond.

19. Let's read again.

19. St: Read.
    T: Continue practice until students can read with acceptable pronunciation, stress and intonation.

20. Optional: Let's write.

20. St: Practice writing the questions and responses for student workbook p. 112.
    T: A master for lined paper is provided on p. 396 of this guide.

Student Workbook   p. 113

VISUALS
all visuals listed for workbook p. 109
on p. 208 of this guide

INSTRUCTION

1. What is (s)he?

2. What are they?

3. Is (s)he a _____ ?

4. Are they _____s?

5. Read this word.

6. What are the 2 words that make "aren't"?

7. Is (s)he a _____ ?

8. Are they _____ ?

9. Is (s)he a _____ ?
   Are they _____ ?

ACTIVITY/RESPONSE

1. T: Review all singular occupational visuals and sight words.
   St: Respond.

2. T: Review all plural occupational visuals and sight words.
   St: Respond.

3. T: Elicit affirmative and negative responses.
   St: Respond.
   T: When the response is negative, ask "What is (s)he?"

4. T: Elicit affirmative and negative responses.
   St: Respond.
   T: When the response is negative, ask "What are they?"

5. T: Hold up the 5 x 8 card or write "aren't" on the board.
   St: aren't

6. St: Respond.

7. T: Hold up visuals. Write these 4 possible responses on sentence strips or on the board:
   Yes, she is.   No, she isn't.
   Yes, he is.   No, he isn't.
   St: Point to or say the correct response.

8. T: Hold up visuals. Write these 2 possible responses on sentence strips or on the board:
   Yes, they are.   No, they aren't.
   St: Point to or select the correct response.

9. T: Hold up visuals. Mix all 6 possible responses.
   St: Point to or say the correct response.

10. Open your books to p. 113.

11. Let's read.

12. Circle the correct answer.

13. Optional:
    Is it a _____ ?
    Are they _____ ?

10. St: Open books.

11. St: Read the questions and respond orally.
    T: Model if necessary.

12. T: Point to the sample box. Demonstrate that the correct response has been circled.
    St: Circle correct responses.
    T: Check student work for accuracy. Be certain that the time has been filled in at the upper right hand corner.

13. T: Using any visual from previous lessons continue to practice yes/no questions in the singular and plural. This also provides practice for previous vocabulary.

Student Workbook   p. 114

INSTRUCTION

1. Is (s)he a _____ ?
   Are they _____ ?

2. (Name) and (name) are students.

3. They aren't teachers.

4. (Mrs. Renshaw) isn't a student.

5. (She's) a teacher.

6. Let's read.

7. Optional: Fix the sentences.

8. Optional: Let's read.

9. Answer the question.

ACTIVITY/RESPONSE

1. T: Review previous learnings as necessary.

2. T: Say the sentence and write it on the board or on sentence strips filling in the name of two students in class.
   St: Listen and read.

3. T: Say the sentence and write it on the board or on sentence strips.
   St: Listen and read.

4. T: Say the sentence and write it on the board or on sentence strips filling in your own name.
   St: Listen and read.

5. T: Say the sentence and write it on the board or on sentence strips.
   St: Listen and read.
   T: Upon completion, these sentences should take the form of a paragraph. See item #1 on workbook p. 114.

6. St: Practice reading the paragraph as frequently as necessary.
   T: Listen for pronunciation, stress and intonation.

7. T: If the sentences are written on the board, erase various words, letters or markings.
   St: Fill them in.
   T: If the sentences are written on sentence strips, cut them into the components.
   St: Rearrange the paragraph.

8. T: For further practice, write more paragraphs on the board or on a ditto using the sight words and substituting various student names.

9. T: Ask "Who/What" and "Is/Are" questions regarding the paragraphs.
   St: Respond.

10. Open your books to p. 114.	10. St: Open books.
11. Look at the picture. His name's Al.	11. T: Point to the visual in #1. St: Listen and repeat.
12. Look at the picture. Her name is Lucy.	12. T: Point to the visual in #1. St: Listen and repeat.
13. Look at the picture. His name is Dick.	13. T: Point to the visual in #1. St: Listen and repeat.
14. What's his (her) name?	14. T: Point to the 3 characters in visual #1. St: Respond.
15. Optional: What does Lucy have? What does Dick have?	15. T: Point to the books and glasses. Model. St: She has books. He has glasses.
16. This is "Dick". What other word has "ick" in it?	16. T: Write "Dick" on the board. Underline the "ick". St: sick St: Assist if necessary.
17. Listen.	17. T: Model the paragraph. St: Listen.
18. Repeat.	18. T: Model the paragraph, sentence by sentence. St: Listen and repeat in chorus and individually.
19. Read.	19. St: Read the paragraph individually, as frequently as necessary. T: Listen for pronunciation, stress and intonation.
20. Answer the questions.	20. T: Ask "Who/What" and "Is/Are questions about the paragraph in items #1. St: Respond.
21. Look at the picture in #2.	21. T: Ask "Who are they?", "What are they?", "What do they have?", "What are they (lockers)?", "What are the locker numbers?". St: Respond.
22. Listen and answer the questions.	22. T: Model the questions. St: Respond orally.
23. Look at the picture in #3. Who (What) is he?	23. St: Respond.
24. Listen and answer the questions.	24. T: Model the questions. St: Respond.

25. Let's read again.

26. Let's write.

27. Optional: Let's write.

25. St: Reread the entire page, responding to the questions orally.

26. St: Answer the questions in items #2 and 3.
    T: Check for accuracy and legibility. Be certain that the time has been filled in at the upper right hand corner.

27. St: Practice writing the paragraph (and variations of it).
    T: A master for writing paper is provided on p. 396 of this guide.

Student Workbook p. 115

VISUALS
all plural visuals listed for student
workbook p. 109 on p. 208 of this guide

INSTRUCTION

1. Listen.

2. Listen and repeat.

3. I am "A" and you are "B".

4. Who will be "A" and "B"?

5. Let's read.

6. Open your books to p. 115.

7. Let's read.

8. Let's write.

9. Optional: Study the words for spelling.

ACTIVITY/RESPONSE

1. T: Write the dailogue in item #1, p. 115 on the board. Tape up or hold up visual 144, students. Model the dialogue.
   St: Listen.

2. T: Model the dialogue line by line.
   St: Repeat in chorus and individually.

3. T: Assume role and reverse upon completion.
   Cl:
   Gr: } Assume role.
   St:

4. T: Seek volunteers or assign roles.
   St: Assume roles.

5. T: Change the visuals and vocabulary items on the board until all visuals and vocabulary presented on p. 115 have been practiced.
   St: Read.

6. St: Open books.

7. T: Assign roles for each dialogue.
   St: Read and respond orally for all dialogues on the page.

8. St: Fill in the responses for items #5-7 and the personal information at the upper right hand corner.
   T: Check for accuracy and legibility.

9. T: Assign all singular and plural occupational sight words for a spelling test.
   St: Study.

Student Workbook   p. 116
Lesson Four, Section II

SIGHT WORDS
where, from, I'm, (Japan/ Japanese, Mexico/Mexican, China/Chinese)*, country, We're

VISUALS
26 map
93 China

INSTRUCTIONAL AIDS
a world map (optional)
yellow 3 x 5 flash cards

STRUCTURE

Where (What country) are you from?
What are you?

I'm (We're) from (country).
My country's (name).
I'm (We're) (nationality).

INSTRUCTION

1. I'm from (country).
   I'm (nationality).

2. Where are you from?

3. Are you (nationality)?

4. Let's read.

5. Ask each other "Where are you from?"

6. Listen.

7. This word is "I'm". I put "I" and "am" together to make "I'm".

ACTIVITY/RESPONSE

1. T: Point to your country on the map or on visual 26.
   St: Listen.

2. T: Model response for each individual student. Point to the map.
   St: Respond individually.

3. T: Point to the map and model response.
   St: "Yes, I am." or "No, I'm not."

4. T: Write the question "Where are you from?" on the board or on a sentence strip. Model.
   St: Listen and repeat in chorus and individually.

5. St: Ask one another "Where are you from?" round-robin fashion and respond.

6. T: Copy the dialogue in item 1 on p. 116 onto the board or on sentence strips. Model the entire dialogue.
   St: Listen.

7. T: Demonstrate and provide example uses of "I'm".
   St: Listen.

*optional

8. Let's read.

9. I'm "A" and you're "B".

10. Let's read.

11. Listen.

12. This word is "country".
    My country's _____ .
    What's your country?

13. Let's read.

14. What country are you from?

15. What are you?

16. Listen.

17. This word is "We're". I put "we" and "are" together to make "we're".

18. Listen and repeat.

8. T: Model the dialogue line by line.
   Cl:
   Gr: Read.
   St:

9. T: Assume role.
   St: Assume role.
   T: For each student, fill in the name of their country and their nationality.

10. T: Pair the students up.
    St: Practice the dialogue and give their own personal information.

11. T: Write the paragraph in item 2 on p. 116 on the board or on sentence strips. Model.
    St: Listen.

12. T: Model response.
    St: My country's _____ .

13. St: Read the paragraph and then reread supplying their own personal information.

14. T: If possible, pair students from the same country. Model response.
    St: We're from _____ .
    T: Continue practice until students understand the use of "we're".

15. T: Model response.
    St: We're (nationality) .

16. T: Write the dialogue in item 3 on p. 116 on the board or on sentence strips. Model.
    St: Listen.

17. T: Demonstrate and provide example uses of "We're".
    St: Listen.

18. T: Model the dialogue line by line.
    Cl:
    Gr: Repeat.
    St:

19. I'm "A" and you are "B".	19. T: Pair up two students if possible from the same country. Assume role. St: Assume role. T: After reading, substitute the student's country and nationality in the appropriate spaces.
20. Optional: Fix the sentences.	20. T: If the dialogues have been written on sentence strips, cut them into components and scramble them. St: Rearrange the sentences (words).
21. Open your books to p. 116.	21. St: Open books.
22. Let's read.	22. T: Model the dialogues and paragraph if necessary. St: Assume roles and read supplying their own personal information in item #4. T: Continue reading practice as necessary. Listen for pronunciation, stress and intonation.
23. Let's write.	23. St: Fill in the responses for item #4 and and their hair color at the upper right hand corner. T: Check for accuracy and legibility.
24. Optional, mechanics: This is a capital letter. We use capital letters for the first word of a sentence and for names.	24. T: Provide instruction for the capitals, questions marks, periods, apostrophes and commas. St: Listen.
25. What two letters say /wh/?	25. St: w - h
26. What word on this page starts with /wh/?	26. St: where T: Repeat strategy for /fr/ from, /st/ first and last, /ch/ China.
27. Let's make some cards.	27. St: Make yellow 3 x 5 cards of all the sight words, writing "I am" on the back of "I'm", the name of their country on the back of "country", and "We are" on the back of "We're". T: Make corresponding 5 x 8 cards.
28. Let's read.	28. St: Read the sight words in chorus and individually.

29. Optional: Let's write.

29. St: Practice writing the sight words and/or the dialogues and paragraphs on p. 116.
    T: A master for lined paper is provided on p. 396 of this guide.

30. Where are you from? What country are you from? What are you?

30. T: Review learnings from this lesson one last time.
    St: Respond.

Student Workbook   p. 117

SIGHT WORD
birthplace

VISUALS
26 map
93 China

INSTRUCTIONAL AIDS
a world map (optional)
a yellow 3 x 5 card

STRUCTURE

What's your birthplace?   It's (country) .

INSTRUCTION

1. I'm from (country) .
   Where are you from?

2. I'm (nationality) . What are you?

3. Where is (student name) from?

4. What is (s)he?

5. Where are (student name) and (student name) from?

6. This word is "country". "What is your country?" is the same as "Where are you from?"

7. This word is "birthplace". It is the same as "country". "What is your country?" is the same as "What is your birthplace?"

8. Let's read this word.

ACTIVITY/RESPONSE

1. T: Review the sight words, visuals, structures and concepts from the previous lesson. Point to the map indicating the countries.
   St: I'm from (country) .

2. St: I'm (We're) (nationality) .
   T: Model if necessary.

3. St: (S)He's from (country) .
   T: Model if necessary. Show visual 93 if you're tutoring an individual student.

4. St: (S)He's (nationality) .

5. T: Ask this question if 2 students are from the same country.
   St: They're from (country) .
   T: Model if necessary.

6. T: Write "country" on the board or hold up the yellow 5 x 8 card of "country".
   St: Listen.

7. T: Write "birthplace" on the board.
   St: Listen.

8. T: Model.
   St: Repeat as frequently as necessary.

9. What's your birthplace?

10. What two letters say /th/ and /pl/?

11. Look at birthplace. Circle the /th/ and /pl/.

12. Optional, compound words: Some words in English are made up of two words such as <u>snow</u> <u>man</u>. "Birthplace" is made up of "birth" and "place".

13. Optional, syllables: How many syllables are there in "birthplace"?

14. Optional, vowels: What are the vowels? What vowel is in "birth" (in "place")?

15. Let's make a card.

16. Open your books to p. 117.

17. Let's read.

18. Let's read.

19. Let's circle the correct answer and write.

9. T: Model.
   St: It's (country).
   T: Repeat question/response practice as frequently as necessary.

10. St: t - h, p - l

11. T: Point to the word "birthplace".
    St: Come to the board and circle the letters.

12. St: Listen and provide other compound words if possible.

13. T: Pound out the syllables on the board or on a table.
    St: Listen and respond.

14. St: a, e, i, o, u; "i" and "a"
    T: Teach this concept if it hasn't been taught yet.

15. St: Make a yellow 3 x 5 card with "birthplace" written on one side and the name of their country on the other.
    T: Make a corresponding yellow 5 x 8 card.

16. St: Open books.

17. T: Model the questions and sample responses for items 1-3.
    St: Repeat and orally select the correct response.

18. St: Read items 4-7 supplying the name of their country and their nationality.
    T: Assist if necessary. Continue practice until all students have had an opportunity to practice and until students understand that 4-6 are asking the same question.

19. T: Demonstrate activity on the board if necessary.
    St: Circle the correct answer. Fill in their country and/or nationality for items 4-6 and fill in their birthplace at the upper right hand corner.
    T: Check for accuracy and legibility.

Student Workbook p. 118
Contractions

INSTRUCTIONAL AIDS
the 5 x 8 sight word flash cards
of the contractions

INSTRUCTION

1. What's your country (birthplace)? Where are you from? What are you?

2. These two words are "I am". I am a teacher. I am a woman (man). I am (nationality), etc. What are you?

3. I can put "I" and "am" together. This is "I'm". The letter "I" in "I am" or "I'm" is always a capital letter.

4. I'm a teacher. I'm a woman (man). I'm (nationality), etc. What are you?

5. Let's read the words.

6. What is the short form for this word?

7. Let's read the words.

8. What is the long form of this word?

ACTIVITY/RESPONSE

1. T: Review concepts, visuals, structure and sight words from the previous lessons.
   St: "It's (country)" or "I'm (We're) from (country)" or "I'm (We're) (nationality)".

2. T: Write "I am" on the board. Model each student's occupation, sex, nationality, etc., if necessary.
   St: I am (a) _____ .

3. T: Demonstrate by erasing the "a" in in "am" and replacing it with an apostrophe.
   St: Observe.

4. St: I'm, (a) _____ .
   T: Repeat instructions 2-3 for the following: you are, are not, he is, she is, it is, is not, we are, they are, what is, name is. Provide sample sentences using the long form. Elicit sentences from the students and demonstrate how the contraction of each is made. Practice the sentences again substituting the long form for the contraction.

5. T: Hold up the side of the flash card with the long form of the contraction.
   St: Read.

6. T: Hold up the side of the flash cards with the long form of the contraction.
   St: I'm, you're, he's, etc.

7. T: Hold up the contraction side of the flash cards.
   St: Read.

8. T: Hold up the contraction side of the flash cards.
   St: I am, you are, he is, etc.

9. Write the short form for these words.

10. Open your books to p. 118.

11. Write the short form of these words.

12. Optional: Study the words for a dictation.

13. Optional: Let's write.

9. T: Write on the board all the words listed on p. 118.
   St: Make the corresponding contractions.

10. St: Open books.

11. T: Allow students to copy samples from the board if necessary.
    St: Write.
    T: Check for accuracy and legibility. Be certain that students have filled in the name of their country in the in the upper right hand corner.

12. St: Study.
    T: Administer a quiz in the following class.

13. St: Practice writing either the contractions or sentences using the contractions on p. 120.
    T: If p. 120 has already been used, a master for lined paper is provided on p. 396 of this guide.

Student Workbook   p. 119

INSTRUCTIONAL AIDS
the 5 x 8 sight word flash cards of the contractions

INSTRUCTION

1. Optional, quiz: Listen and write: I'm, you're, he's, etc.

2. This is "I'm". "I'm" is the same as "I am".

3. I am a teacher. I am a man (woman). I am (nationality), etc. What are you?

4. This is "you're". "You're" is the same as "you are".

5. Let's read the words.

6. What is the long form of this word?

7. Write the long form for these words.

8. Open your books to p. 119.

9. Write the long form of these words.

ACTIVITY/RESPONSE

1. T: Give a dictation quiz of the contractions if they have been assigned for study.

2. T: Write "I'm" and "I am" on the board.
   St: Listen.

3. T: Model "I am" sentences for the students. Model the same sentences again using "I'm".
   St: I am (a) _____ .
       I'm (a) _____ .

4. T: Repeat instruction for all the words listed on p. 119. Provide sample sentences using the long form and repeat them substituting the long form with the contractions. Elicit sentences using the long form, then substituting the long form with contractions.

5. T: Hold up the long form of the contraction flash cards and then the short form.
   St: Read.

6. T: Hold up the contraction side of the flash cards.
   St: I am, you are, he is, etc.

7. T: Write all the contractions listed on p. 119 on the board.
   St: Write the long form.

8. St: Open books.

9. T: Allow students to copy samples from the board if necessary.
   St: Write.
   T: Check for accuracy and legibility. Be certain that students have filled in their birthplace at the upper right hand corner.

10. Optional: Study the words on p. 119 for dictation.

10. St: Study.
    T: Administer a dictation quiz in the following class.

11. Optional: Let's write.

11. St: Practice writing the contractions, the long forms and/or sentences on p. 120.
    T: If p. 120 has already been used, a master for lined paper is provided on p. 396 of this guide.

Student Workbook p. 121
Lesson Five, Section 1
What time is it?

VISUALS
24 Good morning
22 Good afternoon
30 Good evening

INSTRUCTIONAL AIDS
a cardboard clock with movable hands
the sight word flash cards of Good evening, Hello, early, on time and late

STRUCTURE

What time is it?   It's (3) :15.
                         Optional: It's a quarter after _____ .

INSTRUCTION

1. What is this?

2. What does a clock say?

3. What are these?

4. What's this (and this)?

5. What is the short hand for?

6. Optional: How many hours are there in a day?

7. What time is it?

8. You fix the clock. It's _____ o'clock.

ACTIVITY/RESPONSE

1. T: Hold up the clock, point to one or draw one on the board.
   St: (It's a) clock.

2. St: (It says the) time.

3. T: Point to the hands.
   St: (They're) hands.

4. T: Point to the individual hands.
   St: (It's the) short (long) hand.

5. T: Set the clock on the hour.
   St: (It's for the) hour.

6. St: 24
   T: Teach this concept if it was not previously taught.

7. T: Set (or draw) the hour hand at each hour.
   Cl:
   Gr: It's _____ o'clock.
   St:

8. T: Hand the clock to a student and call out the time.
   St: Listens and sets the clock.
   T: Continue practice until students can ask "What time is it?", answer with good pronunciation and set the clock on the hour with accuracy.

9.	What is the long hand for?	9. St:	(It's for the) minutes.
10.	How many minutes are there in an hour?	10. St: T: St:	(There are) 60. Repeat steps 7-8 to review (4):30. Respond.
11.	How do I say "Hi" or "Hello" at this time?	11. T: St:	Hold up visuals 24, 22 and 30. Good morning (afternoon, evening).
12.	If class starts at 8:00 and you are here at 7:00 (8:00, 9:00), you are _____ .	12. St: T:	early, (on time, late) Reteach vocabulary if necessary.
13.	Let's read these words.	13. T: St: T:	Hold up the sight word flash cards listed in the Instructional Aids or write the words on the board. Read. Model and reteach if necessary.
14.	Look at the clock. It's 12:15. What time is it?	14. T: St: T:	Hold up the clock. Count the minutes from 1 to 15 if necessary. It's 12:15. Observe for correct pronunciation of "15". Change the hour hand until all hours have been reviewed at the quarter hour.
15.	What time is it?	15. St:	It's (6):15.
16.	You ask, "What time is it?"	16. T: St:	Hand the clock to a student. Sets the clock and asks the next student "What time is it?". That student responds, sets a new time and asks the next student "What time is it?", and so on.
17.	You fix the clock. It's (7):15.	17. T: St: T:	Hand the clock to a student and call out a time. Listens and sets the clock. Continue practice until students can ask "What time is it?", answer with good pronunciation and set the clock at the quarter hour with accuracy.
18.	Listen.	18. T: St:	Write the first dialogue on p. 121 on the board or on sentence strips. Model. Listen.

19. Listen and read.	19. T: Model the entire dialogue line by line. Cl: Gr: } Repeat. St:
20. I'm "A" and you are "B".	20. T: Assume role and reverse upon completion. Cl: Gr: } Assume role. St:
21. Let's read.	21. T: Pair students up. St: Read and reverse roles.
22. Optional: Fix the sentences.	22. T: Cut up the sentence strips into the components. Shuffle and deal the components out to the students. St: Rearrange the dialogue.
23. Optional, punctuation: This is a comma. I use a comma before saying somebody's name and after "yes" or "no".	23. T: Point to the commas in the dialogue. Give instructions for the capital letters, the question mark, the colon in the time and the periods. Game: Rewrite the dialogue leaving out all the punctuation and capitals. See how many the students can fill in. St: Listen and respond.
24. Open your books to p. 121.	24. St: Open books and write their address at the upper right hand corner.
25. Let's read.	25. T: Ask for volunteers or assign roles. St: Read, roleplay and reverse roles. Continue reading the entire page. T: Be certain that students have accurately filled in their address at the upper right hand corner.
26. Optional, vocabulary development: They're walking and talking.	26. T: Point to the visual on p. 121. St: Listen and repeat.
27. Optional: Let's write.	27. St: Copy the dialogue(s) on p. 121 of the workbook. T: A master for lined paper is provided on p. 396 of this guide.

28. Optional: Listen to the time. Draw the hands on the clock (and write the time). It's 1:15.
Variation: Teacher draws the hands and students write the time.

29. Optional "It's (4):15 is the same as "It's a quarter after (4).

30. Optional: What time do you get up (eat lunch, go to work, etc.)?

28. T: Duplicate the blank clocks on p. 397 of this guide in Appendix C. Provide several examples on the board. Call out times.
St: Draw hands (and write the times if the teacher has requested them to do so).
T: Check for accuracy.

29. St: Listen and practice.
T: Practice as per instructions 14-17.

30. T: Instruct students how to respond and provide a time on the cardboard clock if necessary. Review time on the hour, half hour and quarter hour.
St: I get up at _____ .

Student Workbook   p. 122

SIGHT WORDS
Excuse me

INSTRUCTIONAL AIDS
a cardboard clock with movable hands
the sight word flash cards of
  Thanks, Thank you
a yellow 3 x 5 flash card

INSTRUCTION

1. What time is it?

2. Let's read these words.

3. What two letters say /th/?

4. What do you say?

5. When I do this, I say "Excuse me."

6. Listen.

7. Listen and read.

ACTIVITY/RESPONSE

1. T: Review the time on the hour, half hour and quarter hour.
   St: Respond, set clocks and ask each other "What time is it?"

2. T: Hold up the sight word flash cards for "Thanks" and "Thank you" or write the words on the board.
   St: Read.
   T: Model and reteach as necessary.

3. St: t - h
   T: Point them out in "Thanks" and "Thank you".

4. T: Roleplay, giving students compliments, handing them an object, etc.
   St: "Thanks" or "Thank you".

5. T: Roleplay situations by bumping into someone, interrupting a conversation, etc. Model "Excuse me".
   St: Practice "Excuse me" and make a yellow 3 x 5 card.
   T: Make a corresponding 5 x 8 card.

6. T: Write the first dialogue on p. 122 on the board or on sentence strips. Model.
   St: Listen.

7. T: Model the entire dialogue line by line.
   Cl:
   Gr: } Repeat.
   St:

8. I'm "A" and you are "B".

8. T: Assume role and reverse upon completion.
Cl:
Gr: Assume role.
St:

9. Let's read.

9. T: Pair students up.
St: Read and reverse roles.

10. Optional: Fix the sentences.

10. T: Cut up the sentence strips into the components. Shuffle and deal the components out to the students.
St: Rearrange the dialogue.

11. Optional, punctuation: This is a period. I use a period to finish a sentence.

11. T: Point to the periods in the dialogue. Give instructions for the capital letters, the question mark, the colon in the time and the comma.
Game: Rewrite the dialogue leaving out all the punctuation and capitals. See how many students can fill in.
St: Listen and respond.

12. Open your books to p. 122.

12. St: Open books and write the name of their country at the upper right hand corner.

13. Let's read.

13. T: Ask for volunteers or assign roles.
St: Read, roleplay and reverse roles. Continue reading the entire page.
T: Be certain that students have accurately filled in the name of their country at the upper right hand corner.

14. Optional: Let's write.

14. St: Copy the dialogue(s) on p. 122 of the workbook.
T: A master for lined paper is provided on p. 396 of this guide.

15. Optional: Listen to the time. Draw the hands on the clock (and write the time). It's 4:15.
Variation: Teacher draws the hands and students write the time.

15. T: Duplicate the blank clocks on p. 397 of this guide in Appendix C. Provide several examples on the board. Call out the times.
St: Draw hands and write the times if the teacher has requested them to do so.
T: Check for accuracy.

16. Optional: "It's (5):15" is the same same as "It's a quarter after (5)."

16. St: Listen and practice.
T: Practice as per instructions 14-17.

17. What time do you eat dinner (go to school, go to bed, etc.)?

17. T: Instruct students how to respond and provide a time on the cardboard clock if necessary. Review time on the hour, half hour and quarter hour.
St: I eat dinner at _____ .

Student Workbook   p. 123

SIGHT WORDS
middle (name), Good night,
How time flies.

VISUAL
30 Good evening (night)

INSTRUCTIONAL AIDS
a cardboard clock with movable hands
yellow 3 x 5 cards

STRUCTURE
What time is it?   It's (2):45.

INSTRUCTION

1. What time is it?

2. This word is "middle".

3. Many Americans have a middle name. For example, John Quincy Adams, Lyndon Baines Johnson, Franklin Delano Roosevelt and John Fitzgerald Kennedy were presidents of the United States. Which is the middle (first, last) name?

4. What's your middle (first, last) name?

5. How do I say "Hello" at this time?

6. If I want to say "Goodbye" at this time, I say "Good night".

7. Let's read these words.

ACTIVITY/RESPONSE

1. T: Review the time on the hour, half hour and quarter hour.
   St: Respond, set clocks and ask each other "What time is it?"

2. T: Write "middle" on the board and demonstrate through various examples what position "middle" holds.
   St: Listen and repeat "middle".

3. St: Point to the middle (first, last) name.

4. T: Note: Many foreign people do not have a middle name. Teach them to say "I don't have one."
   St: Respond.

5. T: Hold up visual 30.
   St: Good evening.

6. St: Listen and say "Good night".

7. T: Write "middle" and "Good night" on the board. Model.
   St: Read.

241

8. Sometimes time feels very fast. Americans say "How time flies."

8. T: Provide examples of "How time flies". Write the expression on the board. If necessary, draw a clock on the board with wings on it to demonstrate the concept.

St: Listen and read the expression.

9. Let's make some cards.

9. St: Make yellow 3 x 5 cards of the sight words and expressions. Write a dash, "none" or their middle name on the back of "middle".

10. Let's read.

10. St: Read the sight words in chorus and individually.

11. Look at the clock. It's 12:45. What time is it?

11. T: Hold up the clock or draw one on the board. Count from 30 to 45 if necessary.
St: It's 12:45.

12. It's 1:45.

12. T: Model all the hours at the three quarter hour.
St: Listen, repeat and practice as much as necessary.

13. You ask, "What time is it?"

13. T: Hand the clock to a student.
St: Sets the clock and asks the next student "What time is it?" That student responds, sets a new time and asks the next student "What time is it?" and so on.

14. You fix the clock. It's (8):45.

14. T: Hand the clock to a student and call out a time.
St: Listens and sets the clock.
T: Continue practice until students can ask "What time is it?", answer with good pronunciation and set the clock at the hour, half hour, quarter hour and three quarter hour with accuracy.

15. Listen.

15. T: Write the first dialogue on p. 123 on the board or on sentence strips. Model.
St: Listen.

16. Listen and repeat.

16. T: Model the entire dialogue line by line.
Cl:
Gr: Repeat.
St:

17. I'm "A" and you are "B".

17. T: Assume role and reverse upon completion.
Cl:
Gr: } Assume role.
St:

18. Let's read.

18. T: Pair students up.
St: Read and reverse roles.

19. Optional: Fix the sentences.

19. T: Cut up the sentence strips into the components. Shuffle and deal the components out to the students.
St: Rearrange the dialogue.

20. Optional, punctuation: This is a capital letter. I use capitals for the first word of a sentence or for names.

20. T: Point to the capitals in the dialogue. Give instructions for the question mark, the colon in the time and periods.
Game: Rewrite the dialogue leaving out all the punctuation and capitals. See how many students can fill in.
St: Listen and respond.

21. Open your books to p. 123.

21. St: Open books and fill in their full name.
T: If students do not have a middle name, teach them to write a dash or "none".

22. Let's read.

22. T: Ask for volunteeers or assign roles.
St: Read, roleplay and reverse roles. Continue reading the entire page.
T: Be certain that students have accurately filled in their full name at the upper right hand corner.

23. Optional: Let's write.

23. St: Copy the dialogue(s) on p. 123 of the workbook.
T: A master for lined paper is provided on p. 396 of this guide.

24. Optional: Listen to the time. Draw the hands on the clock (and write the time). It's 12:45.
Variation: Teacher draws the hands and the students write the time.

24. T: Duplicate the blank clocks on p. 397 of this guide. Provide several examples on the board. Call out the times.
St: Draw hands (and write the times if the teacher has requested them to do so).
T: Check for accuracy.

25. Optional: "It's (8):45 is the same as "It's a quarter to (9) ."

25. St: Listen and practice.
T: Practice as per instructions 12-15.

26. Optional: What time do you get home from work (get home from school, get to work, etc.)?

26. T: Instruct students how to respond and provide a time on the cardboard clock if necessary. Review time on the hour, half hour, quarter hour and three quarter hour.
St: I get home from work at _____ .

Student Workbook   p. 124   INSTRUCTIONAL AID
                                                         a cardboard clock with movable hands

---

INSTRUCTION   ACTIVITY/RESPONSE

1. What time is it?   1. T: Review all times on the hour, half hour,
                                                quarter and three quarter hour.
                                            St: Respond.

2. You set the clock. It's   2. T: Call out the times.
   ___:00/ ___:15/ ___:30/ ___:45.   St: Set the clock.

3. Read the words.   3. T: Review sight words with expressions
                                                having to do with time.
                                            St: Read.

4. Open your books to p. 124.   4. St: Open books.

5. Let's read.   5. St: Read all the questions and select
                                                the correct responses orally.

6. Circle the correct answer.   6. T: Point to the sample box in item #1.
                                                Demonstrate the correct answer has been
                                                circled.
                                            St: Circle the answers.
                                            T: Check student work for accuracy.
                                                Be certain that they have written their
                                                middle name, a dash or "none" at the upper
                                                right hand corner.

7. Optional: What time is it?   7. T: Teach students to give all the times
                                                between ___:00 and ___:30.
                                            St; "It's (12:05)" or "It's (5) after (12)."

Student Workbook   p. 125

INSTRUCTION	ACTIVITY/RESPONSE
1. What time is it?	1. T: Review all the times taught up to this point. Review the sight words and sentence strips that relate to time as necessary.
2. Open your books to p. 125.	2. St: Open books.
3. Let's read.	3. St: Read the questions and supply the responses orally.
4. Let's write.	4. St: Write the time and the question as necessary. T: Check for accuracy. Be certain that the area code and telephone number, a dash or "none" have been filled in at the upper right hand corner.
5. Optional: Let's write.	5. T: If students need further practice, p. 397 of this guide provides a master for blank clocks. On a copy, fill in the hands of the clocks and the lines for writing before duplicating the exercise for the students. St: Write "What time is it?" and "It's ___:___."
6. Optional: What time is it?	6. T: Teach students to give all times between ___:31 and ___:59. St: "It's (11:50)" or "It's (10) to (12)."

Student Workbook   p. 126

INSTRUCTIONAL AID
a cardboard clock with movable hands

INSTRUCTION

1. Show me ___:00, ___:15, ___:30, ___:45.

2. Write the time.

3. It's (4:30). Draw the hands.

4. Open your books to p. 126. Draw the hands.

5. Look at the bottom of the page. Listen and write.

ACTIVITY/RESPONSE

1. T: Hand the clock to a student.
   St: Set the clock.
   T: Continue until students have had a good review. Review sight words and sentence strips pertaining to time as necessary.

2. T: Set the clock at various times.
   St: Write the time on the board.

3. T: Draw a clock on the board. Call out the time.
   St: Draw the hands.

4. St: Open books and draw the hands.
   T: Check for accuracy. Be certain students have written the name of their country at the upper right hand corner.

5. T: Dictate any of the following:
   a) times, such as "It's 3:15."
   b) sight words, such as "I'm on time."
   c) expressions, such as "How time flies." and/or
   d) personal information vocabulary where the students are expected to write their own information, such as T: name   St: Jose Gomez.
   St: Write.

Student Workbook   p. 127
Extension
Where are you from?

SIGHT WORDS
married, single

VISUAL
26 map

INSTRUCTIONAL AIDS
a world map (optional)
yellow 3 x 5 cards

INSTRUCTION

1. Open your books to p. 127 and look at the picture in #1.

2. Who's Mr. (Mrs.) Lee? What is he (she)?

3. This word is "married". In the U.S., married men and women usually use the same last name.

4. Are you married?

5. Mr. Lee is from Korea.

6. Where are you from?

7. He's Korean.

8. What are you?

9. Listen.

10. Listen and read.

11. Where is Mrs. Lee from?

ACTIVITY/RESPONSE

1. T: Write the first paragraph on p. 127 on the board, on an overhead projector or on sentence strips. Model the first sentence.
   St: Listen.

2. T: Point to the characters.
   St: He's a doctor.

3. T: Point to "married".
   Note: In some countries, married spouses do not necessarily use the same surname.
   St: Listen.

4. St: "Yes, I am" or "No, I'm not."

5. T: Model the second sentence of the paragraph. Point to Korea on the world map or in visual 26.
   St: Listen.

6. St: I'm from (country).

7. T: Model the third sentence.

8. St: I'm (nationality).

9. T: Model the rest of the paragraph.
   St: Listen.

10. T: Model the entire paragraph, sentence by sentence.
    St: Listen and repeat in chorus and individually.

11. St: She's from France.
    T: Point to France on the map or in visual 26.

247

12. What is she?

13. Let's read.

14. What two letters say /sh/, /fr/ and /ch/?

15. Point to the /sh/, /fr/ and /ch/.

16. Optional, punctuation: I use a period after "Mr." and "Mrs." and at the end of a sentence.

17. Optional, decoding:
    (Fr)<u>ance</u>   (Fr)<u>ench</u>
    dance   bench
    lance   drench
    prance   quench
    stance   trench
    trance

18. Optional, pronouns: I can use "He" for "Mr. Lee", "She" for "Mrs. Lee" and "they" for "Mr. and Mrs. Lee".

19. Optional, compound words: Which word is made of 2 words?

20. Optional: Fix the sentences (words).

21. Look at the picture in #2.

---

12. St: She's French (a housewife).

13. St: Read the paragraph.
    T: Observe for accurate pronunciation, stress and intonation. Repeat reading as frequently as necessary.

14. St: s - h, f - r, c - h

15. St: Point to the s - h in "She's and the f - r and c - h in "French".

16. T: Point to the periods in the paragraph. Provide instructions for capital letters and apostrophe "s".
    Game: Erase all of the punctuation and capital letters (or make a ditto with the same). See how many the students can fill in correctly.
    St: Listen and respond.

17. St: Decode.
    See p. 7 of this guide for discussion and suggestions.

18. T: Demonstrate how pronouns take the place of nouns. Erase the nouns (pronouns) and substitute them for pronouns (nouns).
    St: Listen and make substitutions orally and on the board.

19. St: housewife
    T: Teach the concept if it has not been taught yet.

20. T: If the sentences were written on sentence strips, cut them into components and scramble.
    St: Rearrange the sentence (word) order.

21. T: Write the second paragraph on the board, on an overhead projector or on sentence strips. Model the first sentence.
    St: Listen.

22.	This word is "single". "Single" means "not married".	22. T: St:	Point to the word "single". Listen and repeat "single".
23.	Are you single? Is Joe (Lucy) single?	23. St:	"Yes, I am" or "No, I'm not" and "Yes, he (she) is."
24.	They're from Mexico. Who is from from Mexico?	24. T: St:	Read the second sentence. Lucy and Joe (are from Mexico).
25.	They're Mexican. What are you?	25. T: St:	Read the third sentence. I'm (nationality) .
26.	They're students. What are you?	26. T: St:	Read the fourth sentence. "I'm a student" or "We're students".
27.	Listen and read.	27. T: St:	Model the entire paragraph, sentence by sentence. Listen and repeat in chorus and individually.
28.	Let's read.	28. St: T:	Read the paragraph. Observe for accurate pronunciation, stress and intonation. Repeat reading as frequently as necessary.
29.	Optional, punctuation.	29. T: St:	Repeat instruction 16. Listen and respond.
30.	Optional, pronouns.	30. T: St:	Repeat instruction 18. Listen and make substitutions orally and on the board.
31.	Optional: Fix the sentences.	31. T: St:	Repeat instruction 20. Rearrange the sentence (word) order for the paragraph.
32.	Look at the picture in #3.	32. T: St:	Write the third paragraph on the board, on an overhead projector or on sentence strips. Read the entire paragraph. Listen.
33.	What's her name? Is she married? Where is she from? What is she?	33. T: St:	Ask content questions. Respond.
34.	Listen and read.	34. T: St:	Model the entire paragraph, sentence by sentence. Listen and repeat in chorus and individually.

35. Let's read.

35. St: Read the paragraph.
    T: Observe for accurate pronunciation, stress and intonation. Repeat reading as frequently as necessary.

36. Optional, punctuation.

36. T: Repeat instruction 16.
    St: Listen and respond.

37. Optional: Fix the sentences.

37. T: Repeat instruction 20.
    St: Rearrange the sentences and word order of the paragraph.

38. Let's read #3 again. Use your name.

38. St: Read the third paragraph, substituting their personal information.
    T: Upon completion, have the students fill in their information on the board, overhead projector or sentence strips. If students are capable, have them do the same for the first and second paragraphs, filling in the names of other students, family members, etc.

39. Look at the bottom of the page. Write about yourself or someone else.

39. St: Using paragraph 1, 2 or 3 as a model, students change the names and personal information to write about themselves or others.
    T: Provide oral examples as necessary. Check for accuracy and legibility. Be certain that the present time has been filled in at the upper right hand corner.

40. Let's make some cards.

40. St: Make yellow 3 x 5 cards of "married" and "single".
    T: Make corresponding 5 x 8 cards.

41. Optional: Let's write.

41. St: Copy the paragraph(s) on p. 127 or practice writing the sight words.
    T: A master for writing paper is provided on p. 396 of this guide.

Student Workbook p. 128
Lesson Five, Section II
What day is it?

SIGHT WORDS
month, day, (date, optional),
March, Sunday (Sun.) Monday (Mon.)
Tuesday (Tues.) Wednesday (Wed.)
Thurs (Thur.) Friday (Fri.)
Saturday (Sat.)

VISUAL
74 calendar

INSTRUCTIONAL AID
a calendar

STRUCTURE

What day is it? It's _____ day.

INSTRUCTION

1. This is a calendar. It tells me the month, the day (and the date).

2. Optional: There are 12 months in a year. How many months are there in a year?

3. This month is (March).

4. There are about 4 weeks in a month. This is a week and this is a week, etc. What is this?

5. There are 7 days in a week.

6. Sometimes, on a calendar, we write the days in a short way.

ACTIVITY/RESPONSE

1. T: Write "month", "day" (and "date") on the board. "Date" should be taught on an optional basis.
   St: Listen and repeat "month", "day" ("date").

2. St: Listen and respond "12".

3. T: Show visual 74 or open calendar up to the appropriate month.
   St: Repeat "(March)".

4. T: Point out the 4 weeks in visual 74 or or in the calendar.
   St: Listen and respond "(This is a) week."

5. T: Point to the days in the calendar. Write the names of the days on the board. Model the names.
   St: Repeat the days of the week in chorus and individually.

6. T: Write the abbreviations next to where the days are written.
   St: Listen and observe.

7. Optional: Listen.

7. T: Write the following concepts on the board or on Language Master Cards* if students are capable of digesting the concepts:
1 year = 365 days
1 year = 12 months
1 year = 52 weeks
1 month = about 4 weeks
1 month = about 30 days
1 week = 7 days
1 day = 24 hours
1 hour = 60 minutes
1 minute = 60 seconds
St: Listen, repeat, copy, study and answer questions regarding the information.

8. Listen.

8. T: Write the first dialogue on p. 128 on the board. Hold up visual 74 and model the dialogue pointing to a Tuesday.
St: Listen.

9. Listen and read.

9. T: Model the dialogue line by line.
St: Read in chorus and individually.

10. Read.

10. T: Ask for volunteers or assign roles.
St: Read and reverse roles upon completion.

11. Listen.

11. T: Write the paragraph in item 3 on p. 128 on the board. Hold up visual 74 and model the dialogue pointing to a Thursday. Repeat instructions 9-10.
St: Listen; respond and read.

12. Open your books to p. 128 and write.

12. T: Point to the upper right hand corner.
St: Check either "married" or "single".
T: Check for accuracy.

13. Let's read.

13. T: Model as necessary.
St: Read the entire page.

14. Optional, ordinal numbers:
This is number 1. I say "Sunday, March 1st."

14. T: Teach students how to say the ordinal numbers and how to say the date. Make Language Master Cards.*

*See p. 10 of this guide for suggested uses of the Language Master.

15. Optional, days, dates: What day is the 10th, 20th, etc.?

15. St: Respond.

16. Let's make some cards.

16. St: Make a yellow 3 x 5 card for all the sight words. Have students write abbreviations of the days on the back of the day flash cards.

17. Let's read the words.

17. St: Practice reading the sight words in chorus and individually.

18. What day is today?

18. St: It's _____ day.

19. Let's write.

19. St: Practice writing the days of the week, their abbreviations and the other sight words.
    T: A master for writing paper is provided on p. 396 of this guide.

20. Optional: Fix the words according to the alphabet.

20. St: Alphabetize the sight words.
    T: An additional alphabetizing exercise is provided on p. 398 of this guide for duplication.

21. Optional: Listen and write the date.

21. T: If you have taught students ordinal numbers and dates, dictate various dates.
    St: Write.

22. Optional: Study the days of the week for a spelling test.

22. St: Study.

Student Workbook   p. 129

SIGHT WORDS
today, divorced, widowed

VISUAL
74 calendar

INSTRUCTIONAL AID
a calendar

INSTRUCTION	ACTIVITY/RESPONSE
1. What day is today?	1. T: Write "today" on the board. Explain the meaning. St: It's _____ day.
2. Optional: What's the date?	2. St: It's _____ .
3. How many days are there in a week?	3. St: (There are) 7.
4. What are the days of the week?	4. T: Hold up the sight word flash cards if necessary. St: Say the days of the week.
5. What day is this?	5. T: Hold up the abbreviation side of the flash cards with the days of the week. St: Respond. T: Review as necessary.
6. Optional: What month is this? How many days (weeks) are there in a month? How many months (days, weeks) are there in a year?	6. T: Hold up the calendar or visual 74. St: Respond.
7. Read these words.	7. T: Hold up the 5 x 8 flash cards of "married" and "single" or write them on the board. St: Read the words.
8. Are you married (single)?	8. St: "Yes, I am" or "No, I'm not."
9. This word is "divorced". If you are married and don't want to be married any more, you can get divorced.	9. T: Write "divorced" on the board. Explain the concept. Note: Divorce is not as casual and acceptable in other countries as it is in the U.S. Thus, asking students "Are you divorced?" may be a potentially embarrassing question. Be sensitive to the situation. St: Listen and respond.

10.	This word is "widowed". If you are married and your man (woman) dies, then you are widowed. Are you widowed?	10. T: St:	Write "widowed" on the board. Explain the concept. Listen and respond.
11.	Let's read these words.	11. St:	Read "divorced" and "widowed" in chorus and individually.
12.	Let's make some cards.	12. St: T:	Make yellow 3 x 5 flash cards of "today", "divorced" and "widowed" and practice saying them. Make corresponding 5 x 8 cards.
13.	Open your books to p. 129.	13. St:	Open books.
14.	What are you?	14. T: St: T:	Point to the upper right hand corner. Put an X on or check the box which indicates their marital status. Assist and check for accuracy.
15.	Let's read.	15. T: St:	Model the questions and responses if necessary. Demonstrate that the abbreviation corresponds to the day of the week. Read in chorus and individually.
16.	Let's write.	16. St:	Write the name of the day in item #8.
17.	Optional: Let's write.	17. St: T:	Practice writing the abbreviations of the days of the week. A master for lined paper is provided on p. 396 of this guide.
18.	Optional: Match the day and the short way of writing it.	18. T: St: T:	Devise a match worksheet. Match the day with the abbreviation. Check for accuracy.

Student Workbook p. 130

SIGHT WORD
date of birth

VISUAL
74 calendar

INSTRUCTIONAL AID
a calendar

INSTRUCTION

1. What day is it today?

2. Are you married (single, divorced, widowed)?

3. Let's read.

4. This says "date of birth". My date of birth is (August 26, 1946) or (8/26/46) or (8-26-46).

5. On my date of birth, everybody sings "Happy Birthday" to me.

6. What is your date of birth?

7. Let's make a card.

ACTIVITY/RESPONSE

1. T: Review the days of the week and the abbreviations for the days of the week.
   Optional: Review dates and other concepts taught to this point relating to the calendar.
   St: Respond.

2. St: "Yes, I am" or "No, I'm not."

3. T: Hold up the sight words and sentence strips from workbook p. 128.
   St: Read.

4. T: Point to your date of birth on the calendar. Write the 3 forms on the board.
   St: Listen and observe.

5. T: Teach students to sing "Happy Birthday" if you have not already done so.
   St: Listen and sing.

6. T: Hand the calendar to the students.
   St: Point to their date of birth on the calendar.
   T: Teach them to give their date of birth in written form and orally.

7. St: Make a yellow 3 x 5 card with "date of birth" on one side and their date of birth on the other.
   T: Assist if necessary.

8. Optional: These are the months: January (Jan.), February (Feb.), etc.

9. Optional: Each month has a name and a number. For example, I can write "1" for January.

10. Open your books to p. 130.

11. Let's read.

12. Circle the correct answer.

8. T: Teach the names and abbreviations of the months.
   St: Repeat, memorize, make cards and practice reading and writing the names of the months.

9. T: Teach students how to write dates in numbers only. This concept can be taught through the Language Master. See p. 10 of this guide for suggested uses of the Language Master.
   St: Listen and practice.

10. St: Open books.

11. T: Model the question if necessary.
    St: Read the question and choose the correct response orally.

12. T: Point to the example in box #1. Demonstrate that the correct answer has been circled.
    St: Circle the answers, "X" the day in box #8 and fill in their date of birth at the upper right hand corner using their sight word flash card if necessary.
    T: Check for accuracy.

Student Workbook   p. 131

SIGHT WORD
birthdate

VISUAL
74 calendar

INSTRUCTIONAL AID
a calendar

INSTRUCTION

1. What day is it?

2. Optional: How do you spell _____ day?

3. What is your date of birth?

4. "Date of birth" is the same as "birthdate".

5. What is your birthdate?

6. What two letters say /th/?

7. Optional, compound words: "Birthdate" is made of "birth" and "date". What other words do you know that are made of 2 words?

8. Open your books to p. 131.

9. Let's read.

10. Let's write.

ACTIVITY/RESPONSE

1. T: Hold up the sight word flash cards of the days. Review all calendar concepts and vocabulary taught to this point.
   St: Respond.

2. St: Spell the days of the week orally or write them on the board.

3. T: Write "date of birth" on the board.
   St: Respond orally or in writing on the board.

4. T: Write "birthdate" on the board.
   St: Listen.

5. St: Respond orally or in writing on the board.

6. St: t - h
   T: Point to the t - h in the word "birthdate".

7. T: Underline the two words in <u>birthdate.</u>
   St: Respond.

8. St: Open books.

9. St: Read questions and respond orally.
   T: Assist if necessary.

10. T: Demonstrate how the day has been written in the sample in box #1.
    St: Write the days and fill in their birthdate at the upper right hand corner.
    T: Check for accuracy and legibility.

Student Workbook p. 132
Sentence Scramble

INSTRUCTION	ACTIVITY/RESPONSE
1. Let's read the words.	1. T: Review the sight words, sentence strips and concepts, and readings from workbook p. 101 - 131. St: Read and respond.
2. Look at these words. Fix them.	2. T: Write the scrambled sentences on p. 132 on the board or write the scrambled sentences on sentence strips, cutting them into the components. St: Rearrange the word order and read the sentences aloud.
3. Open your books to p. 132.	3. St: Open books.
4. Look at the sample. Remember that a sentence always begins with a capital letter and ends with a period or a question mark.	4. T: Point to the sample box. Demonstrate how the sentence has been fixed. St: Listen.
5. Let's write.	5. T: Have students work in pairs if necessary. St: Write the sentences and fill in the name of the day at the upper right hand corner. T: Check for accuracy and legibility. The unscrambled sentences are: 　#1 Is he a salesman? 　#2 What day is it today? 　#3 Mr. and Mrs. Lee are married. 　#4 What time is it? 　#5 They're from Mexico. 　#6 Where are you from? 　#7 Her address is 512 Union Ave. 　#8 What's your phone number? 　#9 He isn't a salesman. 　#10 Is it 7:45?
6. Optional: Unscramble the sentences	6. T: Devise a scramble worksheet using sight words and sentences learned to this point. St: Unscramble and write the sentences.

Note: This completes instructions for Lessons 1-5. Provide a thorough review before administering the test pages. See p. 8 and 10 of this guide for ideas and suggestions for the use of the sight word flash cards and sentence strips.

Student Workbook   p. 133-136
   Test of Lessons 1 - 5

OBJECTIVES

Listening Comprehension: To determine if students can:
1. Follow simple oral directions.
2. Comprehend the numbers between 76-100 and 200-1,000 when spoken.
3. Comprehend a dictation exercise based on the sight words and sentences previously introduced.

Reading and Writing: To determine if students can:
1. Complete the personal information requested at the upper right hand corner correctly and without being reminded.
2. Understand and follow directions.
3. Demonstrate comprehension of reading exercises by answering questions correctly.
4. Demonstrate a knowledge of specific vocabulary by matching the visual with the vocabulary item.
5. Tell time and set a clock.
6. Distinguish between the occupations taught in these lessons.
7. Write basic sight words and lesson sentences.
8. Demonstrate an understanding of the contractions.
9. Complete a simple application form.

NOTES TO THE INSTRUCTOR:

1. There are too many test pages to administer in one sitting. Student fatigue may affect results. It is suggested that p. 133-134 and p. 135-136 be completed at different sittings. Allow students as much time as necessary to complete work.

2. This test is designed so that concepts in each lesson between 1-5 are tested.

3. If students cannot understand the directions, provide examples on the board. However, it is expected that by this stage, students would know how to proceed.

4. On p. 136, dictate any vocabulary or sentences you deem important or dictate the following:
   #1 Today is Monday.
   #2 It's 3:00. (o'clock)
   #3 It's 10:45.
   #4 Yes, it is.
   #5 79, 98, 86, 500, 1,000

5. A large number of errors may indicate a full review of Lessons 1 - 5, vision testing or a learning disability. Refer to p. 3 in the Introduction for further discussion.

6. When the test has been completed and corrected, use p. 133-136 as an oral review for the entire class.

Student Workbook p. 137
Lesson Six, Section I
How much is it?

SIGHT WORDS
penny, cent(s), much, nickel, dime, half dollar, dollar

VISUALS
13 ten dollars	61 dime
29 nickel	62 dollar
41 penny	113 quarter
52 five dollars	146 half dollar

INSTRUCTIONAL AIDS
real coins and paper money
yellow 3 x 5 flash cards

STRUCTURE

How much is it?   It's (amount) .

INSTRUCTION

1. It's a penny. What is it?

2. How much is it? It's 1 cent.
   "1 cent" and "a penny" are the same.

3. How much is a penny?

4. This word is "penny". The word "pen" is in "penny".

5. This word is "cent".

6. Sometimes, "c" sounds like /s/ as the letter "s" as in "cent". Sometimes, "c" sounds like /k/ as the letter "k" as in these words: cat, credit card, cook, cup of coffee, etc.

7. What are the two sounds of "c"?

ACTIVITY/RESPONSE

1. T: Hold up a real penny or visual 41.
   St: (It's a) penny.

2. T: Model the question and response.
   St: Listen.

3. St: (It's) 1 cent.

4. T: Write "penny" on the board.
      underline "pen" in "penny".
   St: Listen and repeat "penny".

5. T: Write "cent" on the board.
   St: Listen and repeat "cent".

6. T: Write the examples on the board.
   St: Listen.

7. St: /s/ and /k/
   T: Assist and review as necessary.

261

8. Optional, decoding: This is "cent" and this is "ent". Read the words:

(c)<u>ent</u>

bent	sent
dent	tent
lent	vent
rent	went

9. This word is "much". I say this word in "How much is it?"

10. What two letters say /ch/?

11. What is this? How much is it?

12. Read the words.

13. I can write "1 cent" this way. This says "1 cent" or "1 penny".

14. I can also write "1 cent" this way. This also says "1 cent" or "1 penny".

15. Let's make some cards.

16. Let's read the cards. How much is it?

17. Optional: Let's write.

18. It's a <u>(nickel)</u>. What is it?

8. St: Decode.
   T: See p. 7 of this guide for discussion and suggestions.

9. T: Write "much" on the board.
   St: Listen and repeat "much".

10. St: c - h
    T: Under line the "ch" in the word "m<u>uch</u>".

11. T: Hold up a penny or visual 41.
    St: (It's a) penny. (It's) 1 cent.

12. T: Point to "penny", "1 cent" and "much" on the board.
    St: Read the words.

13. T: Write "1¢" on the board.
    St: Listen and observe.

14. T: Write "$.01" on the board.
    St: Listen and observe.

15. St: Make a yellow 3 x 5 card for "penny" with "$.01" on the back, another for "1 cent" with "1¢" on the back and another for "much".
    T: Make corresponding 5 x 8 cards.

16. T: Hold up the 5 x 8 cards showing both sides of the money cards.
    St: Read the words and respond.

17. St: Practice writing "penny", "1 cent", "1¢" and "$.01".
    T: A master for writing paper is provided on p. 396 of this guide.

18. T: Repeat same strategies in instructions 1-18 for nickel, dime, half dollar and dollar (five and ten dollars, optional). Hold up the correct amount or the corresponding visual.
    St: It's a <u>(nickel)</u>.

19. How much is it? It's (5) cents.
    A (nickel), (5) cents and (5) pennies are the same.

20. How much is a (nickel)?

21. This word is (nickel).

22. Optional, phonics:
    For nickel: "c" and "k" together say /k/ as in ni<u>ck</u>el, si<u>ck</u>, che<u>ck</u> out, clo<u>ck</u>, bla<u>ck</u> and tru<u>ck</u>.
    For dime: The letter "i" is a vowel. Sometimes a vowel says its own name, as in d<u>i</u>me, H<u>i</u>, fr<u>i</u>es, kn<u>i</u>fe, wr<u>i</u>te, t<u>i</u>me, <u>I</u>'m and Fr<u>i</u>day.

23. What's this? How much is it?

24. I can write (nickel) this way or this way.

25. Let's make some cards.

26. Let's read the cards. How much is it?

27. Optional: Let's write.

28. Open your books to p. 137 and write.

29. Let's read.

---

19. T: Model the question and response. Put a (nickel) on the table and (5) pennies next to it. Note: Of course, we never say "100¢" in English. It is listed for comprehension.
    St: Listen and observe.

20. St: It's (5) cents.

21. T: Write (nickel) on the board.
    St: Listen and repeat (nickel).

22. T: Write the examples on the board.
    St: Listen.

23. T: Hold up a (nickel) or the corresponding visual.
    St: (It's a) (nickel). It's (5) cents.

24. T: Write (5)¢ and $(.05) on the board.

25. St: Make yellow 3 x 5 cards for each amount, writing the ___ ¢ and $. ___ form on the back.
    T: Make corresponding 5 x 8 cards.

26. T: Hold up the 5 x 8 cards showing both sides of each card.
    St: Read the words and respond.

27. St: Practice writing the words and the amounts.
    T: A master for writing paper is provided on p. 396 of this guide.

28. T: Point to the upper right hand corner.
    St: Fill in the day.
    T: Check for accuracy and legibility.

29. T: Model the questions and responses.
    St: Read in chorus and individually.
    T: Pair the students.
    St: Read and reverse lines upon completion.

30. Look at the bottom of the page. This is "equals". It is the same as "is". I can say "a penny equals (is) 1 cent".

31. Optional: Match.

32. Optional, syllables: How many syllables are there in "penny" "nickel", "dime", etc.

33. Optional: This is a quarter. I can make 25¢ with 2 dimes and a nickel or 2 dimes and 5 cents or 1 dime and 3 nickels, etc.

30. T: Write "=" on the board.
    St: Observe and then read and study the equivalents in the workbook.

31. T: Write the equivalents on sentence strips. Cut them into the component parts. Shuffle and deal them out to the students.
    St: Match the equivalents.

32. T: Pound out the sounds on the board or a table.
    St: Respond.

33. T: Hold up a real quarter or visual 113. Make change for a quarter in as many ways as possible.
    St: Observe, count and make change.
    T: Do the same for a dime, half dollar and dollar.

Student Workbook p. 138

SIGHT WORD
signature

INSTRUCTIONAL AID
plenty of change (optional)
a yellow 3 x 5 flash card

INSTRUCTION	ACTIVITY/RESPONSE
1. What is it? How much is it?	1. T: Review the visuals, sight words and equivalents from the previous lesson. St: Respond.
2. How do you write (25) cent(s)?	2. St: Write (25) ¢ and $.(25). T: Review all amounts from the previous lesson.
3. Optional: How many (pennies) are there in a (nickel)?	3. St: Respond.
4. Optional: Show me 25¢ (10¢, 50¢, $1.00).	4. T: Hand the change to the students. St: Point to the coin or make equivalent change.
5. My name is (Kay Renshaw).	5. T: Print your name on the board. St: Listen.
6. Sometimes I have to write my name like this.	6. T: Sign your name below your printed name on the board.
7. This is my signature.	7. T: Point to your signature. St: Listen and repeat "signature".
8. This word says "signature".	8. T: Write "signature" on the board. St: Repeat "signature" in chorus and individually.
9. When you see this word, you write your name like this.	9. T: Point to the word "signature" and and to your own signature. St: Listen and observe.

10. Practice writing your signature.

10. T: This may be a good time to introduce Part 4 of the workbook, "Transition to Cursive Writing". Otherwise, hand each student a sheet of writing paper. A master for lined paper is provided on p. 396 of this guide. Provide a model for the student's signature at the top of the page.
    St: Practice writing their signature as frequently as necessary.
    T: Check for accuracy and legibility.

11. Let's make a card.

11. St: Print "signature" on one side of a yellow 3 x 5 card and sign their name on the other side.
    T: Make a corresponding 5 x 8 card.

12. Open your books to p. 138 and sign your name.

12. T: Point to the upper right hand corner.
    St: Open books and sign their name.

13. Look at the picture. What is this and this?

13. T: Point to all the objects in the visual.
    St: (It's a) garage, car, woman, table, etc.

14. This says "Garage Sale". Americans sometimes sell old or unneeded things in a garage sale.

14. T: Point to the words in the visual or write them on the board.
    St: Listen.

15. Look at the hat (book, spoon, glass, etc.). How much is it?

15. St: "(It's a) half dollar." or "(It's) 50¢." etc.

16. Let's read.

16. T: Model all the questions if necessary.
    St: Read the questions and respond orally.

17. Let's write.

17. St: Fill in the amounts on the price tags.
    T: Check for accuracy and legibility.

18. Optional: Let's have a garage sale.

18. St: Roleplay a garage sale, "selling" various classroom objects and making price tags.
    T: With a large class, set up several garage sales. Use real money and appoint a cashier for each garage sale. Teach expressions such as "That's too much."
    St: Pay for the items and count their change.

Student Workbook p. 139-140						INSTRUCTIONAL AID

								plenty of change

INSTRUCTION

1. What is it? How much is it?

2. How do you write (50) cents?

3. This is 75¢.

4. Show me _____ ¢.

5. This is a dollar and this is a dime. Together they are one dollar and 10 cents.

6. How much is this? Write it on the board.

7. Open your books to p. 139.

8. Look at the picture. Where are they?

9. Listen.

10. Listen and read.

ACTIVITY/RESPONSE

1. T: Review all visuals, sight words and equivalents relating to money.

2. St: Write (50) ¢ or $.(50).

3. T: Make 75¢ with a half dollar and a quarter, 3 quarters, 7 dimes and a nickel, etc.
   St: Observe.

4. T: Hand the change to the students.
   St: Count the money to make the amount requested.

5. T: Hold up the money or visuals 61 and 62. Write $1.10 on the board.
   St: Repeat "one (a) dollar and 10 cents".

6. T: Teach students how to "read" various monetary amounts over $1.00. Optional: Write the monetary amounts on Language Master Cards and record the amount. See p. 10 of this guide for further suggestions.
   St: Say the amount and write it on the board.
   T: Continue practice until students are fairly competent in counting change and writing monetary amounts.

7. St: Open the books.

8. St: (They're in a) restaurant.

9. T: Model the entire dialogue.
   St: Listen.

10. T: Model the dialogue line by line.
    Cl:
    Gr: Read.
    St:

11. I am "A" and you are "B".

12. Let's read.

13. Let's write.

11. T: Assume role and reverse upon completion.
    Cl:
    Gr: Assume role.
    St:

12. T: Ask for volunteers or assign roles for the dialogues on p. 139-140.
    St: Read and supply the monetary amounts orally.

13. St: Count the change and write the following amounts:
    #1 95¢ or $ .95
    #2 55¢ or $ .55
    #3 40¢ or $ .40
    #4 $1.10
    #5 45¢ or $ .45
    #6 30¢ or $ .30
    #7 $2.30
    #8 50¢ or $ .50
    #9 $1.50
    Check for accuracy and legibility. Be certain that the students have filled in their social security number at the upper right hand corner of p. 139 and the name of their country at the upper right hand corner of p. 140.

269

Student Workbook   p. 141
Review

INSTRUCTION

1. What's this? How much is it?

2. Open your books to p. 141.

3. Listen and write.

4. Circle the correct answer.

ACTIVITY/RESPONSE

1. T: Review all previous learnings regarding money.
   St: Respond, read and write amounts and count money as necessary.

2. St: Open books.

3. T: Provide examples on the board if necessary. Call out various monetary amounts or dictate the following, stating each amount only 2 times, forcing students to listen:

#1	50¢
#2	5¢
#3	10¢
#4	$1.00
#5	1¢
#6	25¢

   St: Write either "____ ¢" or "$ ____".

4. T: Point to the sample in box #1. Demonstrate that correct answer has been circled.
   St: Circle the correct answer.
   T: Allow students as much time as necessary. Check for accuracy and legibility. Be certain that the day has been filled in at the upper right hand corner.
   Note: The results of this review will indicate to you if:
   a) the students have achieved the objectives of this lesson
   b) a full review is required
   c) students can proceed to extension p. 142-143.

Student Workbook   p. 142-143

SIGHT WORD
separated

INSTRUCTION

1. Are you married (single, divorced, widowed)?

2. Sometimes, a man and a woman want to be divorced. When they live in different houses before the divorce, they are separated.

3. Optional, syllables: How many syllables are there in "separated"?

4. Optional, vowels: What are the vowels? Each syllable has a vowel.

5. Are you separated?

6. What's this? How much is it?

7. Open your books to p. 142.

8. Let's read.

ACTIVITY/RESPONSE

1. St: "Yes, I am" or "No, I'm not".

2. T: Write "separated" on the board.

3. T: Pound out the syllables as you say the word.
   St: 4

4. St: a, e, i, o, u
   T: Point out the vowel in each syllable.
   St: Listen and observe.

5. T: Note: Divorce and separation are not as casual and acceptable in other countries as in the U.S. Thus, this may be a potentially embarrassing question. Be sensitive to the situation.
   St: "Yes, I am", "No, I'm not" or "I'm single".

6. T: Review all previous learnings regarding money.
   St: Respond, read, write amounts and count money as necessary.
   T: Extend teaching to include concepts presented on p. 142-143.

7. St: Open books.

8. St: Read the questions and provide the responses orally.

9. Circle the correct answer.

9. T: Point to the sample in box #1. Demonstrate that the correct answer has been circled.
   St: Count the money and circle the following:
   #2 It's $1.75
   #3 It's 36¢.
   #4 It's 41¢.
   #5 It's $3.09.
   #6 It's 60¢.
   #7 It's 85¢.
   #8 It's $2.50.
   #9 It's $10.45.
   T: Check for accuracy. Review and reteach as necessary. Be certain that students have correctly checked their marital status at the upper right hand corner.

10. Open your books to p. 143.

10. St: Open books.

11. Let's read.

11. St: Read the questions and provide the responses orally.

12. Circle the correct answer.

12. T: Point to the sample in box #1. Demonstrate that the correct answer has been circled.
   St: Count the money and circle the following:
   #2 It's $15.35.
   #3 It's $5.71.
   #4 It's $2.73.
   #5 It's $1.48.
   #6 It's $10.55.
   T: Check for accuracy. Review as necessary. Be certain that students have filled in their city and state at the upper right hand corner.

Student Workbook p. 144
Lesson Six, Section II
What this/that?

SIGHT WORDS
Marital Status, this, that

VISUALS
147 This is a cup of coffee.
    That's a hot dog.
148 This is a map.
    That's a mop.
149 This is a clock.
    That's a watch.

INSTRUCTIONAL AIDS
an application form or a copy of the
    form on p. 399 or 400 of this guide
yellow 3 x 5 flash cards

STRUCTURE

What's this/that?   This is a _____ ⟩ It's a _____ .
                                   That's a _____ ⟋

INSTRUCTION

1. Sometimes I see these words on an application or identification form.

2. Which word do I use when the man or the woman died?

3. These words are your "marital status". "Marital status" is: Are you married (single, divorced, separated, widowed)?

4. What is your marital status?

5. Let's make a card.

ACTIVITY/RESPONSE

1. T: Hold up the 5 x 8 cards or write the following words on the board.
   married   single
   divorced   widowed
   separated
   Point to the words on an application or identification form.
   St: Listen and observe.

2. T: Review the meaning of each word.
   St: Respond or point to the word.

3. T: Write "Marital Status" on the board.
   St: Listen and observe.

4. T: Model responses.
   St: I'm (single).
   T: Review concept as necessary.

5. St: Make a yellow 3 x 5 card with "Marital Status" on one side and "I'm (single) on the other.
   T: Make a corresponding 5 x 8 card.

6. What is "marital status"?

6. St: Are you married (single, divorced, separated, widowed, etc.)?
   T: Assist to insure comprehension of the concept.

7. Listen. What's this?

7. T: Point to a common classroom object that is nearby.
   St: (It's a) _____ .

8. When one thing is close and I can touch it, I say "this".

8. T: Touch the object. Write "this" on the board.
   St: (It's a) _____ .

9. Let's practice.

9. T: Touch several classroom objects and say "This is a (my, your, his, her) (adjective) _____ .
   St: Repeat and give original sentences if possible.

10. What's this?

10. T: Point to classroom objects.
    St: This is a (my, your, his, her) (adjective) _____ .

11. You ask "What's this?"

11. St: Ask each other the question and respond.

12. When the question is "What's this?", I can answer "This is a _____ " or "It's a _____ ."

12. T: Model both responses.
    St: Practice both responses.
    T: Continue practice until concept is achieved.

13. When one thing is far and I can't touch it, I say "that".

13. T: Point to a far away object. Write "that" on the board.
    St: Repeat "that".

14. What's that?

14. T: Point to a classroom object that is out of your reach.
    St: (It's a) _____ .

15. Let's practice.

15. T: Point to several classroom objects that are far away and say "That's a (my, your, his, her) (adjective) _____ .
    St: Repeat and give original sentences if possible.

16. What's that?

16. T: Point to classroom objects.
    St: That's a (my, your, his, her) (adjective) _____ .

17. You ask "What's that?"

17. St: Ask each other the question and respond.

18. When the question is "What's that?", I can answer "That's a _____." or "It's a _____."

19. Let's read the words.

20. What is this word?

21. Let's make some cards.

22. Look at the pictures. What is it?

23. What's this?

24. What's that?

25. Is this a cup of coffee?

26. Is that a hot dog?

27. Is this (that) a _____ ?

18. T: Model both responses.
    St: Practice both responses.
    T: Continue practice until concept is achieved.

19. T: Point to "this" and "that" on the board.
    St: Read.

20. T: Cover the "th" in both words.
    St: is, at

21. St: Make a yellow 3 x 5 card of "this" and "that".
    T: Make corresponding 5 x 8 cards.

22. T: Hold up visuals 147, 148, and 149. Point to the objects.
    St: (It's a) _____ .
    T: Review vocabulary as necessary. Optional: Point out or review the hard "c" in cup, coffee, clock; the /cl/ in clock and /ch/ in watch; the pronunciation contrast between map/mop; the spelling of any or all of the words, etc.

23. T: Hold up visual 147.
    St: "This is a cup of coffee" or "It's a cup of coffee."

24. St: "That's a hot dog" or "It's a hot dog."
    T: Repeat practice for visuals 148-149.

25. T: Hold up visual 147. Point to the cup of coffee.
    St: Yes, it is.

26. T: Point to the hot dog.
    St: Yes, it is.
    T: Repeat practice for visuals 148-149.

27. T: Point to the visuals and elicit a negative response.
    St: No, it isn't.
    T: Continue practice until students are firm on the usage of "this" and "that".

28.	Open your books to p. 144 and write.	28. T: St: T:	Point to the upper right hand corner. Open their books and put an X or ✓ in the box indicating their marital status. Check for accuracy.
29.	Look at the picture in #1. Where are they?	29. T: St:	Point to the visual. (They're in a) restaurant.
30.	Optional: How much is the (milk)? (K) means (ketchup).	30. T: St:	Review the visual carefully adding vocabulary to the students' repertoire. Listen, respond, repeat.
31.	Listen.	31. T: St:	Model the entire dialogue. Listen.
32.	Listen and repeat.	32. T: Cl: Gr: Repeat. St:	Model the dialogue line by line.
33.	I'm "A" and you are "B".	33. T: Cl: Gr: Assume role. St:	Assume role and reverse upon completion.
34.	Read.	34. T: St:	Pair the students up. Read the lines and reverse roles upon completion.
35.	Look at the picture in #2.	35. T: St: T:	Repeat instruction 29-34 for the rest of p. 144. Respond. Practice readings as necessary.
36.	Optional, punctuation: This is is a question mark, I use it after a question.	36. T: St:	Point out all the question marks, periods, apostrophes and capital letters in the dialogues. Listen.
37.	Optional: Fix the sentences.	37. T: St:	Write the dialogue(s) on sentence strips. Cut the sentences (words) into the components. Scramble the sentences (words) and hand them out to the students. Fix the sentences (word) order.
38.	Optional: Let's write.	38. St: T:	Practice writing any or all of the dialogues or sight words. A master for writing paper is provided on p. 396 of this guide.

Student Workbook   p. 145-146

VISUALS
147 This is a cup of coffee.
     That's a hot dog.
148 This is a map.
     That's a mop.
149 This is a clock.
     That's a watch.

INSTRUCTION

1. Let's read.

2. When one thing is close and I can touch it, I say "this".

3. When one thing is far away and I can't touch it, I say "that".

4. What's this/that?

5. Optional: Let's read.

6. Open your books to p. 145. Let's read.

7. Circle the correct answer.

ACTIVITY/RESPONSE

1. T: Hold up the sight word flash cards from the previous lesson.
   St: Read.

2. T: Provide and elicit several sentences using the "This is a _____." structure.
   St: Listen and respond.

3. T: Provide and elicit several sentences using the "That's a _____." structure.
   St: Listen and respond.

4. T: Show visuals and point to classroom objects.
   St: Respond.

5. St: Reread the dialogues on workbook p. 144.

6. St: Open books and read questions and appropriate responses orally for p. 145 and p. 146.
   T: Workbook p. 146 challenges students to select the correct spelling.

7. T: Point to the sample box. Demonstrate that the correct response has been circled.
   St: Circle the correct answer.
   T: Check for accuracy. Be certain that students have completed the personal information that has been requested at the upper right hand corner of each page.

Student Workbook   p. 147-148

SIGHT WORD
place of birth

VISUALS

6 hamburger	76 cap
10 table	90 chair
32 notebook	94 watch
45 lamp	113 quarter
57 door	121 clock
62 dollar	

INSTRUCTIONAL AID
a yellow 3 x 5 flash card

STRUCTURE

Is this (that) a (noun) ?   Yes, it is.
   No, it isn't.

INSTRUCTION

1. Look at the word and give me the answer.

2. "What is your country?", "Where are you from?" and "What is your birthplace?" all ask the same question.

3. "Place of birth" also asks the same question.

4. What is your place of birth?

5. Let's make a card.

ACTIVITY/RESPONSE

1. T: Hold up the sight word flash cards for these words or write them on the board:

day	marital status
(month)	height
(date)	weight
birthdate	country
date of birth	birthplace

   St: Respond providing their own personal information.
   T: Repeat instruction as necessary.

2. T: Ask the 3 questions of various students.
   St: Respond by naming their country.

3. T: Write "place of birth" on the board.
   St: Listen.

4. St: Name their country.
   T: Practice as necessary.

5. St: Make a yellow 3 x 5 card with "place of birth" written on one side and the name of their country written on the other.
   T: Make a corresponding 5 x 8 card.

6. Let's read the card.

7. What is your place of birth?

8. What is it?

9. Is it a hot dog?

10. What is it?

11. Is this a hot dog?

12. What is it?

13. Is that a chair?

14. What is it?

15. Let's read.

16. Optional: Fix the words.

17. Open your books to p. 147. Let's read.

18. Let's write.

6. St: Read "place of birth".

7. St: Respond.

8. T: Hold up visual 6, hamburger.
   St: It's a hamburger.

9. T: Hold up visual 6, hamburger.
   St: No, it isn't.

10. T: Repeat instructions 8-9 for all of the visuals.
    St: Respond.

11. T: Hold up visual 6, hamburger.
    St: No, it isn't.

12. St: It's a hamburger.

13. T: Place visual 45, lamp, out of your reach and point to it.
    St: No, it isn't.

14. St: It's a lamp.
    T: Continue practice until students can orally produce the questions and responses presented on p. 147-148 with good pronunciation, stress and intonation.

15. T: Copy the first dialogue on p. 147 on the board, sentence strips or overhead projector. Model.
    St: Repeat in chorus and individually.

16. T: Cut the sentence strips into components, shuffle and deal them out to the students.
    St: Rearrange the dialogue.

17. St: Open books and read all of the exercises on p. 147-148 filling in the missing words orally.

18. T: Reproduce the exercises from the workbook onto the board.
    St: Come to the board and write.

19. Let's write.

20. Optional: Let's talk.

21. Optional: Let's write.

19. St: Write in their books and copy from the board if necessary.
    T: Check for accuracy and legibility. Be certain that the personal information has been properly completed at the upper right hand corner of each page.

20. T: Pair students up.
    St: Practice the questions and responses on p. 147-148 using the visual side of their flash cards.

21. St: Practice writing some or all of the dialogues on p. 147-148.
    T: A master for lined paper is provided on p. 396 of this guide.

Student Workbook p. 149
Lesson Seven, Section I
It's a/an _____ .

SIGHT WORDS
orange, lemon, banana, pepper,
apple, onion, ea. (each)

VISUALS
101 orange   42 pepper
 46 lemon   21 apple
150 banana   100 onion
                  151 Is that
                       an orange?

INSTRUCTIONAL AIDS
old magazines or copies of the
   orange, lemon, banana, pepper,
   apple and onion on p. 382 of this guide
yellow 3 x 5 flash cards

INSTRUCTION

1. It's a lemon (banana, pepper).

2. What's this (that)?

3. It's an orange (apple, onion).

4. What's this (that)?

5. What is it?

6. What letter does lemon start (end) with?

7. What letter says /ĕ/ as in lemon?

8. What's the next letter in lemon?

9. The other letter in lemon is "o".

ACTIVITY/RESPONSE

1. T: Hold up the respective visuals.
   St: Repeat.

2. T: Hold up the visuals (or point to them).
   St: "It's a (lemon)." or "This is a (banana)."
       or "That's a (pepper)."

3. T: Hold up the respective visuals.
   St: Repeat.

4. T: Hold up visuals (or point to them).
   St: "It's an (orange)." or "This is an (apple)."
       or "That's an (onion)."

5. T: Hold up visual 46.
   St: It's a lemon.

6. St: "l" (n)
   T: Write "l   n" on the board.

7. St: "e"
   T: Write "le   n" on the board.

8. St: "m"
   T: Fill in the "m".

9. T: Complete writing lemon.
   St: Practice reading the word in chorus and individually.

10. What is it?	10. T:	Repeat strategies in instruction 5-9 for the remaining sight words.
	St:	Respond and practice reading the sight words.
11. Let's make some cards.	11. St:	Make a yellow 3 x 5 card for each sight word. Staple or tape a magazine picture or a copy of orange, lemon, banana, pepper, apple, onion on p. 382 of this guide to back of the respective cards.
	T:	Make corresponding 5 x 8 cards.
12. Both "a" and "an" mean one: "a lemon" is one lemon; "an orange" is one orange.	12. T:	Write "a" and "an" on the board.
	St:	Listen.
13. I use "an" with words that begin with the vowels. What are the vowels?	13. St:	a, e, i, o, u
	T:	Review as necessary and demonstrate that orange, apple and onion start with vowels.
14. "a" or "an"?	14. T:	Hold up various visuals from this and previous lessons.
	St:	a (an) (noun).
15. Optional: Match the word with the picture.	15. St #1:	Places his sight word cards visual side up on a table.
	St #2:	Matches the visual with the word using his set of sight word cards.
	St #1,2:	Check for accuracy.
16. Look at the picture. Where are they? What is (s)he? What is it?	16. T:	Hold up visual 151, point to the people and objects.
	St:	Respond.
17. Look at this: "ea" means "each".	17. T:	Point to the "15¢ ea." and "20¢ ea". in visual 151 and write them on the board. Demonstrate the concept of "each".
18. How much is a banana (lemon)?	18. St:	It's 15¢ (20¢).
19. Listen.	19. T:	Write the dialogue on p. 149 on the board, sentence strips or an overhead projector. Model the entire dialogue.
	St:	Listen.
20. Listen and repeat.	20. T:	Model each line separately.
	St:	Listen and repeat in chorus and individually.

21. I am "A" and you are "B".

22. Let's read again.

23. Optional, punctuation: This is a question mark. I use it after a question.

24. Optional: Fix the sentences (words).

25. Open your books to p. 149 and write.

26. Let's read.

27. Let's make a card.

21. T:
    Cl: ⟩ Assume roles and reverse upon completion.

22. Gr:
    Gr: ⟩ Assume roles and reverse upon completion.

    St:
    St: ⟩ Assume roles and reverse upon completion.

23. T: Provide instruction also for the comma, apostrophes, periods and capital letters.
    St: Listen.

24. T: Cut the sentence strips into component parts, shuffle and deal them out to the students.
    St: Rearrange the sentences (words).

25. St: Open books and fill in their full name and check "M" or "F" at the upper right hand corner.
    T: Check for accuracy.

26. St: Read the dialogue, assuming roles and finish reading p. 149.
    T: Model as necessary. Repeat and review as necessary.

27. St: Make a yellow 3 x 5 card with "ea." on one side and "each" on the other.
    T: Make a corresponding 5 x 8 card. See p. 8 of this guide for suggested uses of the flash cards.

Student Workbook   p. 150

VISUALS
101 orange   42   pepper
46   lemon   21   apple
150 banana   100 onion
                    151 Is that an orange?

INSTRUCTIONAL AIDS
the sight word flash cards
from the previous lesson

INSTRUCTION

1. What's this (that)?

2. What's this (that)?

3. How many is "a" and "an"?

4. When do you use "an"?

5. Let's read.

6. Is that an orange?

7. Open your books to p. 150 and read.

8. Circle the answer.

ACTIVITY/RESPONSE

1. T: Hold up the visuals (or point to them).
   St: "It's a (lemon)." or "This is a (banana)." or "That's a (pepper)."

2. T: Hold up the visuals (or point to them).
   St: "It's an (orange)." or "This is an (apple)." or "That's an (onion)."

3. St: one

4. St: with the vowels.
   T: Review vowels as necessary.

5. T: Hold up the sight word cards from the previous lessons.
   St: Read.

6. T: Hold up visual 151. Review the dialogue on p. 149.
   St: Respond and reread the dialogue.

7. St: Read the questions and correct responses orally.

8. T: Demonstrate activity if necessary.
   St: Circle the correct answer.
   T: Check for accuracy. Be certain that the day and time have been filled in at the upper right hand corner.

Student Workbook   p. 151

SIGHT WORDS
sign here

VISUALS

101 orange	42 pepper
46 lemon	21 apple
150 banana	100 onion
	151 Is that an orange?

INSTRUCTIONAL AIDS
the sight word flash cards of orange, lemon, banana, pepper, apple, onion any form (application or identification) or a copy of the form on p. 399 or 400 of this guide

---

INSTRUCTION	ACTIVITY/RESPONSE
1. This word is "signature".	1. T: Hold up the 5 x 8 card of "signature" or write it on the board.
2. Show me your signature.	2. St: Put their signature on the board or on paper.
3. This word says "sign".	3. T: Draw a box around "sign" in the word [sign]ature.
4. When you see "sign" or "sign here", you write your signature.	4. T: Point out the words "sign here" on the application form. St: Listen and observe.
5. Open your books to p. 151 and sign here.	5. St: Open books and sign their names at the upper right hand corner. T: Check for accuracy and legibility.
6. Close your books. Let's make a card.	6. St: Close books and make a 3 x 5 card with "sign here" on one side and their signature on the other. T: Make a corresponding 5 x 8 card.
7. What's this (that)?	7. T: Review visuals, structures, sight words and concept of "this/that, a/n" and "each". St: Respond.
8. Listen.	8. T: Write dialogue #1 from p. 151 on the board, sentence strips or an overhead projector. Place visual 100, onion, nearby and visual 42, pepper, far away. Model. St: Listen.

9. Listen and repeat.

10. I am "A" and you are "B".

11. Let's read.

12. Optional, punctuation: This is a comma. I use a comma after "yes" and "no".

13. "Isn't" is "is" and "not" together.

14. Optional: Fix the sentences (words).

15. Listen.

16. Open your books to p. 151. Let's read.

17. Optional: Let's write.

18. Optional: Match the word with the picture.

9. T: Model the dialogue line by line.
   St: Listen and repeat in chorus and individually.

10. T: ⎱ Assume roles and reverse upon completion.
    Cl: ⎰

11. Gr: ⎱ Assume roles and reverse upon completion.
    St: ⎰

12. T: Point out the use of the question marks, periods, capital letters and apostrophes also.

13. T: Demonstrate how the abbreviation is formed.
    St: Listen and observe.

14. T: If the dialogue was written on sentence strips, cut and scramble the sentences (words).
    St: Rearrange the dialogues.

15. T: Write dialogue #2 from p. 151 on the board, sentence strips or an overhead projector. Place visual 101, orange, nearby and visual 21, apple, far away. Model. Repeat instructions 8-14. Do the same for dialogue #3. Place visual 46, lemon, nearby and visual 150 banana, far away.
    St: Listen, repeat, assume roles (and rearrange dialogues).

16. St: Open books and read.
    T: Continue practice until all students can read and carry on the dialogue with regard to classroom items.

17. St: Practice writing any or all of the dialogues on p. 151.
    T: A master for lined paper is provided on p. 396 of this guide.

18. T: Using the visuals provided on p. 382 of this guide, devise an exercise sheet similar to the one suggested on p. 74 of this guide.
    St: Match.

Student Workbook   p. 152

VISUALS

101 orange	42 pepper
46 lemon	21 apple
150 banana	100 onion

INSTUCTIONAL AIDS

the sight word flash cards of orange, lemon, banana, pepper, apple, onion

---

INSTRUCTION	ACTIVITY/RESPONSE
1. What is it?	1. T: Hold up visuals and sight words listed above. St: It's a _____ .
2. What's this (that)?	2. T: Review concept of "this (that)" and usage via the visuals. St: "This is a (n) _____ ." or "That is a (n) _____ ."
3. How many is "an"?	3. T: Review the usage of "an" with the vowels. St: one
4. Is this an onion?	4. T: Using the visuals, duplicate the questions and answers on workbook p. 152 orally. St: Respond. T: Continue practice until students can speak with confidence, acceptable pronunciation, stress and intonation.
5. Let's read.	5. T: Reproduce some or all of the exercises on workbook p. 152 on the board. St: Fill in the blanks orally and then in writing.
6. Open your books to p. 152 and read.	6. St: Open books and read, filling in the blanks orally.
7. Let's write.	7. St: Fill in the blanks, copying from the board if necessary. T: Check student work for accuracy and legibility. Be certain that students have filled in their social security number into the boxes at the upper right hand corner.

8. Optional: Spell _____ .

8. T: Name any or all of the words on p. 152.
   St: Work in pairs or individually and spell the words aloud or on paper.
   T: Assign troublesome words for study.

Student Workbook   p. 153

VISUALS

101 orange	21 apple
46 lemon	100 onion
150 banana	103 vegetables
42 pepper	152 fruits and vegetables

INSTRUCTIONAL AIDS

the sight word flash cards of orange, lemon, banana, pepper, apple, onion
real fruit and vegetables (optional)

INSTRUCTION

1. What is it?

2. They're (bananas).

3. What are they?

4. If I have one (lemon), I say "a" (an). I can say "It's a (n)(lemon)."

5. If I have two or many (peppers), I say "They're (peppers)."

6. Optional: Let's practice.

ACTIVITY/RESPONSE

1. T: Review all visuals, sight words, concepts, sentence strips and dialogues as necessary from workbook p. 149-152.
   St: Respond.

2. T: Hold up visual 152. Model "They're (bananas)." for each item in the visual.
   St: Listen and repeat.

3. St: They're (_____).

4. T: Review singular visuals of the orange, lemon, banana, pepper, apple and onion. Write "It's a(n)_____." on the board. Remind students that "is" is used with one.
   St: Listen.

5. T: Review plural with visual 152. Write "They're (peppers)" on the board. Remind students that "are" and plural "s" are used when referring to more than one.
   St: Listen.

6. T: Review singular and plural occupations with the students to re-establish the difference between singular and plural. Gather classroom items and have students create sentences about them in the singular and plural.
   St: It's a (pen).
   They're (pens).

7. Read this word. How many is it?	7. T: Write "ea." (each) on the board. St: each, one
8. Look at the picture. How much is a (n) _____ ?	8. T: Hold up visual 152. St: It's ____ ¢. T: Ask the same question for every item in the visual.
9. Optional: How much are the _____s?	9. St: They're ____ ¢ each. T: Ask the same question for every item in the visual.
10. Open your books to p. 153 and read.	10. St: Open books and read the questions and responses orally.
11. Let's write.	11. St: Write the responses. T: Students may write "It's 30¢." or "It's 30 cents." Check for accuracy and legibility. Be certain that students have filled in their last name and the name of their country at the upper right hand corner.
12. Optional, pronunciation contrast: This is 30¢ and this is 13¢.	12. T: Write both figures on the board. St: Say each amount. T: Which one? Cover your mouth and say 13¢ (30¢). St: Point to the amount they hear.
13. Optional: They're vegetables.	13. T: Hold up visual 103 or bring a pepper, carrot, onion, etc. to class. St: Practice "They're vegetables."
14. Optional: They're fruit.	14. T: Hold up the visuals of the orange, lemon, banana, etc. or bring a banana, apple, orange, etc. to class. St: Practice "They're fruit."
15. Optional: Is this a fruit or a vegetable?	15. T: Point to various items via the visual or realia. St: fruit (vegetable) T: Optional: If there is a market nearby, take the class to the produce department and teach the names of the various fruits and vegetables. Teach them "price/lb." and how to weigh their produce. Use this field experience to add vocabulary to their repertoire.

Student Workbook   p. 154

SIGHT WORDS
food, drink, coins, out of order

VISUALS
  7 hot dog   75 cup of coffee
19 soft drink   101 orange
21 apple   153 doughnut
                   154 vending machine

INSTRUCTIONAL AIDS
yellow 3 x 5 cards

INSTRUCTION

1. What is it?

2. It's a doughnut.

3. What's the first (last) letter in "doughnut"?

4. This is food.

5. What's this?

6. What's the first (last) letter in "food"?

7. Read this word.

8. What is it?

9. This is a drink and this is a drink.

10. What's this?

11. What two letters say /dr/ drink? What's the last letter in "drink"?

ACTIVITY/RESPONSE

1. T: Show visuals 7, 21, 101.
   St: It's a (n) hot dog (apple, orange).
   T: Review as necessary.

2. T: Show visual 153. This is a new vocabulary item.
   St: Listen and repeat.

3. St: "d" (t)

4. T: Gather visuals 7, 21, 101, 153 and and any other food visuals you may wish to review.

5. St: It's food.

6. St: "f" (d)
   T: Write "food" on the board.

7. St: food

8. T: Show visuals 19 and 75.
   St: It's a soft drink (cup of coffee).
   T: Review as necessary.

9. T: Refer to visuals 19 and 75.

10. T: Hold up visuals 19 (75).
    St: It's a drink.

11. St: d - r, k
    T: Write "drink" on the board.
    St: Read "drink".

12. What other word(s) start(s) with /dr/?	12. St: dress (drive, dry)

13. Optional, decoding
(dr)<u>ink</u>
  fink   sink
  kink   tink
  link   wink
  mink   blink
  pink   stink
  rink   think
	13. St: Decode.

14. Look at this picture. Sometimes I can get food or a drink from a machine.	14. T: Hold up visual 154. St: Listen.
15. What is the food?	15. St: Name the food items in the vending machine.
16. What can you drink?	16. St: Name the drink items.
17. This word is "coins".	17. St: Listen and repeat "coins".
18. "Coins" are pennies, nickels, dimes and quarters. This is where I put my money.	18. T: Establish the fact that coins are money but not paper money. Roleplay inserting money. St: Listen and observe.
19. This is a sign. It says "Out of order".	19. T: Point to the sign on the vending machine. St: Listen and repeat "Out of order".
20. "Out of order" means the machine is no good. It isn't working. Don't put your money in it.	20. St: Listen.
21. Read the words.	21. St: Read "food, drink, coins, Out of order".
22. Let's make some cards.	22. St: Make a yellow 3 x 5 flash card of each sight word. T: Make a corresponding 5 x 8 card. Read and review as necessary.
23. How much is the _____ ?	23. St: It's ___ ¢. T: Ask the question for all food and drink items in the vending machine.
24. Open your book to p. 154 and read.	24. St: Open books and read the questions supplying the responses orally.

25. Let's write.

26. Optional: Look at the machine. What's food (drink)? How much is the _____ ?

25. T: Optional: Have capable students write the sentences on the board and have other students copy them if necessary.
    St: Write the sentences.
    T: Check for accuracy and legibility. Be certain that students have filled in their home phone, a dash or "none" at the upper right hand corner.

26. T: If possible, take the class to a nearby vending machine. Ask questions and discuss the items.
    St: Respond and make purchases.

Student Workbook p. 155
Lesson Seven, Section II
What are these/those?

SIGHT WORDS

carrots, cabbages, peppers, oranges, onions, lemons, these, those, give, me, one, please

VISUALS

155 carrots	159 onions
156 cabbages	160 lemons
157 peppers	103 vegetables
158 oranges	

INSTRUCTIONAL AIDS

real fruit and vegetables (optional)
old magazines or copies of the
   carrots, cabbages, peppers, oranges,
   onions and lemons on p. 383 of
   this guide
yellow 3 x 5 flash cards

STRUCTURE

What are these (those)?

They're _____ s.
These (Those) are _____ s.

INSTRUCTION

1. They're carrots.

2. What are they?

3. This is "carrots".
   I write "s" because I have more than one carrot.

4. Read this word.

5. This letter "c" has 2 sounds:

/s/	/k/
city	cat
circle	code
cent	closed
pencil	doctor

6. They're _____ s.

ACTIVITY RESPONSE

1. T: Hold up visual 155.
   St: Repeat.

2. St: They're carrots.

3. T: Write "carrots" on the board.
   St: Listen.

4. St: carrots

5. St: Listen and supply additional vocabulary from their group of sight word flash cards.

6. T: Hold up the remaining visuals. Repeat strategies in instruction 1 - 5. For "cabbages", point out the hard "c" and soft "g".
   St: Listen, repeat, respond.

7. Let's make some cards.

7. St: Make a yellow 3 x 5 card with carrots, cabbages, peppers, oranges, onions, lemons on one side. Stapel or tape a magazine picture or a copy of the visuals on p. 383 of this guide.

8. Let's read.

8. St: Read the sight word flash cards.
   T: Continue practice until students have a firm grasp of the plural vocabulary.

9. When two or more things are close and I can touch them, I say "these".

9. T: Touch the visuals. Write "these" on the board.
   St: Repeat "these".

10. These are _____ s.

10. T: Hold up the visuals.
    St: Listen and repeat.

11. What are these?

11. St: "These are _____ s." or "They're _____ s."

12. Let's practice.

12. T: Touch several classroom items and say "These are (my, your, his, her) (adjective) _____ s."
    St: Repeat and give original sentences if possible.

13. What are these?

13. T: Point to classroom objects.
    St: These are (possessive adjective) (adjective) _____ s.

14. You ask, "What are these?"

14. St: Ask each other the question and respond.

15. When the question is "What are these?", I can say "These are _____ s" or "They're _____ s."

15. T: Write the questions on the board. Model both responses.
    St: Practice both responses.
    T: Continue practice until concept is achieved.

16. When two or more things are far and I can't touch them, I say "those".

16. T: Repeat instructions 9 - 15, substituting "those" for "these".
    St: Listen, repeat, respond.

17. Optional, decoding:
    th<u>ose</u>
       hose   chose
       nose   close
       pose   prose
       rose

17. St: Decode.

18. Let's make cards.

19. Listen.

20. Give me one (a pen), please.

21. Listen and repeat.

22. I'm "A" and you are "B".

23. Let's read.

24. Optional: Fix the sentence (words).

25. Optional, decoding:
    a) "Give" has a hard "g" and sounds like "live".
    b) The "e" in "me" says it's own name as in "Lee".
    c) "Please" starts with /pl/. What other words start with /pl/?

26. Let's make some cards.

27. Open your books to p. 155 and write.

28. Let's read.

18. St: Make a yellow 3 x 5 card of "these" and "those".
    T: Make a corresponding 5 x 8 card.

19. T: Write dialogue #1 from p. 155 on the board, sentence strips or an overhead projector. Hold up visuals 155, carrots, and 156, cabbages, or use visual 103, vegetables. Model.
    St: Listen.

20. T: Repeat the line and have students hand you a pen, pencil, book, etc.
    St: Practice saying "Give me one, please." with one another.

21. T: Model the dialogue line by line.
    St: Repeat in chorus and individually.

22. T:
    Cl: Assume roles and reverse upon completion.

23. Gr:
    St: Assume roles and reverse upon completion.

24. T: If the dialogue was written on sentence strips, cut and scramble the components.
    St: Rearrange the sentences (words).

25. St: a) Listen and provide other hard "g" words if possible such as "get, gas"
    b) Listen
    c) plant, place (plate, play)

26. St: Make yellow 3 x 5 cards of "give, me, one".
    T: Make corresponding 5 x 8 cards.

27. T: Point to the upper right hand corner. Point out the /th/, /pl/.
    St: Fill in the name of their country.
    T: Check for accuracy and legibility.

28. St: Read the entire page.
    T: Model as necessary.

29. Optional: Let's write.

29. T: Using the visuals on p. 383 of this guide, devise a worksheet whereby students will write sentences. For example:

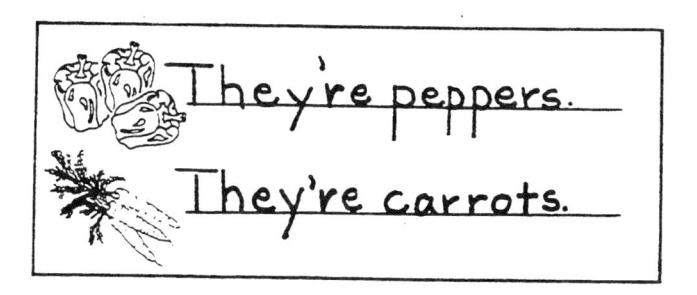

> They're peppers.
> They're carrots.

30. Let's read.

30. T: Hold up all the flash cards from this lesson. See p. 8 of this guide for suggested uses of the flash cards.
    St: Read.

Student Workbook   p. 156

SIGHT WORD
apples

VISUALS

101 orange	158 oranges
46 lemon	160 lemons
150 banana	37 bananas
42 pepper	157 peppers
100 onion	159 onions
21 apple	161 apples

INSTRUCTIONAL AIDS
the sight word flash cards of the visuals listed above
copies of the exercises in Appendix C, p. 401-2 (optional)
a yellow 3 x 5 flash card

INSTRUCTION

1. This (That) is an orange.
   These (Those) are oranges.

2. What is it?
   What's this (that)?

3. What are they?
   What are these (those)?

4. This (That) is an <u>apple</u>.
   These (Those) are <u>apples</u>.

5. Let's make a card.

6. Let's read.

ACTIVITY/RESPONSE

1. T: Hold up visuals 101 and 158.
      Compare the singular and plural.

2. St: Practice the responses.
      It's a (n) _____.
      This (That) is a (n) _____ .

3. St: Practice the responses.
      They're _____ s.
      These (Those) are _____ s.

4. T: Continue until all visuals have been practiced, contrasting singular and plural.

5. St: Make a 3 x 5 card with "apples" written on one side and staple or tape the visual of apples from p. 383 of this guide to the other side.
   T: Make a corresponding 5 x 8 card.

6. T: Hold up all the sight word flash cards for the vocabulary listed above.
   St: Read.

7. Optional: Let's write.

7. T: Hand out a copy of Appendix C, p. 401 to each student. Students can write the singular and plural nouns under the visuals. For example:

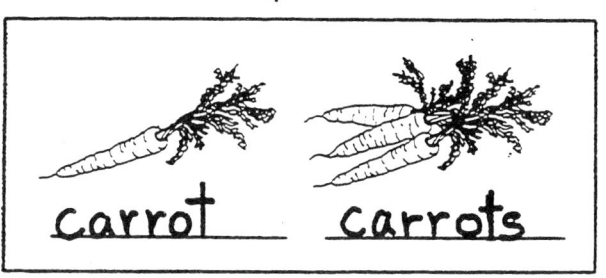

   carrot   carrots

8. Optional: Let's write.

8. T: Hand out a copy of Appendix C, p. 401 to each student.
   St: Write "It's a(n) _____ ." and/or "This is a(n) _____ ." for the singular visuals. Write "They're _____ s." and/or "These are _____ s." for the plural visuals.
   T: Check for accuracy and legibility.

9. Optional: Let's write.

9. T: Hand out a copy of Appendix C, p. 402 to each student.
   St: Write "It's a(n) _____ ." and/or "That's a(n) _____ ." for the singular visuals. Write "They're _____ s." and/or "Those are _____ s." for the plural visuals.
   T: Check for accuracy and legibility.

10. Open your book to p. 156 and read.

10. St: Open books and read the questions providing the responses orally.

11. Circle the correct answer.

11. T: Demonstrate if necessary.
    St: Circle the correct answer.
    T: Check for accuracy, Be certain students have filled in their city, state and zip at the upper right hand corner.

299

Student Workbook   p. 157

SIGHT WORD
50¢/lb.

VISUALS
all visuals listed on p. 298 of this guide

INSTRUCTIONAL AIDS
a scale (optional)
a 3 x 5 yellow flash card
copies of the exercise in Appendix C,
   p. 401 of this guide (optional)

INSTRUCTION

1. What is it (this, that)?
   What are they (these, those)?

2. Sometimes when I buy food, it's
   "___ ¢ each" or "___ ¢/lb."

3. This is a pound.

4. If you buy 2 pounds of carrots
   and they are 50¢/lb., how much do
   you pay?

5. Let's make a card.

6. Open your books to p. 157 and read.

7. Optional, pronunciation contrast:
      19, 90
      15, 50
      13, 30

8. Let's write.

ACTIVITY/RESPONSE

1. T: Review all visuals, sight words,
      structures and concepts presented
      between workbook p. 155-156.
   St: Respond.

2. T: Write both forms on the board.
   St: Listen.

3. T: Point to the "lb.", write "pound"
      and demonstrate how much a pound is
      on the scale. Explain that "per" means
      "for each" pound.
   St: Listen.

4. T: Provide various examples for
      the students.
   St: Calculate their bill.

5. St: Make a 3 x 5 card with "50¢/lb." on one
       side and "50¢ for each pound" on
       the other.
   T: Make a corresponding 5 x 8 card.

6. St: Open books and read the questions
       supplying the responses orally.

7. St: Practice saying the numbers.
   T: Cover your mouth and say a number.
   St: Point to the number they hear.

8. St: Write the answers for items #1-2 and
       the questions and answers for item #3.
   T: Check for accuracy and legibility.
      Be certain that the day has been filled
      in at the upper right hand corner.

9. Optional: Let's write how much.

10. Optional: Match the word with the picture.

9. T: Distribute a copy of p. 401 in Appendix C to each student. Have the class decide upon a good price for the items.
   St: Write "It's ____ ¢" or "They're ____ ¢ each" or "They're ____ ¢/lb."
   T: Check for accuracy and legibility.

10. St #1: Lays all of his singular and plural sight word cards from this lesson visual side up.
    St #2: Matches the visuals with her set of sight words.
    St #1,2: Check for accuracy.

Student Workbook   p. 158

SIGHT WORDS
all right, You're welcome

VISUALS
151 Is that an orange?
152 fruits and vegetables

INSTRUCTIONAL AIDS
yellow 3 x 5 flash cards

INSTRUCTION

1. What is it (this, that)?
   What are they (these, those)?

2. Listen.

3. This says "all right". It is the same as OK.

4. Optional, decoding:
all	(r)ight
ball	fight
call	light
fall	might
hall	night
mall	tight
stall	blight
	bright
	flight
	fright
	plight
	slight

5. This says "You're welcome." When somebody says "Thank you", you say "You're welcome".

6. Let's make some cards.

ACTIVITY/RESPONSE

1. T: Review all visuals, sight words, structures and concepts presented between workbook p. 155-157.
   St: Respond.

2. T: Copy the dialogue on p. 158 on the board, sentence strips or an overhead projector. Substitute the word "cabbages" and "89¢" for whatever you refer to using visuals 151 and 152.
   St: Listen.

3. T: Point to the words in the dialogue.
   St: Listen and repeat "all right".

4. St: Decode.

5. T: Point to the words in the dialogue.
   St: Listen and repeat "You're welcome".

6. St: Make a yellow 3 x 5 card of "all right" on one side and "OK" on the other, and a card for "You're welcome".
   T: Make corresponding 5 x 8 cards.

7. Listen and repeat.

8. I'm "A" and you are "B".

9. Read.

10. Optional, punctuation: This is a question mark. I use it after a question.

11. Optional: Fix the sentences (words).

12. Open your books to p. 158 and read.

13. Let's write.

14. Optional: Let's read these words.

7. T: Model the dialogue line by line.
   St: Repeat in chorus and individually.

8. T:
   Cl: ⟩ Assume role and reverse upon completion.
   Gr:
   St: ⟩ Assume role and reverse upon completion.

9. T: Pair the students up. Point to varying objects in visuals 151 and 152.
   St: Read the lines and reverse the roles upon completion.

10. T: Point to the question mark. Provide instruction for the periods, capitals and apostrophes.
    St: Listen.

11. T: If the dialogue was written on sentence strips, cut them into components and scramble.
    St: Rearrange the sentences (words).

12. St: Open books and read the dialogue in #1. Complete dialogue #2 orally.

13. St: Copy and complete dialogue #2.
    T: Check for accuracy and legibility. Be certain that students have filled in the name of their country at the upper right hand corner.

14. T: In addition to "You're welcome", this may be a good time to review other polite expressions learned to this point, including: Thank you, thanks, I'm sorry and Excuse me. Roleplay situations where the expressions might be used.
    St: Read and practice using the polite expressions.

Student Workbook   p. 159

VISUALS

37 bananas	158 oranges
155 carrots	159 onions
156 cabbages	160 lemons
157 peppers	161 apples

STRUCTURE

Are these (those) _____ ?   Yes, they are.
                                No, they aren't.

INSTRUCTION

1. Are these (those) _____ ?

2. Are these (those) _____ ?

3. Listen.

4. Listen and repeat.

5. I'm "A" and you are "B".

6. Optional: Fix the sentences (words).

7. Open your books to p. 159 and write.

8. Let's read.

ACTIVITY/RESPONSE

1. T: Show visuals. Elicit positive responses. Model "Yes, they are."
   St: Respond.

2. T: Show visuals. Elicit negative responses. Model "No, they aren't."
   St: Respond.

3. T: Hold up visuals 155 carrots and 156 cabbages. Copy dialogue #1 from p. 159 on the board, sentence strips or an overhead projector. Model.
   St: Listen.

4. T: Model the dialogue line by line.
   St: Repeat in chorus and individually.

5. T: Assume role and reverse upon completion.
   Cl:
   Gr: Assume role.
   St:

6. T: If the dialogue was written on sentence strips, cut them into components and scramble.
   St: Rearrange the sentences (words).

7. T: Point to the upper right hand corner.
   St: Complete the personal information.
   T: Check for accuracy.

8. St: Practice reading the dialogues on p. 159.

Student Workbook   p. 160

VISUALS
37 bananas   159 onions
155 carrots   160 lemons

INSTRUCTIONAL AIDS
the sight word flash cards of the visuals listed above

INSTRUCTION	ACTIVITY/RESPONSE

1. Are these onions?

   1. T: Hold up visual 159.
      St: Yes, they are.
      T: Model as necessary.

2. How much are they?

   2. T: Write "15¢ each" on the board and point to it.
      St: They're 15¢ each.

3. Are those lemons?

   3. T: Point to visual 160.
      St: Yes, they are.

4. How much are they?

   4. T: Write "20¢ each" on the board and point to it.
      St: They're 20¢ each.

5. Are these apples?

   5. T: Hold up visual 37, bananas.
      St: No, they aren't.
      T: Model as necessary.

6. What are they?

   6. St: They're bananas.

7. How much are they?

   7. T: Point to "15¢ each".
      St: They're 15¢ each.

8. Are those peppers?

   8. T: Hold up visual 155, carrots.
      St: No, they aren't.

9. What are they?

   9. St: They're carrots.

10. How much are they?

    10. T: Write "50¢/lb." on the board and point to it.
        St: They're 50¢/lb.
        T: Model as necessary.

11. Let's read these words.

    11. T: Hold up the sight word flash cards of the visuals listed above.
        St: Read.

12. Open your books to p. 160. Let's read.

    12. St: Open books and read the exercises providing the missing words orally.

13. Let's write.

14. Optional: Let's talk.

13. T: If necessary, have capable students complete the exercises on the board.
    St: Write or copy responses from the board.
    T: Check for accuracy and legibility. Be certain that students have filled in their area code and phone number, a dash or "none" at the upper right hand corner.

14. T: Have students practice the structure on this workbook page substituting the names of classroom objects for the names of the produce and supply their own prices.

Student Workbook p. 161
Odd Man Out

INSTRUCTION	ACTIVITY/RESPONSE
1. Let's read these words.	1. T: Copy the sample box on p. 161 onto the board. St: Read.
2. Put an X on the word that is different.	2. T: Explain that all the words are the abbreviations for days of the week except "It's" and therefore it is different. St: Listen and put an X on "It's".
3. Look at the words. Put an X on the word that is different.	3. T: The Odd Man Out game is extremely difficult. Provide the following examples explaining why each answer is chosen:

160	162	~~165~~	167	169
cat	~~door~~	hat	bat	mat
STOP	QUIET	DON'T WALK	SLOW	~~Hello~~
?	.	,	~~Yes~~	'
~~b~~	a	e	i	o

St: Respond.

| 4. Open your books to p. 161. | 4. T: Have students work as a class, in small groups, in pairs or individually.
St: Put an X on the one that is different.
T: Check for accuracy. The answers are:
  1. time   7. baker
  2. 7:15   8. desk
  3. cents   9. market
  4. chalkboard   10. apple
  5. 30¢   11. Sam
  6. onion   12. middle
Be certain students have filled in their birthdate at the upper right hand corner. |
| 5. Optional: Put an X on the one that is different. | 5. T: Devise a worksheet similar to the one on p. 161 using any of the sight words learned up to this point or have the students devise some exercises.
St: Put an X on the one that is different.
T: Check for accuracy. |

Student Workbook p. 162
Sentence Scramble

INSTRUCTION

1. Unscramble the sentence.

2. Open your books to p. 162.

3. Let's write.

ACTIVITY/RESPONSE

1. T: Write the sample scrambled sentence from p. 162 on the board or on a sentence strip. Remind students that sentences always start with a capital letter and end with a period or question mark. If the sentence is on a sentence strip, cut it into the components.
   St: Unscramble the sentence.
   T: Provide as many examples as necessary.

2. St: Open books and read the sentences in proper order orally.
   T: If necessary, put each scrambled sentence on a sentence strip and have students reorganize the sentences.

3. St: Work in pairs or individually writing the following sentences:
   1. How much are the peppers?
   2. Is this a hot dog?
   3. That's a cup of tea.
   4. She's a secretary.
   5. How much is a soft drink?
   6. Give me one, please.
   7. What day is it?
   8. They're 25¢ each.
   9. A banana is 15 cents.
   T: Check for accuracy and legibility. Be certain students have signed their name at the upper right hand corner.

Student Workbook p. 163
Lesson Eight, Section I
He's at the _____ .

SIGHT WORDS
bank, barber shop, post office, department store, beauty shop, laundromat, airport, market, hospital

VISUALS
28 market	165 department store
47 laundromat	
162 bank	166 beauty shop
163 barber shop	167 airport
164 post office	168 hospital

INSTRUCTIONAL AIDS
copies for each student of the visuals on p. 384 of this guide which correspond to the sight words
yellow 3 x 5 flash cards

INSTRUCTION

1. All of these are places.

2. It's a market.

3. What is it?

4. It's a (laundromat).

5. What is it?

6. Read this word.

7. Listen.

ACTIVITY/RESPONSE

1. T: Fan out the lesson visuals.
   St: Listen.

2. T: Hold up visual 28.
   St: Listen and repeat.

3. St: It's a market.

4. T: Hold up the appropriate visual.
   St: Listen and repeat.

5. St: It's a (laundromat).
   T: Continue practice until students can identify the visual locations orally.

6. T: Write "where" on the board.
   St: Respond.
   T: Remind students of the question "Where are you from?" if necessary.

7. T: Model the question "Where is (s)he?" or "Where are they?" for each of the lesson visuals and also model "(S)He's at the _____ ." or "They're at the _____ ." Write "_____ at the _____" on the board to provide a model sentence for the students.

309

8. "Where is (s)he?" or "Where are they?"

8. T: Hold up each of the lesson visuals. Point to the model sentence "_____ at the _____." if necessary.
   St: "(S)He's at the _____" or "They're at the _____."
   T: Continue practice until students can respond with ease and accuracy using good pronunciation, stress and intonation.

9. This is a market. What is the first (last) letter in "market"?

9. T: Hold up visual 28.
   St: m, t
   T: Write "m   t"

10. What other letters are in "market"?

10. St: Respond if possible.
    T: Complete writing "market".

11. Read this word.

11. St: market

12. Optional: How many vowels (syllables) are in market?

12. T: Pound out the sounds on the board or on a desk.
    St: Respond.

13. Let's make a card.

13. St: Make a yellow 3 x 5 card with "market" written on one side and staple or tape a copy of the visual of a market from p. 384 of this guide to the back of the card.
    T: Make a corresponding 5 x 8 card.

14. This is a (laundromat). What is the first (last) letter in (laundromat)?

14. T: Repeat instructions 9 - 13 for each of the remaining sight words.
    St: Respond, read and make cards.

15. Optional, decoding:

(b)<u>ank</u>	(sh)<u>op</u>
Hank	bop
rank	cop
sank	hop
tank	mop
yank	top
blank	chop
crank	crop
drank	drop
Frank	prop
prank	stop
spank	
stank	(st)<u>ore</u>
thank	bore
	lore
	more
(p)<u>ost</u>	sore
host	tore
most	wore
	chore
	shore
	snore
	swore

15. T: See p. 7 for a discussion about decoding.
    St: Decode.

16. Open your books to p. 163 and write.

16. T: Point to the upper right hand corner.
    St: Open their books and fill in the time.
    T: Check for accuracy.

17. Let's read.

17. St: Read the questions and responses.
    T: Model if necessary. Continue practice until students can read with good pronunciation, stress and intonation.

18. Optional: Fix your cards according to the alphabet.

18. T: Have the students say the alphabet and write it on the board.
    St: Alphabetize their sight word flash cards* from this lesson.

19. Optional: Match the picture with the word.

19. St #1: Lays the flash cards visual side up.
    St #2: Matches the visual with the sight word.
    St #1,2: Check for accuracy.

20. Optional: (S)He's (They're) at school (home, work, church).

20. T: Explain that with some words we don't say "the" after "at". Model.
    St: Listen, repeat and practice.

*See p. 8 of this guide for suggested uses of the sight word flash cards and p. 10 for the suggested uses of the Language Master.

21. You ask "Where is (s)he?" or "Where are they?"

21. St #1: Holds up either the visual or word side of a flash card and asks one of the questions.
    St #2: Responds and asks St #3 a question and so on.

22. Optional: Let's write.

22. St: Practice writing the questions and answers on p. 163.
    T: A master for lined paper is provided on p. 396 of this guide.

23. Optional: What is (s)he? What is it?

23. T: When students have a firm grasp of the vocabulary and structure for this lesson, you may wish to point to as many visuals on p. 163 asking the questions.
    St: She's a teller (saleslady, nurse, etc.). He's a barber (clerk). It's a chair (letter, washing machine, etc.).

24. Optional: Do you go to the _____?

24. T: Teach the response and any additional vocabulary students can digest.
    St: Yes, I do (every week).
    No, I don't.

25. Optional: Where do you go when you want to get food (are sick, etc.)?

25. St: Looking at the visuals on p. 163, respond "I go to the market (hospital)."

Student Workbook   p. 164

VISUALS
all visuals listed for the previous lesson

INSTRUCTIONAL AIDS
all the 5 x 8 sight word flash cards from the previous lesson

---

INSTRUCTION	ACTIVITY/RESPONSE
1. What is it?	1. T: Hold up each visual and ask the question. St: It's a _____ .
2. Where is (s)he? Where are they?	2. T: Hold up each visual and ask the question. St: "(S)He's at the _____ ." or "They're at the _____ ."
3. Let's read.	3. T: Hold up the 5 x 8 flash cards from the previous lesson. St: Read. T: Review all learnings from the previous lesson.
4. Open your books to p. 164. Let's read.	4. St: Open books and read the questions, supplying the correct responses orally.
5. Circle the correct answer.	5. St: Circle the correct answer. T: Check for accuracy. Be certain that students have filled in their date of birth at the upper right hand corner.
6. Optional: Learn to spell _____ .	6. T: Assign some or all of the sight words to be learned for a spelling quiz. St: Study.
7. Optional: What is (s)he? What is it?	7. T: Develop vocabulary and conversation as suggested in the optional instructions 23-25 for the previous lesson. St: Respond.

Student Workbook   p. 165

SIGHT WORDS
Ht., Wt.

VISUALS
28 market   165 department s
47 laundromat   166 beauty shop
162 bank   167 airport
163 barber shop   168 hospital
164 post office

INSTRUCTIONAL AIDS
all the sight word flash cards of the
  visuals listed above
any identification (application) form
  or a copy of the form on p. 399 or 4(
  this guide
yellow 3 x 5 flash cards

INSTRUCTION

1. What is your <u>personal information</u>?

2. Optional: Let's write.

3. Read the words.

4. This word is "height". I can write this word in a short way.

5. If you see "Ht." on an application, you write your height.

6. This word is "weight". I can write this word in a short way.

ACTIVITY/RESPONSE

1. T: Review as much personal information vocabulary as time allows including age, height and weight.
   St: Respond.

2. T: Hold up 5 x 8 cards of personal information vocabulary.
   St: Number their paper and write their personal information.

3. T: Hold up the 5 x 8 cards of personal information including age, height and weight.
   St: Read.

4. T: Write "height" and "Ht." on the board.
   St: Listen.

5. T: Point to "Ht." on the board. Show how "Ht." is requested on a (identification or application) form.
   St: Listen and write their height on the board or on paper.

6. T: Write "weight" and "Wt." on the board.
   St: Listen.

7. If you see "Wt." on an application, you write your weight.

7. T: Point to "Wt." on the board.
   Show how "Wt." is requested on a(n) (identification or application) form.
   St: Listen and write their weight on the board or on paper.

8. Let's make some cards.

8. St: Make a yellow 3 x 5 flash card with Ht. (Wt.) on one side and their height (weight) on the other
   T: Make corresponding 5 x 8 cards.

9. Open your books to p. 166 and write.

9. T: Point to the upper right hand corner.
   St: Fill in their age, height and weight.
   T: Check for accuracy.

10. Close your books.
    Is (s)he at the _____ ?
    Are they at the _____ ?

10. T: Hold up the visuals listed above. Elicit positive response.
    St: "Yes, (s)he is." or "Yes, they are."

11. Is (s)he at the _____ ?
    Are they at the _____ ?

11. T: Hold up the visuals. Elicit a negative response.
    St: "No, (s)he isn't." or "No, they aren't."

12. I can use "she" or a woman's name:
    She's at the _____ .
    (Student name's) at the _____ .

12. T: Write the two sentences on the board.
    St: Listen.

13. I can use "he" or a man's name:
    He's at the _____ .
    (Student name's) at the _____ .

13. T: Write the two sentences on the board.
    St: Listen.

14. Where is (s)he?

14. T: Distribute the visuals to the students. Point to a particular student.
    St: (S)He's at the _____ .

15. Where's (student name)?

15. T: Point to a particular student.
    St: (Student name's) at the _____ .

16. Is (student name) at the _____ ?

16. St: "Yes, (s)he is" or "No, (s)he isn't."

17. Listen.

17. T: Copy the dialogue on p. 165 onto the board, on sentence strips or an overhead projector. Hold up visual 162, bank and 167, airport. Model.

18. Listen and repeat.

18. T: Model the dialogue line by line.
    St: Repeat in chorus and individually.

19. I am "A" and you are "B".

20. Who will be "A" (B)?

21. Optional: Fix the sentences (words).

22. Open your books to p. 165. Let's read.

23. Let's read.

24. To make a question, I move "is" to the front of the sentence (capitalize "is", change the capital to a small letter and add a question mark).

25. Let's write.

26. Optional: Let's write.

27. Optional: Let's make questions.

19. T: Assume role and reverse upon completion.
    Cl:
    Gr: Assume role.
    St:

20. T: Seek volunteers, assign roles or pair all students up.
    St: Read and reverse roles.

21. T: If the dialogue was written on sentence strips, cut them into components and scramble the sentences (words). Refer to p. 14 of this guide for suggested uses of the sentence strips.
    St: Rearrange the sentences (words).

22. St: Open books and read the dialogue.

23. T: Point to the second exercise.
    St: Read the sentences.

24. T: Demonstrate the concept on the board or with the sentence strips. Do several examples on the board.
    St: Convert sentences into questions on the board.
    T: Continue practice until students are secure in the process.

25. St: Change the sentences on p. 165 into questions.
    T: Check for accuracy and legibility.

26. St: Practice writing the dialogue, sentences and/or questions from p. 165.
    T: A master for lined paper is provided on p. 396 of this guide.

27. T: Devise a worksheet similar to the exercise on p. 165.
    St: Make questions.
    T: Check for accuracy and legibility.

Student Workbook p. 166   VISUALS
                                             all visuals listed for the previous lesson

---

INSTRUCTION   ACTIVITY/RESPONSE

1. Is (student name) at the _____ ?   1. T: Distribute the visuals to the students.
                                                St: "Yes, (s)he is" or "No, (s)he isn't."
                                                T: Review learnings from the previous lesson.

2. Change the sentences into questions.   2. T: Write several sentences on the board.
                                                St: Change the sentences into questions on
                                                    the board.
                                                T: Review as necessary.

3. I can use "they" for two or more   3. T: Write the two sentences on the board.
   names: St: Listen.
   They're at the _____ .
   Tom and Ben are at the _____ .

4. Where are they?   4. T: Redistribute the visuals so that there's
                                                    one visual between two or more
                                                    students. Point to a pair of students.
                                                St: They're at the _____ .

5. Where are (student name) and   5. T: Point to a pair of students.
   (student name) ?   St: They're at the _____ .

6. Are (student name) and (student   6. St: "Yes, they are" or "No, they aren't.
   name) at the _____ ?

7. Listen.   7. T: Copy the dialogue on p. 166 onto the
                                                    board, sentence strips or on an
                                                    overhead projector. Hold up visual 163.
                                                    Model.

8. Listen and repeat.   8. T: Model the dialogue line by line.
                                                St: Repeat in chorus and individually.

9. I am "A" and you are "B".   9. T: Assume role and reverse upon
                                                    completion.
                                                Cl:
                                                Gr: Assume role.
                                                St:

10. Who will be "A" (B)?   10. T: Seek volunteers, assign roles or pair
                                                    all students up.
                                                St: Read and reverse roles.

11. Optional: Fix the sentences (words).

12. Open books to p. 166. Let's read.

13. Let's read.

14. To make a question, I move "are" to the front of the sentence (capitalize the "are", change the capital to a small letter and add a question mark).

15. Let's write.

16. Optional: Let's write.

17. Optional: Let's make questions.

11. T: If the dialogue was written on sentence strips, cut them into components and scramble the sentences (words).
    St: Rearrange the sentences (words).

12. St: Open books and read the dialogue.

13. T: Point to the second exercise.
    St: Read the sentences.

14. T: Demonstrate the concept on the board or with sentence strips. Do several examples on the board.
    St: Convert the sentences into questions on the board.
    T: Continue practice until students are secure in the process.

15. St: Change the sentences on p. 166 into questions.
    T: Check for accuracy and legibility. Be certain students have filled in their middle name, a dash or "none".

16. St: Practice writing the dialogue, sentences and/or questions from p. 166.
    T: A master for lined paper is provided on p. 396 of this guide.

17. T: Devise a worksheet similar to the exercise on p. 166.
    St: Make questions.
    T: Check for accuracy and legibility.

Student Workbook   p. 167-168

VISUALS
- 28 market
- 47 laundromat
- 162 bank
- 163 barber shop
- 164 post office
- 165 department store
- 166 beauty shop
- 167 airport
- 168 hospital

INSTRUCTIONAL AIDS
all the sight word flash cards
 of the visuals listed above

INSTRUCTION

1. Where is (s)he (student name) ?
   Where are they (student names) ?
   Is (s)he (student name) at the _____ ?
   Are they (student names) at the _____ ?

2. Write the words in the blank.

3. Listen and write.

ACTIVITY/RESPONSE

1. T: Review the vocabulary structures, readings and learnings from workbook p. 163 on.
   St: Respond.

2. T: Copy the dialogues on workbook p. 165 and 166 on the board, an overhead projector or on a ditto. Blank out some words. For example:
   A: ____ Tom at the bank?
   B: Yes, ____ is.
   A: Is Lucy ____ ____ beauty shop?
   B: No, she ____ .
   St: Read the dialogue silently and fill in as many words as possible or listen to the teacher read and then fill in the blanks.
   T: This excellent review of reading and writing can be used to review previous lessons.

3. T: Copy the dialogue on workbook p. 167 on the board or an overhead projector. Read the dialogue once at a natural pace, point to each word as you read it, but not writing in the words in the blanks.
   St: Listen and write the words that belong in the blanks if possible.
   T: Read the dialogue again saying the words which belong in the blanks.
   St: Complete the exercise.

4. Open your books to p. 167. Listen and write.

5. Close your books. You ask a "Where" question. Say "Where's" for one person and "Where are" for two or or more people.

6. You ask a question beginning with "Is" (Are).

7. Open books to p. 167. Look at the pictures and let's read. Remember, "is" is used for one and "are" is used for two or more.

8. Let's write.

9. Optional: Let's write.

10. Optional: Write a "Where" (Is, Are) question.
Variation: Students listen to the teacher ask questions and write the answer.

4. T: Read the dialogue only twice if possible.
   St: Listen and write the following in the blanks: time, It's, the, He's, shop.

5. T: Hand out the lesson visuals.
   St: Ask "Where is (s)he (name)?" or "Where are they (names)?" Another student responds.

6. St: Ask "Is (s)he (name) at the _____ ?" or "Are they (names) a the _____ ?" Another student responds.

7. St: Read and supply the questions and responses orally.
   T: Model if necessary. Have capable students write the questions and responses on the board.

8. T: Note to the students the "where" questions on p. 167 give a name of a place as an answer and the "Is, Are" questions on p. 168 give a "Yes-No" answer.
   St: Complete the questions and responses copying from the board or working in pairs if necessary.
   T: Check for accuracy and legibility. Be certain that students have checked their marital status at the upper right hand corner of p. 167 and their sex at the upper right hand corner of p. 168.

9. St: Practice writing the questions and answers on workbook p. 167-168.
   T: A master for lined paper is provided on p. 396 of this guide.

10. T: Hold up lesson visuals.
    St: Write questions (or answers).
    T: Check for accuracy and legibility.

Student Workbook p. 169
Lesson Eight, Section II
He's here/there

SIGHT WORDS
here, there

VISUALS
147 This is a cup of coffee.
     That's a hot dog.
148 This is a map.
     That's a mop.
149 This is a clock.
     That's a watch.
any or all the visuals listed for
  workbook p. 155 - 168

INSTRUCTIONAL AIDS
yellow 3 x 5 flash cards

STRUCTURE

Where's the (noun)?   It's here (there).
Where is (s)he (name)?   (S)He's here (there).
Where are they (names)?   They're here (there).

INSTRUCTION

1. Listen. Where's the cup of coffee
   (map, clock)? It's here.

2. Where's the _____ ?

3. If I ask the question "Where's the
   (book)?" and the (book) is
   close and I can touch it, I say, "It's
   here".

4. Where's the _____ ?

5. Where's (student name)?

6. You ask a "Where" question.

7. This word is "here".

ACTIVITY/RESPONSE

1. T: Hold up visuals 147, 148 and 149.
       Model the question and response.
   St: Listen.

2. T: Ask the question regarding singular
       classroom items or singular visuals
       that are nearby. Model the response.
   St: Listen and repeat "It's here".

3. St: Listen and practice.

4. T: Ask the question of items or visuals
       that are close to the students.
   St: It's here.

5. T: Model "(S)He's here."
   St: Listen and repeat.

6. St: Ask "Where's (the object/student name)?"
       of one another and respond.

7. T: Write "here" on the board.
   St: Listen and read "here".

8. Listen. Where's the hot dog (map, watch)? It's there.

9. Where's the _____ ?

10. If I ask the question "Where's the _____ ?" and the _____ is far away and I can't touch it, I say "It's there."

11. Where's the _____ ?

12. Where's (student name)?

13. You ask a "Where" question.

14. This word is "there".

15. Let's make some cards.

16. Listen to the question. Hold up the the "here" (there) card when something is "here" (there). Where's the _____ ?

17. Listen. Where are the _____s? They're here.

18. If there are two or more things or people, I say "They are" or "They're". Where are (student names)?

19. Where are the _____s?

20. Listen. Where are the _____s? They're there.

---

8. T: Hold up visuals 147, 148 and 149. Model the question and response.
   St: Listen.

9. T: Ask the question regarding singular classroom items or singular visuals that are far away. Model the response.
   St: Listen and repeat "It's there."

10. St: Listen and practice.

11. T: Ask the question of items or visuals that are far away from the students.
    St: It's there.

12. T: Model "(S)He's there."
    St: Listen and repeat.

13. St: Ask "Where's (the object/student name)? of one another and respond.

14. T: Write "there" on the board.
    St: Listen and read "there".

15. St: Make a yellow 3 x 5 card of "here" and "there".
    T: Make corresponding 5 x 8 cards.

16. T: Demonstrate the activity if necessary.
    St: Hold up the "here" (there) card in response to the questions.

17. T: Hold up any or all of the plural visuals.
    St: Listen.

18. T: Model the response.
    St: Listen and repeat "They're here."

19. T: Ask the question regarding plural classroom items or plural visuals which are nearby. "They're here."

20. T: Hold up any or all of the plural visuals.
    St: Listen.

21. "They're" means two or more things or people. It means "They are".

22. Where are the _____s?

23. Where are (student names)?

24. Listen to the question. Tell me the number of the answer.
Where's the _____ ?
Where's (student name) ?
Where are the _____s?
Where are (student names) ?

25. Open your books to p. 169 and write.

26. Look at the picture.

27. Let's read.

28. Optional: Let's write.

21. T: Write "They're" on the board and write "there"
    St: Listen.

22. T: Ask the question regarding plural classroom items or plural visuals which are far away.
    St: They're there.

23. St: They're there.

24. T: Write these 8 sentences on the board:
    1. It's here.
    2. He's here.
    3. She's here.
    4. They're here.
    5. It's there.
    6. He's there.
    7. She's there.
    8. They're there.
    St: Respond by saying the correct number.

25. T: Point to the upper right hand corner.
    St: Fill in their social security number.
    T: Check for accuracy.

26. T: Analyze each picture before reading. Ask content questions regarding the visuals.
    St: Respond.

27. T: Model the dialogues if necessary.
    St: Assume and reverse roles and read.
    T: Continue practice reading and speaking until students can distinguish between "here/there" in the singular and plural.

28. St: Practice writing the 8 sentences in instruction 24.
    T: A master for lined paper is provided on p. 396 of this guide.

Student Workbook p. 170	VISUAL
	169 here/there

INSTRUCTION | ACTIVITY/RESPONSE

1. Where's the _____ ?
   Where's (student name) ?

   1. T: Review structure, visuals, sight words and learnings from the previous lesson.
      St: It's here (there).
      (S)He's here (there).

2. Where are the _____ ?
   Where are (student names) ?

   2. T: Continue reviewing.
      St: They're here (there).

3. Look at the picture. What's this (that)?

   T: Hold up visual 169. Refer to all things close to the boy as "this" and all things away from him as "that".
   St: It's a lamp (bed, cat, etc.)

4. Optional: He is in the bedroom.
   They're curtains (pillows). It's a rug.

   4. T: Add additional vocabulary to the students' repertoire if they are capable. Provide appropriate decoding, reading and writing exercises.
      St: Respond, read and write.

5. Where's the _____ ?
   Where are the _____ ?

   5. T: Ask all of the questions which are presented on p. 170.
      St: Respond orally.

6. Write the answer.

   6. T: Repeat the questions on p. 170.
      St: Write the answers on the board.
      T: Continue practice until students are able to respond with confidence and good pronunciation.

7. Open your books to p. 170. Let's read.

   7. St: Open books. Read the questions and provide the responses orally.

8. Let's write.

   8. St: Write the answers:
      #1 It's here.
      #2 It's there.
      #3 They're there.
      #4 They're here.
      #5 It's there.
      #6 They're here.
      #7 He's here.
      #8 They're there.
      T: Check for accuracy and legibility. Be certain students have filled in their address at the upper right hand corner.

9. Optional: Let's write.

10. Optional: Let's make a story.
    What's his name?
    What is he?
    How old is he?
    Where does he live?
    Where is he from?
    What day/date is it?
    What time is it?
    Where is he?
    What's he doing? etc.

9. St: Practice writing the questions and and answers again.
   T: A master for lined paper is provided on p. 396 of this guide.

10. T: Hold up visual 169. Ask these questions and create additional ones. As the students respond, write the sentences in paragraph form. For example:
    This is Ken. He's a student. Ken is 18 years old. He lives in (Chicago). He's from (country). Today is (day), (date), 198 __ . It's ___ : ___ and Ken is in his bedroom. He's reading (etc.).
    a) Use the story for a reading exercise and spelling review.
    b) In the next class, present the exact story on a ditto with every (5)th word blanked out. Have students fill in the blanks.
    c) On another ditto, ask the same questions listed above in random order. Have students use their story to give the answers.
    d) Have the students copy the story.
    e) Dictate sentences from the story for a quiz.
    f) Cut the story up into individual sentences. Scramble them and have students reorganize the story.
    g) Have students read the story into a tape recorder and listen to themselves. Work on an individual basis with the students focusing on their pronunciation problems.
    h) Have students look at any lesson visual to create their own stories orally. Write these on paper, making no grammatical changes. Each student will have his own reading exercise. Repeat any of the suggested activities for the individual stories.

Student Workbook   p. 171

SIGHT WORD
egg

VISUALS
any singular and plural visuals you wish to review

INSTRUCTIONAL AIDS
a yellow 3 x 5 flash card

STRUCTURE

Where's the _____ ?   Here (There) it is.
Where are the _____ s ?   Here (There) they are.

INSTRUCTION

1. Where's the _____ ?

2. What are the 2 words in "It's"?

3. I can say "It's here" and I can say "Here it is."

4. Where's the _____ ?

5. I can say "It's there" and I can say "There it is."

6. Where's the _____ ?

7. Where are the _____ s?

ACTIVITY/RESPONSE

1. T: Hold up singular visuals or name singular classroom items. Review previous structures, sight words and learnings.
   St: It's here (there).

2. St: "It" and "is".

3. T: Write both forms on the board. Demonstrate how "Here it is" has the same 3 words as "It's here" only in reverse and without a contraction.
   St: Listen and repeat "Here it is."

4. T: Point to or name nearby items or visuals.
   St: Here it is.
   T: Continue practice as necessary.

5. T: Write both forms on the board. Demonstrate how "There it is" has the same words as "It's there", only in reverse and without a contraction.
   St: Listen and repeat "There it is."

6. T: Point to or name far away singular items or visuals.
   St: There it is.
   T: Continue practice as necessary.

7. T: Hold up plural visuals or name plural classroom items.
   St: They're here (there).

8.	What are the 2 words in "They're"?	8. St:	"They" and "are".
9.	I can say "They're here" and I can say "Here they are".	9. T:	Write both forms on the board. Demonstrate how "Here they are" has the same 3 words as "They're here" only in reverse and without a contraction.
		St:	Listen and repeat "Here they are."
10.	Where are the _____ s ?	10. T:	Point to or name nearby plural items or visuals.
		St:	Here they are.
		T:	Continue practice as necessary.
11.	I can say "They're there" and I can say "There they are."	11. T:	Write both forms on the board. Demonstrate how "There they are" has the same 3 words as "They're there", only in reverse and without a contraction.
		St:	Listen and repeat "There they are."
12.	Where are the _____ s?	12. T:	Point to or name faraway plural items or visuals.
		St:	There they are.
		T:	Continue practice as necessary.
13.	Listen to the question and say the answer.	13. T:	Mix questions for near and far, singular and plural items and visuals.
		St:	Here (There) it is. Here (There) they are.
14.	Open your books to p. 171 and write.	14. T:	Point to the upper right hand corner.
		St:	Fill in their city and state.
		T:	Check for accuracy.
15.	Look at the picture in #1. Where are they? What is (s)he (it)?	15. T:	Have students carefully study each visual before reading.
		St:	Respond.
16.	Let's read.	16. T:	Point out the new sight word "egg" and explain it's meaning. Model the dialogue if necessary.
		St:	Read.
		T:	Point out that either response is acceptable.
17.	Let's make a card.	17. St:	Make a yellow 3 x 5 card of "egg".
		T:	Make a corresponding 5 x 8 card.
18.	Look at the picture in #2, 3, 4.	18. T:	Continue to ask content questions regarding each exercise.
		St:	Respond.

19. Let's read.

20. Optional: Let's write.

21. Optional: Listen and write the answer.

19. T: Model dialogues if necessary.
    St: Read.

20. St: Copy any or all of the dialogues on on p.171.
    T: A master for lined paper is provided on p. 396 of this guide.

21. T: Write these four responses. on the board.
    1. Here it is.
    2. There it is.
    3. Here they are.
    4. There they are.
    Ask several questions regarding near and far, singular and plural classroom items and visuals.
    St: Listen and respond to each question by writing one of the four sentences.

Student Workbook   p. 172

INSTRUCTIONAL AIDS
a copy of p. 403 and/or p. 404 of Appendix C for each student
scissors (optional)

INSTRUCTION

1. Open your books to p. 172. Look at the pictures in #1.
   What is (s)he?
   Where is (s)he?

2. Listen.

3. Listen and write.

4. Read.

5. Look at the pictures in #2.
   What is (s)he?
   Where is (s)he?

ACTIVITY/RESPONSE

1. St: Open books and answer questions regarding each visual in the first exercise.

2. T: Read the paragraph filling in the following words in the blanks orally:
   are
   They're
   at the
   isn't
   He's
   is
   isn't
   a
   St: Listen.

3. T: Reread the paragraph.
   St: Listen and fill in the words in the blanks.
   T: Check for accuracy.

4. St: Read the paragraph.
   T: Listen for correct pronunciation, stress and intonation.

5. T: Repeat instructions 1-4 for the second paragraph filling in the following words in the blanks:
   are barbers
   barber shop
   is at
   He's a
   at the
   store
   is a
   St: Respond, listen, write and read.
   T: Check for accuracy and legibility. Be certain students have filled in the day at the upper right hand corner.

6. Optional: Let's write.

6. St: Copy the paragraphs on p. 172.
   T: Point out the capital letters for the beginning of each sentence and for names. Point out the periods at the end of each sentence and the apostrophes for the contractions. A master for lined paper is provided on p. 396 of this guide.

7. Optional: Study story #1 (#2) for dictation.

7. St: Study.
   T: Dictate sentences from the story randomly.
   St: Listen and write.

8. Optional: Listen and circle the word.

8. T: Distribute a copy of p. 403 in Appendix C. Call out one word for each numbered row.
   St: Circle the word.
   T: Check for accuracy. The next time you distribute a copy of the same page, call out a different word for each numbered row. This time students can X, underline, or ✓ the word. Each time you present this exercise, dictate the words at a quicker pace expecting students to read more rapidly.

9. Optional: Cut out every word on this paper. Make some sentences. Write each sentence on paper.

9. T: Distribute a copy of p. 404 in Appendix C.
   St: Cut out the words and work in pairs or individually creating sentences. Write each sentence on paper.
   T: Collect the written sentences and make a ditto with as many different sentences as possible and use that as reading exercise in another class. This activity can be done several times.

Student Workbook p. 173

SIGHT WORDS
grow, Yummy!, good

VISUALS
170 Tom and Ken are gardeners.
171 Mrs. Lee and Linda are cooks.
172 It's Saturday.

INSTRUCTIONAL AIDS
yellow 3 x 5 flash cards

INSTRUCTION	ACTIVITY/RESPONSE
1. Look at the picture. What is it? What are they?	1. T: Hold up visual 170. Ask content questions regarding the visual. St: Respond. T: Optional: Add the following vocabulary to the students' repertoire: hose, planting
2. Listen.	2. T: Read the story from p. 173 that corresponds to visual 170 twice. Write "grow" and "Yummy!" on the board and explain the concept of each.
3. Who are they? What are they? What do they grow? Where are the carrots? What color are they? Where are the peppers? What color are they?	3. St: Answer the questions as best as possible based on the visual and previous learnings.
4. Listen.	4. T: Write the story on the board, sentence strips or an overhead projector. Model. St: Listen.
5. Let's read.	5. T: Model the story line by line. St: Read in chorus and individually.
6. Read.	6. St: Read the story. T: Listen for correct pronunciation, stress and intonation.
7. Optional: Fix the sentences (words).	7. T: If the story was written on sentence strips, scramble the sentences (words). See p. 14 of this guide for suggested uses of the sentence strips. St: Reorganize the sentences (words).

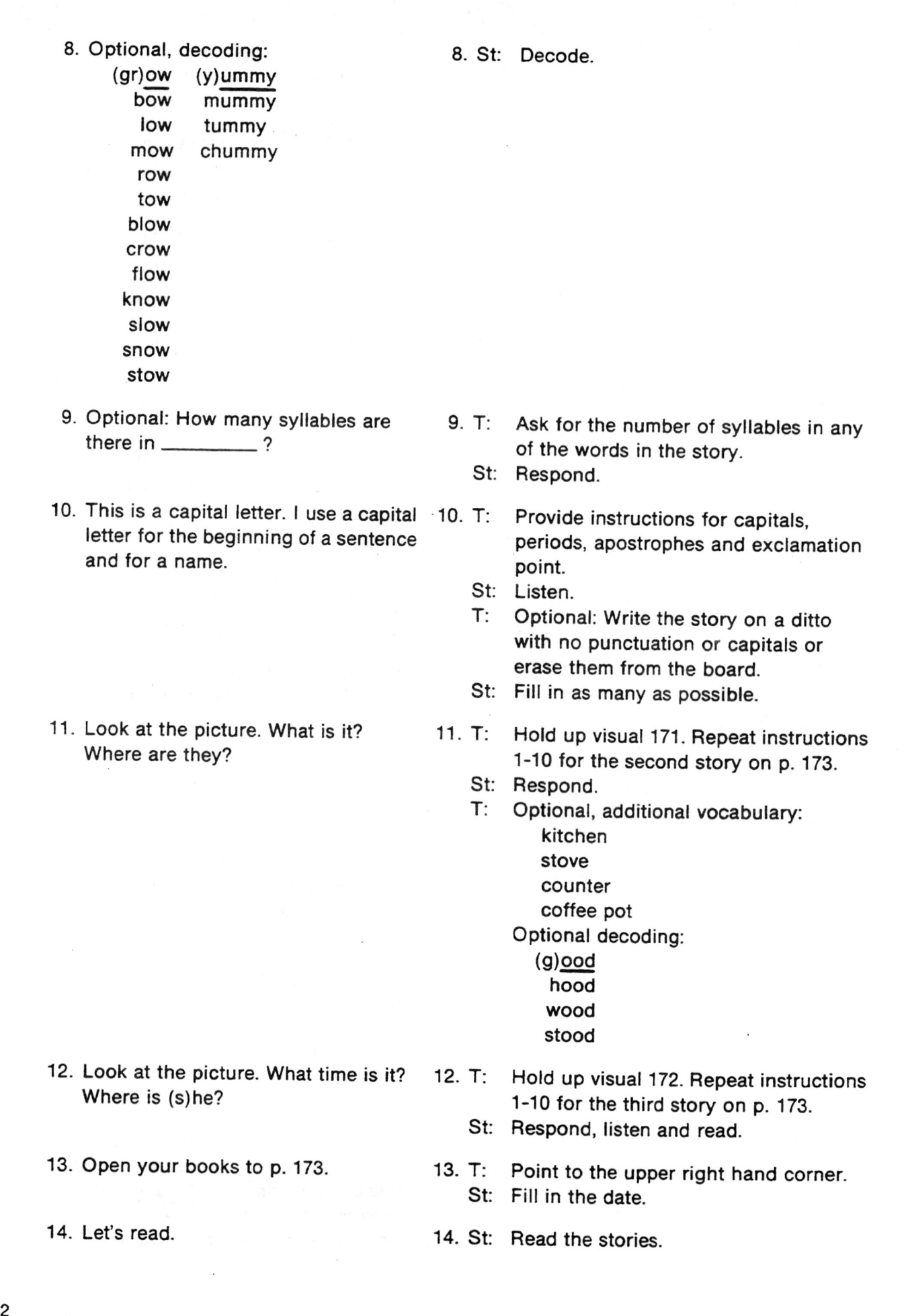

8. Optional, decoding:
   (gr)<u>ow</u>   (y)<u>ummy</u>
     bow   mummy
     low   tummy
     mow   chummy
     row
     tow
     blow
     crow
     flow
     know
     slow
     snow
     stow

8. St: Decode.

9. Optional: How many syllables are there in _____?

9. T: Ask for the number of syllables in any of the words in the story.
   St: Respond.

10. This is a capital letter. I use a capital letter for the beginning of a sentence and for a name.

10. T: Provide instructions for capitals, periods, apostrophes and exclamation point.
    St: Listen.
    T: Optional: Write the story on a ditto with no punctuation or capitals or erase them from the board.
    St: Fill in as many as possible.

11. Look at the picture. What is it? Where are they?

11. T: Hold up visual 171. Repeat instructions 1-10 for the second story on p. 173.
    St: Respond.
    T: Optional, additional vocabulary:
       kitchen
       stove
       counter
       coffee pot
    Optional decoding:
       (g)<u>ood</u>
       hood
       wood
       stood

12. Look at the picture. What time is it? Where is (s)he?

12. T: Hold up visual 172. Repeat instructions 1-10 for the third story on p. 173.
    St: Respond, listen and read.

13. Open your books to p. 173.

13. T: Point to the upper right hand corner.
    St: Fill in the date.

14. Let's read.

14. St: Read the stories.

15. Let's make some cards.

16. Optional: Let's write.

17. Optional: Study the story for dictation.

18. Optional: Listen and write the word in the blank.

19. Optional: Answer the questions.

20. Optional, fluency:
    Read the story on the tape recorder.

21. Optional: Make some sentences.

22. Optional: Let's make our own story.

15. St: Make a yellow 3 x 5 card of the sight words.
    T: Make a corresponding 5 x 8 card. See p. 8 of this guide for suggested uses of the sight word flash cards.

16. St: Copy any or all of the stories on p. 173.
    T: A master for lined paper is provided on p. 396 of this guide.

17. T: Assign one (or more) story to be studied for dictation.
    St: Study.

18. T: Copy the stories on p. 173 onto a ditto, leaving every (5)th word blank. Read.
    St: Listen and fill in the missing words.

19. T: Make a ditto asking a content question for each sentence of a paragraph. For example: What are Tom and Ken?
    St: Write the answers.

20. St: Read into a tape recorder and listen to themselves.
    T: Focus on individual pronunciation, stress and intonation problems.

21. T: Distribute a copy of p. 404 in Appendix C.
    St: Create and write sentences.

22. T: Using the lesson visuals, stimulate students to create their own class story. Write it on the board or ditto and use it as a reading exercise. See p. 325 for further suggestions.

Student Workbook   p. 174

SIGHT WORD
pay

VISUAL
28 market

INSTRUCTIONAL AID
a yellow 3 x 5 flash card

INSTRUCTION	ACTIVITY/RESPONSE
1. Look at the picture. What time is it? What is she? What is it? What are they? How much are they? How many (wo)men are there?	1. T: Hold up visual 28. Ask as many content questions about the visual as possible. St: It's 10:30. She's a cashier. It's a scale. They're (bananas). They're ____ ¢. (There are) 2.
2. Look at the words. Read them.	2. T: Point to the "Pay here" in the visual. See if a student can decode the words. St: Decode.
3. "Pay" means give your money. You pay the cashier.	3. St: Listen and repeat "pay".
4. Optional, decoding: (p)ay bay say day way gay clay hay gray jay play Kay pray lay stay May sway ray tray	4. St: Decode.
5. Let's make a card.	5. St: Make a yellow 3 x 5 flash card of "pay". T: Make a corresponding 5 x 8 card.
6. Listen to the story.	6. T: Read the story that corresponds to visual 28 on p. 174 two times. Point to the characters as you refer to them. St: Listen.

7. What's his (her) name?
   What is (s)he?
   Is (s)he at the _____?
   What day is it?
   Where are they?
   How much are the _____ ?
   Where's the (salesman) ?

8. Let's read the story. Find the word and write it in the blank.

9. Optional: Fix the sentences (words).

10. Open your books to p. 174. Let's read the story.

11. Let's write.

12. Optional: Let's write.

13. Optional: Write the words in the blanks.

7. T: Ask as many content questions about the story as possible.
   Read the story as frequently as necessary.
   St: Respond.

8. T: Copy the story from p. 174 on the board, sentence strips or an overhead projector. It is suggested that you review the story several times with the class, blanking out different words each time. Always provide a word bank. Teach students to:
   a) Read all the words in the bank.
   b) Read the selection entirely before writing.
   c) Choose words for the blanks, checking them off or crossing them out.
   d) Re-read the selection upon completion to check for accuracy.
   St: Read, select and write.

9. T: If the story was written on sentence strips, hand out one sentence (word) to each student.
   St: Reorganize the sentences (words).

10. St: Open books and read the story filling in the missing words orally.

11. St: Fill in the blanks and the name of their country at the upper right hand corner.
    T: Check for accuracy.

12. St: Copy the story.
    T: A master for lined paper is provided on p. 396 of this guide.

13. T: Rewrite the story on a ditto, blanking out different words. Do not provide a word bank. See how many words the students can fill in correctly. As a last resort, do provide a word bank on a separate piece of paper.

14. Optional: Fix the story.

14. T: Provide a mini-set of scrambled sentences (words) in a baggie or envelope to each (pair of) student(s). See p. 14 of this guide for suggested uses of sentence strips.
    St: Rearrange the story and check themselves by looking at p. 174.

15. Optional: Write the answer.

15. T: Make a worksheet incorporating questions as listed in instruction 1 and 7.
    St: Write the answers in full sentences.

16. Optional: Match the answer with the question.

16. T: On a ditto, write a list of questions and another list of answers.
    St: Match the answer to the question.

17. Optional: Write the question.

17. T: This is an extremely difficult exercise. Reserve this for the most capable students. Write a list of answers regarding the story on p. 174 on a worksheet. Leave a blank above the answer.
    St: Write the question.

18. Optional, fluency: Read the story into the tape recorder.

18. St: Tape their reading.
    T: Work with each student on their pronunciation, stress and intonation problems.

19. Optional: Let's re-write the story.

19. St: Rewrite the story changing the names and occupation of the characters, the day, the prices of the items, etc.
    T: Write the story on the board or on a ditto. Use it as a follow up reading exercise.

Student Workbook   p. 175
Lesson Nine, Section I
Where are they?

SIGHT WORDS
bedroom, (bed, lamp) dresser
wallet, purse, money, glasses, pillows, shoes

VISUAL
173 a bedroom

INSTRUCTIONAL AIDS
copies for each student of the visuals corresponding to the sight words on p. 385 of this guide
yellow 3 x 5 flash cards

INSTRUCTION

1. Look at the picture. This is a bedroom.

2. It's a (dresser).

3. How do you spell "bed"?

4. What's the first (last) letter in room?

5. This is "bedroom".

6. Optional, compound words: Sometimes I can make one word by putting two words together. For example, "bed" and "room" together say "bedroom".

7. What are the first two letters in /dr/ dresser/? What other words start with /dr/?

8. This is "dresser". What word do you see in "dresser"?

9. Read these words.

ACTIVITY/RESPONSE

1. T: Hold up visual 173.
   St: Repeat "This is a bedroom".

2. T: Point to all the numbered objects in the visual. Refer to p. 175 if necessary. Drill the vocabulary.
   St: Listen, repeat and practice until they're familiar with all of the vocabulary.

3. St: b - e - d

4. St: r - m

5. T: Write "bedroom" on the board. Remind students of the sight word "restrooms".
   St: Read both words.

6. T: Underline the two words in bedroom. Elicit other compound words students may recall.
   St: Listen and respond.

7. St: d - r; drink, dress

8. T: Write "dresser" on the board.
   St: dress

9. St: bedroom, dresser

337

10.	Spell "lamp".	10. T:	This is a previous sight word.
		St:	l - a - m - p
		T:	Assist as necessary.
11.	Remember the words "small, mall, tall, ball". What letters say "all"?	11. St:	a - l - l
12.	What letter says /w/? Spell "wall".	12. St:	w; w - a - l - l
13.	Remember the words "jet, pet, get". What letters say "et"? Spell "wallet".	13. St:	e - t; w - a - l - l - e - t
14.	Read these words.	14. St:	bedroom, dresser, wallet
15.	What letter does "purse" start with? What other word sounds like "purse"?	15. St:	p; nurse
16.	This is "purse".	16. T:	Write "purse" on the board.
		St:	Read.
17.	What letter does "money" start with? This is "money".	17. St:	m
		T:	Write "money" on the board.
18.	Read these words.	18. St:	bedroom, dresser, lamp, wallet, purse, money
19.	What two letters say /gl/ as in "glasses"? This is "glasses". What word do you see in "glasses"?	19. St:	g - l
		T:	Write "glasses" on the board.
		St:	Read "glasses"; glass
20.	Spell "ill"; pill. The word "pill" is in "pillows".	20. St:	i - l - l; p - i - l - l
		T:	Write "pillows" on the board.
		St:	Read "pillows".
21.	What 2 letters say /sh/ as in "shoes"? This is "shoes". What other words start with /sh/?	21. St:	s - h
		T:	Write "shoes" on the board.
		St:	Read "shoes"; ship, she
22.	Read the words.	22. St:	Read the sight words for this lesson.
23.	Point to the word.	23. T:	Hold up visual 173. Point to the numbered items.
		St:	Point to the word that corresponds to the item.
24.	Let's make some cards.	24. St:	Write the sight words on one side of a yellow 3 x 5 card and staple or tape a corresponding visual from p. 385 of this guide to the back.
		T:	Make corresponding 5 x 8 cards.

25. Optional, alphabetizing: Put your cards in alphabetical order.	25. St: Alphabetize their 3 x 5 cards. T: An additional alphabetizing worksheet is available on p. 398 of this guide.
26. Optional, syllables: How many syllables are there in (bedroom) ? What are the vowels? What's the vowel in the first (second) syllable?	26. T: Ask the same questions for each of the of the sight words. St: Respond.
27. Read these words.	27. T: Write "this, that, these, those" on the board. Re-practice their usage. St: Respond.
28. Open your books to p. 175 and write.	28. T: Point to the upper right hand corner. St: Check their marital status. T: Check for accuracy. Review as necessary.
29. Let's read.	29. St: Read all of p. 175, twice.
30. Optional: Let's write.	30. St: Practice writing the sight words or the sentences from p. 175.
31. Optional: Study the words (sentences) for spelling (dictation).	31. St: Study. T: Administer a quiz in the following class.

Student Workbook   p. 176

SIGHT WORDS
(in, on) under

VISUALS
79 in   169 here/there
99 on   173 a bedroom

INSTRUCTIONAL AIDS
yellow 3 x 5 flash cards

STRUCTURE

It's (They're) { in / on / under } the _____ .

INSTRUCTION

1. Where's the (wallet) ?
   It's in the (purse) .

2. Where are the (bed and dresser) ?
   They're in the (bedroom) .

3. Where's the _____ ?

4. Where are the (shoes) ?
   They're on the (bed) .

5. Spell "in" (on).

ACTIVITY/RESPONSE

1. T: Hold up visual 79. Teach usage of the preposition "in". Model question and response.
   St: Repeat "It's in the (purse) .
   T: Ask several "Where's the _____ ?" questions with regard to visuals 169, 173 and classroom objects.
   St: It's in the _____ .

2. T: Hold up visual 169 (173). Model the question and response.
   St: Repeat "They're in the (bedroom)".
   T: Ask several "Where are the _____ ?" questions with regard to the visuals and classroom objects.
   St: They're in the _____ .

3. T: Hold up visual 169 (173). Teach the usage of the prepositions "on" and "under". Repeat instruction #1.
   St: "It's on (under) the _____ ."

4. T: Hold up visual 99. Repeat instruction #2.
   St: "They're on (under) the _____ ".
   T: Continue practice with "in, on, under" with singular and plural items until students are secure in the structure.

5. T: These are previous sight words.
   St: i - n; o - n
   T: Write them on the board.

6. Spell "un" as in "under". This is "under".

6. St: u - n
   T: Write "under" on the board.

7. Read these words.

7. St: in, on, under

8. Optional, decoding:

in	on	under
bin	con	blunder
fin	Ron	plunder
gin		thunder
kin		
pin		
sin		
tin		
win		
chin		
grin		
spin		
thin		
twin		

8. St: Decode.

9. Let's make a card.

9. St: Make a card for "under" only if cards have already been made for "in, on".
   T: Make a corresponding 5 x 8 card.

10. Open your books to p. 176 and write.

10. T: Point to the upper right hand corner. Review personal information, sight words, as necessary.
    St: Fill in height, weight, color of hair and eyes.
    T: Check for accuracy.

11. Let's read.

11. T: Model questions and responses.
    St: Repeat and read.

12. Optional: Let's write.

12. St: Practice writing the sentences on p. 176.
    T: A master for lined paper is provided on p. 396 of this guide.

13. Optional:
    The _____ is { above / next to the / behind } _____ .

    The ____s are { in front of / to the right of the / to the left of } _____ .

13. T: Hold up any appropriate visuals and singular and plural classroom objects. Teach usage of as many prepositions you deem appropriate and have time for.
    St: Repeat, practice and respond.

341

Student Workbook   p. 177

VISUALS

79 in	169 here/there
99 on	173 a bedroom

INSTRUCTION

1. Read these words.

2. Where's the _____ ?
   Where are the _____s?

3. Open your books to p. 177.
   Let's read.

4. Circle the correct answer.

5. Optional: Circle the correct answer.

ACTIVITY/RESPONSE

1. T: Review all the sight words from workbook p. 175 on.
   St: Read the words.

2. T: Hold up visuals. Refer to classroom items.
   St: Respond using "in, on, under".

3. St: Open books, read the questions and select the responses orally.

4. T: Demonstrate that the correct answer in sample box #1 has been circled.
   St: Circle the correct answer and sign their name at the upper right hand corner.
   T: Check for accuracy.

5. T: If you have taught other prepositions, devise an exercise similar to that on p. 177.
   For example:

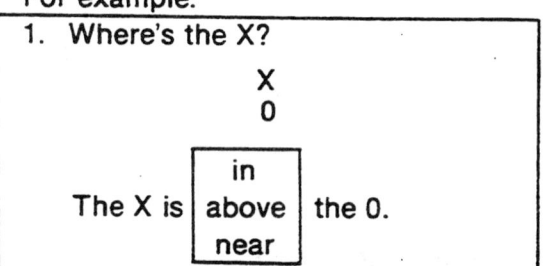

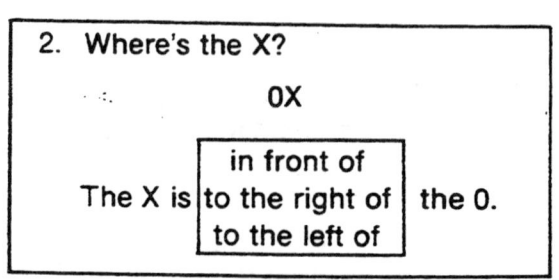

1. Where's the X?
X
O
The X is | in / above / near | the O.

2. Where's the X?
OX
The X is | in front of / to the right of / to the left of | the O.

   St: Circle the correct answer.

Student Workbook p. 178

SIGHT WORD
box

VISUALS
174 Where's my wallet?
175 Where are the cabbages?

INSTRUCTIONAL AID
a yellow 3 x 5 flash card

INSTRUCTION	ACTIVITY/RESPONSE
1. Where's the _____ ?	1. T: Hold up any singular visuals or name any singular classroom items. Place these near and far. St: It's here (there). Here (There) it is. T: Review both responses thoroughly.
2. Look at this picture. What's this?	2. T: Hold up visual 174. Ask as many content questions regarding the visual as possible. St: It's a dresser (wallet, pen, table, etc.)
3. Optional: What time is it? Where's he going? What's his (her) name? etc.	3. T: Ask questions which help to set a mood but whose answers are not found in visual 174. St: Respond.
4. Listen.	4. T: Tape the visual above your head on the board. Stand by the man (woman) when modeling "A's" (B's) words. Read the first dialogue on p. 178 twice. St: Listen.
5. Listen and repeat.	5. T: Write the dialogue on the board, sentence strips or on an overhead projector. Model the dialogue line by line. St: Repeat each line in chorus and individually.
6. I'm "A" and you are "B".	6. T: Assume role and reverse upon completion. Cl: Gr: Assume role. St:

343

7. Who's "A" (B)?	7. T: Seek volunteers or pair all students up. St: Assume roles and reverse upon completion.
8. This is a comma. When I call a name, I use a comma.	8. T: Point to the comma. Provide instruction for the capital letters, apostrophes, contractions, periods, question marks and the exclamation point.
9. Optional: Fix the sentences (words).	9. T: If the dialogue was written on sentence strips, cut and scramble sentences (words). St: Rearrange the sentences (words).
10. Optional: Let's play a game.	10. T: Collect a personal item from a student. Have him leave the room. Place the item in a visible location in the classroom. To retrieve the object, the student must ask "Where's my _____?" Other students will say "It's (on) the _____." The first student must say "Oh, yes, here (there) it is." If he cannot produce the structure, he must leave the room and try again. St: Play.
11. Where are the _____s?	11. T: Hold up any plural visuals or name any plural classroom items. Place these near and far. St: They're here (there). Here (There) they are. T: Review both responses thoroughly.
12. Look at the picture. Where are they?	12. T: Hold up visual 175. Repeat instructions 2-10 for the second dialogue on p. 178. This time, however, all referrants are plural. St: Respond, listen, read and play.
13. This word is "box".	13. T: Point to the word "box" in the story. Draw a box on the board. St: Repeat "box".
14. Let's make a card.	14. St: Make a yellow 3 x 5 flash card with "box" written on it. T: Make a corresponding 5 x 8 card.

15. Optional, decoding:
   (b)<u>ox</u>
     fox
     lox
     sox
     boxer
     boxing

15. St: Decode.

16. Optional, new vocabulary:
   For visual 174:
     shirt
     pants
     belt
   For visual 175:
     shopping cart
     clerk

16. St: Practice and write.

17. Open your books to p. 178 and write.

17. T: Point to the upper right hand corner.
    St: Write the name of the day.
    T: Check for accuracy.

18. Let's read.

18. St: Assume roles and read both dialogues.

19. Optional: Read into the tape recorder.

19. T: Assign pairs to practice a dialogue together and speak into a tape recorder. Correct individual errors in pronunciation, stress and intonation.
    St: Read.

20. Optional: Let's write.

20. St: Copy either or both of the dialogues on p. 178.
    T: A master for lined paper is provided on p. 396 of this guide.

21. Optional: Fix the sentences.

21. T: Copy the dialogues onto a ditto, leaving out all punctuation and capital letters.
    St: Fill in as many periods, commas, question marks, etc. as possible.

22. Optional: Listen and write.

22. T: Copy the dialogues onto a ditto, leaving out every (5)th word. Read the dialogues.
    St: Listen and fill in the missing words.

Student Workbook p. 179

INSTRUCTION

1. Where's the _____ ?

2. Where are the _____ s?

3. Say the number of the correct answer.
   Where's the _____ ?
   Where are the _____ s?

4. Open your books to p. 179. What is it?

5. Let's read.

6. Circle the correct answer.

7. Optional: Let's write.

ACTIVITY/RESPONSE

1. T: Select any singular visuals you wish to review. Place them near and far.
   St: Here (There) it is.

2. T: Select any plural visuals you wish to review. Place them near and far.
   St: Here (There) they are.

3. T: Write these sentences on the board and number them:
   1. Here it is.
   2. There it is.
   3. Here they are.
   4. There they are.
   St: Call out the correct number.

4. T: Point to each visual.
   St: Identify the items in each visual.

5. St: Read the questions and select the correct answer orally.
   T: Explain that contractions are never used at the end of a sentence.

6. T: Demonstrate that the correct answer has been circled in the sample box.
   St: Circle the correct answer and fill in their social security number.
   T: Check for accuracy.

7. St: Copy the questions and correct answers for practice.
   T: A master for lined paper is provided on p. 396 of this guide.

Student Workbook   p. 180

SIGHT WORDS
kitchen, sink, stove, cabinet, counter, refrigerator

VISUALS

18 sink	97 refrigerator
17 stove	176 cabinet
77 kitchen	177 counter

INSTRUCTIONAL AIDS
copies for each student of the visuals corresponding to the sight words on p. 386 of this guide
yellow 3 x 5 flash cards

INSTRUCTION

1. What is it?

2. It's a cabinet. I put boxes and cans of food in a cabinet.

3. It's a counter.

4. Look at this picture. What is it?

5. This is "kitchen".

6. Optional, decoding:
   "itch" as in "kitchen"
      (k)<u>itch</u> (en)
        bitch   pitch
        ditch   witch
        hitch   snitch
        Mitch   switch

7. What's this?

8. What's the first (last) letter in sink?

9. This is "sink".

ACTIVITY/RESPONSE

1. T: Hold up visuals 18, 17, 77 and 97.
   St: It's a sink (stove, kitchen, refrigerator).
   T: These words were presented orally in Part 2, Literacy.

2. T: Hold up visual 176.
   St: Listen and repeat "It's a cabinet".

3. T: Hold up visual 177.
   St: Repeat.

4. T: Hold up visual 77.
   St: It's a kitchen.

5. T: Write "kitchen" on the board.
   St: Read "kitchen".

6. T: Underline the "itch".
   St: Decode.

7. T: Point to the sink in visual 77.
   St: It's a sink.

8. St: s - k

9. T: Write "sink" on the board.
   St: Read "sink".

10. Optional, decoding:
 (s)ink
 fink   wink
 kink   blink
 mink brink
 pink   drink
 rink   stink
           think

10. St: Decode.

11. What's this?

11. T: Point to the stove in visual 77.
    St: It's a stove.

12. What two letters say /st/ as in stove? What other words start with /st/?

12. St: s - t; stop, store, state

13. This is "stove".

13. T: Write "stove" on the board.
    St: Read "stove".

14. Optional, decoding:
 (st)ove
 cove clove
 dove drove
 rove   grove
 wove

14. St: Decode.

15. What's this?

15. T: Point to the cabinet in visual 77.
    St: It's a cabinet.

16. What's the first (last) letter in "cabinet"?

16. St: c - t

17. How do you spell "cab" (net). What letter says /i/?

17. St: c - a - b; n - e - t; i

18. This is "cabinet".

18. T: Write "cabinet" on the board.
    St: Read "cabinet".

19. I see three words in "cabinet".

19. T: Point out the "cab, in, net" in "cabinet".

20. What's this?

20. T: Point to the counter in visual 77.
    St: It's a counter.

21. This is "counter".

21. T: Write "counter" on the board.
    St: Read "counter".

22. What's this?

22. T: Point to the refrigerator in visual 77.
    St: It's a refrigerator.

23. What's the first (last) letter in "refrigerator"?

23. St: r - r

24. This is "refrigerator".	24. T: Write "refrigerator" on the board. St: Read "refrigerator".
25. Let's read these words.	25. St: Read the sight words in chorus and individually.
26. Point to the word.	26. T: Hold up each of the lesson visuals. St: Point to the word that corresponds to the item.
27. Let's make some cards.	27. St: Write the sight words on one side of a yellow 3 x 5 card and staple or tape a corresponding visual from p. 386 of this guide to the back. T: Make corresponding 5 x 8 cards.
28. Optional, alphabetizing: Put your cards in alphabetical order.	28. St: Alphabetize the sight word cards from this lesson. T: An additional alphabetizing worksheet is available on p. 398 of this guide.
29. Optional, syllables: How many syllables are there in (kitchen) ? What are the vowels? What's the vowel in the first (second, third, etc.) syllable?	29. T: Ask the same questions for each sight word.
30. Open your books to p. 180 and write.	30. T: Point to the upper right hand corner. St: Check their age. T: Check for accuracy.
31. Let's read.	31. St: Read all of p. 180. T: Have students re-read as frequently as necessary.
32. Optional: Let's write.	32. St: Practice writing the sight words and/or the sentences from p. 175.
33. Optional: Study the words (sentences) for spelling (dictation).	33. St: Study. T: Administer a quiz in the following class.

Student Workbook   p. 181

SIGHT WORD
maiden (name)

VISUALS
all visuals listed for the previous lesson and

| 43 purse | 108 wallet |
| 45 lamp | 173 a bedroom |

INSTRUCTIONAL AIDS
all the sight word flash cards from the the previous lesson and of the visuals listed above
a yellow 3 x 5 flash card

INSTRUCTION	ACTIVITY/RESPONSE
1. What is your (first, last, middle, name?	1. St: Respond.
2. Read the word and give me the answer.	2. T: Write "name, first, last, middle" on the board. Point to the words randomly. St: Give the corresponding information.
3. Read this.	3. T: Write "maiden" on the board. Cover up the "mai". St: den
4. Can you read this word?	4. T: Remind students of the "a - i" sound in "waiter". St: Decode "maiden".
5. In the United States, when a woman is married, she usually uses the man's last name. Her name when she was single is her maiden name. For example: Mrs. (Nancy Reagan) is married to Mr. (Ronald Reagan). (Reagan) is her married name. Her single name was (Nancy Davis). (Davis) is her maiden name. What's your maiden name?	5. T: Ask the question of the women. St: (name) or "I don't have one." T: Explain that men and single women should write a dash when "maiden name" is requested on a form.

6. Let's make a card.

6. St: Make a 3 x 5 card with "maiden" written on one side and their maiden name on the other. Single women and men can write a dash on the other side.
   T: Make a corresponding 5 x 8 card.

7. What is it?

7. T: Hold up each of the visuals.
   St: It's a kitchen (counter, lamp, etc.)

8. Read these words.

8. T: Hold up each of the sight word cards corresponding to the visuals.
   St: Read.

9. Optional: Hold up your word card when I show the picture.

9. T: Hold up the visuals in random order.
   St: Hold up the corresponding 3 x 5 flash cards.

10. Optional: Spell _____ .

10. St: Spell various sight words.

11. Open your books to p. 181. Let's read the words.

11. St: Open books and read the words at the top of the page.

12. What is it?

12. St: Identify each visual orally.

13. Let's write.

13. T: Demonstrate the response has been written in the sample box. Point to the capital letter, apostrophe and period. Show students how the word "lamp" has been checked off at the top.
    St: Write the sentences and write their maiden name or a dash at the upper right hand corner.
    T: Check for accuracy and legibility.

14. Optional: Let's write.

14. St: Practice writing the sentences on p. 181.
    T: A master for lined paper is provided on p. 396 of this guide.

15. Optional: Put on the names of these things at home.

15. T: Suggest to the students that they label bedroom and kitchen items at home. Using visuals 78 and 173, students determine what labels to make.
    St: Attach labels at home.

351

Student Workbook   p. 182

VISUAL
178 May's in the kitchen

INSTRUCTION

1. Look at this picture. What is it?
   What are they?

2. Where's the (woman)?
   Where are the (soft drinks)?

3. Listen.

4. Where's May?

5. Listen.

6. Let's read.

7. Read.

8. Optional: Read.

9. Read the words.

10. Find (counter) (/dr/, a word with 2 syllables, a compound word).

11. Optional: Fix the sentences (words).

ACTIVITY/RESPONSE

1. T: Hold up visual 178. Thoroughly review the names of all the items.
   St: It's a (sink).
       They're (soft drinks).

2. St: (She's) (in the kitchen).
       They're (under the sink).

3. T: Read the paragraph on p. 182 that corresponds to the visual twice.
   St: Listen.

4. T: Ask each of the questions listed on p. 182.
   St: Respond.

5. T: Write the paragraph from p. 182 on the board, sentence strips or an overhead projector. Model.
   St: Listen.

6. T: Model the paragraph line by line.
   St: Repeat in chorus and individually.

7. St: Read the paragraph.

8. T: Erase or cut out every (5)th word.
   St: Read, filling in the blanks orally and then in writing.
   T: Make a ditto doing the same for the following class.

9. T: Point to the words in random order as rapidly as possible.
   St: Read as quickly as possible.

10. T: Ask for various words, sounds, etc.
    St: Point to it.

11. T: If the paragraph was written on sentence strips, cut them into components and scramble.
    St: Rearrange the sentences (words).

12. Open your books to p. 182 and read.	12. St:	Open books and read the paragraph and the questions, supplying the answers orally.
13. Let's write.	13. T:	If necessary, have capable students write the answers on the board.
	St:	Write (copy) the responses and fill in their birthdate at the upper right hand corner.
	T:	Check for accuracy and legibility.
14. Optional: Let's write.	14. St:	Practice writing the paragraph.
	T:	Have students indent. A master for lined paper is provided on p. 396 of this guide.
15. Optional: Study the sentences for dictation.	15. St:	Study.
	T:	Dictate sentences in random order in the following class.
16. Optional: Read into the tape recorder.	16. St:	Read.
	T:	Work with students on individual pronunciation, stress and intonation problems.

Student Workbook   p. 183

INSTRUCTION	ACTIVITY/RESPONSE
1. What is it? What are they?	1. T: Provide review of visuals, sight words and structures as necessary. St: Respond.
2. Open your books to p. 183 and look at the picture. What is it? What are they?	2. St: Open books and identify the items.
3. Where's the coffee? Where are the doughnuts (soft drinks, hamburgers)?	3. St: It's on the stove. They're (in the cabinet).
4. Let's read.	4. St: Read and complete the sentences orally in chorus and individually.
5. Let's write.	5. St: Complete the sentences on the board and in the workbook. T: Check for accuracy and legibility. Be certain students have filled in their names at the upper right hand corner.
6. Optional: Answer the questions.	6. T: Devise a worksheet (similar to that on p. 182) asking several questions about the paragraph on p. 183. St: Write the answers in full sentences.
7. Optional: Let's write.	7. St: Practice writing the paragraph.
8. Optional: Let's make the story longer. What's Bob? Where's he from? How old is he? What time is it?	8. T: Ask questions so that the responses can be used to create a story: Bob is a salesman. He's 55 years old. It's 6:30. His wife is at work. Bob cooks on Mondays, etc. St: Write the story on the board. T: Write it on a ditto as a follow up reading exercise:

Student Workbook   p. 184

SIGHT WORDS
United States

INSTRUCTIONAL AIDS
yellow 3 x 5 flash cards

INSTRUCTION

1. Open your books to p. 184. Where do you live?

2. This is "United States".

3. What country is this?

4. "United States" is the same as "U.S.A.".

5. Let's make a card.

6. Where do you live?

7. Optional, decoding:
   (w)est
   - best   rest
   - fest   test
   - jest   vest
   - lest   chest
   - nest   crest
   - pest   quest

8. Where do you live?

9. Let's write.

ACTIVITY/RESPONSE

1. St: Open books.
   T: Model the first sentence.
   St: Repeat.

2. T: Write "United States" on the board.
   St: Listen and repeat.

3. St: United States.

4. T: Write "U.S.A." on the board.
   St: Listen.

5. St: Make a 3 x 5 card with "United States" written on one side and "U.S.A." on the other.

6. T: Model the remaining sentences.
   St: Repeat.

7. St: Decode.

8. St: Re-read the sentences inserting the name of their own state, city, street and address, and continue practicing as necessary.

9. St: Complete the sentences filling in their own state, city, street and address.
   T: Check for accuracy and legibility. Be certain that the day has been filled in at the upper right hand corner.

Student Workbook p. 185
Lesson Ten, Section I
He's Mr. Lee's son.

SIGHT WORDS
family, husband, wife, son
mother, daughter, brother, sister

VISUAL
  53 (The Lee) family
  54 father/son
179 husband/wife
180 mother/daughter
181 brother/sister

INSTRUCTIONAL AIDS
copies for each student of the visuals corresponding to the sight words on p. 387 of this guide

---

INSTRUCTION

1. This is a family. This is the Lee family.

2. What is it?

3. They are married. He is Mr. Ben Lee. She is Mrs. May Lee. They are Mr. & Mrs. Lee.

4. Ben is the husband. May is the wife.

5. What's his (her) name?

6. What is Ben (May)? What are they?

7. Ben is the father. Joe is the son.

8. What's his name?

9. What is he? What are they?

10. May is the mother. Linda is the daughter.

11. What's her name?

12. What is she? What are they?

ACTIVITY/RESPONSE

1. T: Hold up visual 53.
   St: Repeat "This is a family".

2. St: (It's a) family.

3. T: Hold up visual 179.
   St: Listen.

4. St: Listen and repeat.

5. St: Ben (May) Lee.

6. St: He's the husband. She's the wife. They're husband and wife.

7. T: Hold up visual 54.
   St: Listen and repeat.

8. St: Ben (Joe) Lee.

9. St: He's the father (son). They're father and son.

10. T: Hold up visual 180.
    St: Listen and repeat.

11. St: May (Linda) Lee.

12. St: She's the mother (daughter). They're mother and daughter.

13. Joe is the brother. Linda is the sister. They're brother and sister.

14. What's his (her) name?

15. What is (s)he? What are they?

16. What's his (her) name (first, last)?

17. What is he (she)? What are they?

18. What's the first letter in "family"?

19. This is a family and this is "family".

20. What word do you see in family?

21. Read this word.

22. What's the first (last) letter in _____ ?

23. Optional, decoding:

(w)i<u>fe</u>	(M)<u>ay</u>	
life	bay	way
knife	day	clay
	gay	gray
	hay	play
	jay	pray
	Kay	slay
	lay	stay
	pay	sway
	ray	tray

13. T: Hold up visual 181.
    St: Listen and repeat.

14. St: Joe (Linda) Lee.

15. St: He's the brother. She's the sister. They're brother and sister.

16. T: Hold up visual 53. Review the names of all the family members.
    St: Respond.

17. T: Hold up the respective visuals. Review all the relationships.
    St: Respond.
    T: Continue practice until students are secure in the vocabulary and pronunciation.

18. St: f

19. T: Hold up visual 53 and write "family" on the board.
    St: Repeat "family".

20. St: am

21. St: family

22. T: Present the rest of the sight words on the board. Point out the "er" in fath<u>er</u>, moth<u>er</u>, daught<u>er</u>, broth<u>er</u>, sist<u>er</u>, (wait<u>er</u>, garden<u>er</u>, lawy<u>er</u>, teach<u>er</u>, bak<u>er</u>).
    Point out the "ther" in fa<u>ther</u>, mo<u>ther</u>, bro<u>ther</u>.
    St: Repeat and practice reading.

23. St: Decode.

24. Let's make some cards.

24. St: Make a yellow 3 x 5 card with the sight words written on one side corresponding visuals from p. 387 to the back.
    T: Make corresponding 5 x 8 cards.

25. What is he (she)?

25. T: Hold up the lesson visuals.
    St: Hold up the corresponding card.
    T: Continue practice until students can read the words with ease and match them to visuals.

26. Sometimes I see these words on an application. If you are a wife, you write your husband's name. If you are a husband, you write your wife's name. If you are single (divorced, widowed) you write a dash or "none".

26. T: Write "name of spouse" on the board.
    St: Listen and repeat "name of spouse".

27. What is the name of your spouse?

27. St: Give the name or say "I don't have one".

28. Open your books to p. 185 and write.

28. T: Point to the upper right hand corner.
    St: Open books and fill in the name of the spouse, a dash or "none".

29. Let's read.

29. T: Model if necessary.
    St: Read in chorus and individually.

30. Let's make a card.

30. St: Make a yellow 3 x 5 card with "spouse" on one side and the name, a dash or "none" on the other.
    T: Make a corresponding 5 x 8 card.

31. Optional, decoding:
    (sp)<u>ouse</u>
        house
        louse
        mouse
        blouse

31. St: Decode.

32. Optional, alphabetizing:
Fix your sight word cards from this lesson according to the alphabet.

32. St: Alphabetize their cards.

33. Optional, syllables:
How many syllables are there in _____ ?

33. St: Give the number of syllables in each of the sight words.

34. Optional: Let's write.

34. St: Practice writing the sight words or sentences that appear on p. 185.

35. Optional: Study the words (sentences) for spelling (dictation).

35. St: Study.
    T: Provide a spelling (dictation) quiz in the following class.

Student Workbook   p. 186

VISUALS
all visuals listed for the previous lesson

INSTRUCTIONAL AIDS
all sight word flash cards from the the previous lesson

INSTRUCTION

1. What's his/her (first, last) name?

2. What is he(she)?
   What are they?

3. Read these words.

4. Open your books to p. 186.

5. Circle the correct answer.

6. Optional, vocabulary development:
   Ben and May Lee are parents.
   Ben is the dad and May is the mom.
   Linda is a child. Joe and Linda are children (kids).

ACTIVITY/RESPONSE

1. T: Hold up visual 53.
   St: Name all of the family members.

2. St: Name all of the family relationships.

3. St: Read all of the sight words from the previous lesson.

4. St: Open books, read the questions and supply the answers orally.

5. St: Circle the correct answer and fill in the name of their spouse, a dash or "none".

6. T: Introduce and explain the usage of the vocabulary.
   St: Repeat, read, practice writing and make cards.

Student Workbook   p. 187

SIGHT WORDS
How do you do?

VISUALS
182 This is my family.
 54 father/son   180 mother/daughter
179 husband/wife 181 brother/sister

STRUCTURE
Who is (s)he?   (S)He's (name's) (relation).

INSTRUCTION

1. This is the Lee family at home.
   This is Bob. Bob is here to say "Hello".

2. Listen.

3. "How do you do?" is the same as "Hello". I say it when I meet somebody the first time.

4. Listen.

5. Let's read.

6. Find (wife).

7. I am "A" and you are "B".

8. Who's "A" (B)?

ACTIVITY/RESPONSE

1. T: Hold up visual 182.
   St: Listen.

2. T: Tape the visual on the board. Stand by Ben's side of the visual when modeling A's words. Stand by Bob's side of the visual when modeling B's words.
   St: Listen.

3. St: Listen and repeat "How do you do?"

4. T: Write the dialogue on the board, sentence strips or an overhead projector. Model the dialogue.
   St: Listen.

5. T: Model the dialogue line by line.
   St: Repeat in chorus and individually.

6. T: Name various sight words.
   St: Point to them in the dialogue.

7. T: Assume role and reverse upon completion.
   Cl:
   Gr: Assume role.
   St:

8. T: Seek volunteers or pair students up.
   St: Assume roles and reverse upon completion.

9. Optional: Let's talk.

10. Optional: Read.

11. She's Mr. Lee's wife.

12. This " 's" says "is".

13. This " 's" says "his" wife.

14. He's Mrs. Lee's husband.

15. Open your books to p. 187.

16. Let's read.

17. Optional: Read into the tape recorder.

18. Optional, Language Master: Who is (s)he?

9. T: Group 5 students. Hand 4 students the 5 x 8 cards of "husband, wife, daughter, son". Have each take turns introducing their "family" to the 5th student.
   St: Practice introductions.

10. T: Erase every (5)th word from the dialogue.
    St: Fill in the missing vocabulary orally and then in writing.
    T: Make a ditto with every (5)th word blanked out to be completed in the following class.

11. T: Hold up visual 179.
    St: Listen and repeat.

12. T: Write "She's Mr. Lee's wife." on the board. Point to the " 's" in "She's".
    St: Listen.

13. T: Point to the " 's" in "Lee's". Review the possessive " 's" as per instructions for student workbook p. 86 on p. 175 of this guide.

14. T: Provide instructions for each of the sentences on p. 187. Write each on the board and discuss the differences between the verbal -s and possessive -s thoroughly.
    St: Listen, repeat, respond and read.

15. T: Point to the upper right hand corner.
    St: Open books and write "11:00."
    T: Check for accuracy.

16. St: Assume roles for the dialogue and read sentences 2-7 as necessary.
    T: Listen for the pronunciation of all the final "s".

17. St: Read the dialogue/sentences.
    T: Work on individual pronunciation, stress and intonation problems.

18. T: Clip the visuals of the family relations onto Language Master cards.
    St: (S)He's (name's) (relation) and check tape for accuracy.
    T: See p. 10 of this guide for suggested uses of the Language Master.

19. Optional: Let's write.

20. Optional: Study the sentences for dictation/writing.

19. St: Practice writing the dialogue/sentences on p. 187.

20. T: Assign specific sentences to be studied for dictation. In next class, dictate the sentences or ask "Who is (s)he?
St: Study and write "(S)He's (name's) (relation)."

Student Workbook   p. 188

INSTRUCTION	ACTIVITY/RESPONSE
1. Open your books to p. 188. Look at the picture. Where are they? What's on the stove?	1. T: Ask content questions regarding the visual. St: Open books, analyze the visual and respond.
2. Listen.	2. T: Model the paragraph. St: Listen.
3. Listen and repeat.	3. T: Model the paragraph line by line. St: Repeat individually and in chorus.
4. Let's read.	4. St: Read. T: Practice reading as frequently as necessary.
5. Who's Mrs. Lee?	5. T: Ask questions 1-6 from p. 188. St: Respond.
6. Let's read the questions.	6. St: Read and respond orally.
7. Let's write.	7. St: Write the answers in complete sentences and sign their name at the upper right hand corner. T: Check for accuracy and legibility.
8. Optional: Let's write.	8. St: Practice writing the paragraph that appears on p. 188.
9. Optional: Fill in the blanks.	9. T: Make a ditto with every (5)th word blanked out. St: Fill in the blanks.
10. Optional: Fix the words.	10. T: Write the paragraph on a ditto. Cut each individual word. Hand the collection to a student or a pair of students in an envelope or baggie. St: Rearrange the story.
11. Optional, alphabetizing: Put the words in alphabetical order.	11. St: After rearranging the stories, alphabetize the individual words.
12. Optional, syllables: Put all the words with 1, 2 or 3 syllables in separate groups.	12. St: Using their individual paragraph words, group words according to number of syllables.

Student Workbook p. 189

VISUALS
54 father/son
179 husband/wife
180 mother/daughter
181 brother/sister

INSTRUCTION	ACTIVITY/RESPONSE
1. Who is (s)he?	1. T: Hold up the visuals. St: He's (name). He's (name's) (relation). T: Review possessive and verbal "s". Review sight words, structures and concepts introduced from workbook p. 185 on.
2. Open your books. Who are they?	2. St: Open books and state "(S)He's (name's) (relation)." for each visual.
3. Let's write.	3. St: Write the responses on the board and then in the workbook. T: Check for accuracy and legibility. Be certain students filled in the name of their spouse, a dash or "none" at the upper right hand corner.
4. Who are you?	4. T: Have students explore their relationship to various members of their family. For example: I'm Kong's wife. I'm Phet's sister. I'm Malay's mother. I'm Bounmy's daughter. St: Respond orally and then in writing at the bottom of p. 189. T: Check for accuracy and legibility.
5. Optional: Your mother's mother and your father's mother is your grandmother.	5. T: Teach some or all of the following additional family relations: grandmother, grandfather, aunt, uncle, niece, nephew, brother (sister)-in-law, cousin, etc. St: Read, repeat, make cards, answer questions, etc.

Student Workbook   p. 190

INSTRUCTIONAL AIDS
all the family relations sight word cards
a photograph of the teacher's family
a photograph of each student's family
(optional)

INSTRUCTION

1. Read these words.

2. Who is your mother (father, wife, husband, sister, brother)?

3. Optional: Who's your grandmother (grandfather, cousin, aunt, uncle, etc.)?

4. This is my family, the (Renshaw) family. This is my _____ and my _____ .

5. Bring a picture of your family to class.

6. Who's this?

7. Write about your family.

ACTIVITY/RESPONSE

1. St: Read the sight word flash cards of family members.

2. St: (Name's) my (relation).

3. St: (Name's) my (relation).

4. T: Show the photograph of your family and tell who your relations are.
   St: Listen.

5. St: Bring a photograph and attach it to p. 190 with tape, corners or a paper clip. In lieu of a photo, students may wish to sketch in stick figures of their family members.

6. St: Tell who their family relations are.

7. St: Fill in their family name under the photograph (picture) and write about their relationship to family members.
   T: Check for accuracy and legibility. Be certain students have filled in their social security number at the upper right hand corner.

GENERAL REVIEW

The following are a few suggestions for a general review.

1. Hold up any or all 182 visuals for an oral review.

2. Review all the sounds of the alphabet, blends and digraphs, and alphabetical order.

3. Have students say the numbers between 1-100. Dictate various numbers and monetary amounts.

4. Hold up the 5 x 8 flash cards of any or all of the 339 sight words and have students read them.

5. Have students group their sight word cards in any or all of the following groups:
    a. known/unknown words (students practice the unknown words).
    b. personal information, occupation, place, food, color, household, etc. categories.
    c. words having 2, 3, 4 syllables.
    d. words having the same vowel sound.

6. Reread any of the dialogues and paragraphs (sentence strips and Language Master cards).

7. Make reading packets. Put at least 10 visuals together and write a word or sentence about each on a card. Students match the cards with the pictures.

8. Administer spelling and dictation quizzes.

9. As a listening and reading exercise, you may wish to have students "follow directions". Have them open their books to any page having a dialogue or paragraph. Instruct students to circle (word), put an X on the (/ /) sound, underline the opposite of (word), etc.

Student Workbook p. 191-194
Test of Lessons 6-10

OBJECTIVES

Listening Comprehension: To determine if students can:
1. Follow simple oral directions.
2. Comprehend various monetary amounts when spoken.
3. Comprehend a dictation exercise based on sight words and sentences previously introduced.

Reading and Writing: To determine if students can:
1. Complete the personal information requested at the upper right hand corner correctly and without being reminded.
2. Understand and follow simple directions.
3. Demonstrate comprehension of reading exercises by answering questions correctly and matching visuals with corresponding sentences.
4. Write various monetary amounts.
5. Write basic sight words and lesson sentences.
6. Use a capital letter at the beginning of a sentence, a comma in a short answer, a question mark and apostrophe for contractions.
7. Complete a simple application form and sign their names.

NOTES TO THE INSTRUCTOR

1. There are too many test pages to administer in one sitting. Student fatigue may affect results. It is suggested that p. 191-192 and p. 193-194 be completed at different sittings. Allow students as much time as necessary to complete work.

2. This test is designed so that concepts in each lesson between 6-10 are tested.

3. If students cannot understand the directions, provide examples on the board. However, it is expected that by this stage, students would know how to proceed.

4. If the responses on p. 193 prove to be too difficult, have students provide the responses orally first and then in writing.

5. On p. 194, dictate monetary amounts for items 1-4 and vocabulary/sentences you deem important for items 5-7. The following are suggestions:
   1. 15¢   5. He's at the bank.
   2. 80¢   6. How much is it?
   3. 50¢   7. My family isn't here.
   4. $1.25

6. A large number of errors may indicate a full review of Lessons 6-10, vision testing or a learning disability. Refer to p. 3 in the Introduction for further discussion.

7. When the test has been completed and corrected, use p. 191-194 as an oral review for the entire class.

Part 4 - Transition to Cursive Writing

Part 4: Transition to Cursive Writing
Student Workbook   p. 195

OBJECTIVES

Reading and Writing: The students will be able to:
1. Form the letters accurately in cursive.
2. Match the lower case letters with their capitals.
3. Read the letters, basic sight words and sentences written in cursive.
4. Put letters together to form words (sentences) legibly.

NOTES TO THE INSTRUCTOR

The cursive alphabet is included as a model for correct letter formation. Individual differences in handwriting are to be expected and acceptable as long as letters are not ambiguous.

In presenting the lessons, call each letter by name. Write it on the board and have students identify it. Point out that the letters have been grouped according to the initial stroke. Explain what the arrows mean and demonstrate how the letter is formed. Student volunteers can come to the board and copy the letter. After any discussion and further clarification, students practice forming the letters (words, sentences) in the workbook. For additional practice, students can copy sight words, dialogues and paragraphs from Part 3 of the workbook in cursive writing.

APPENDIX A

Visuals For Duplication

Visuals for Student Workbook p. 31

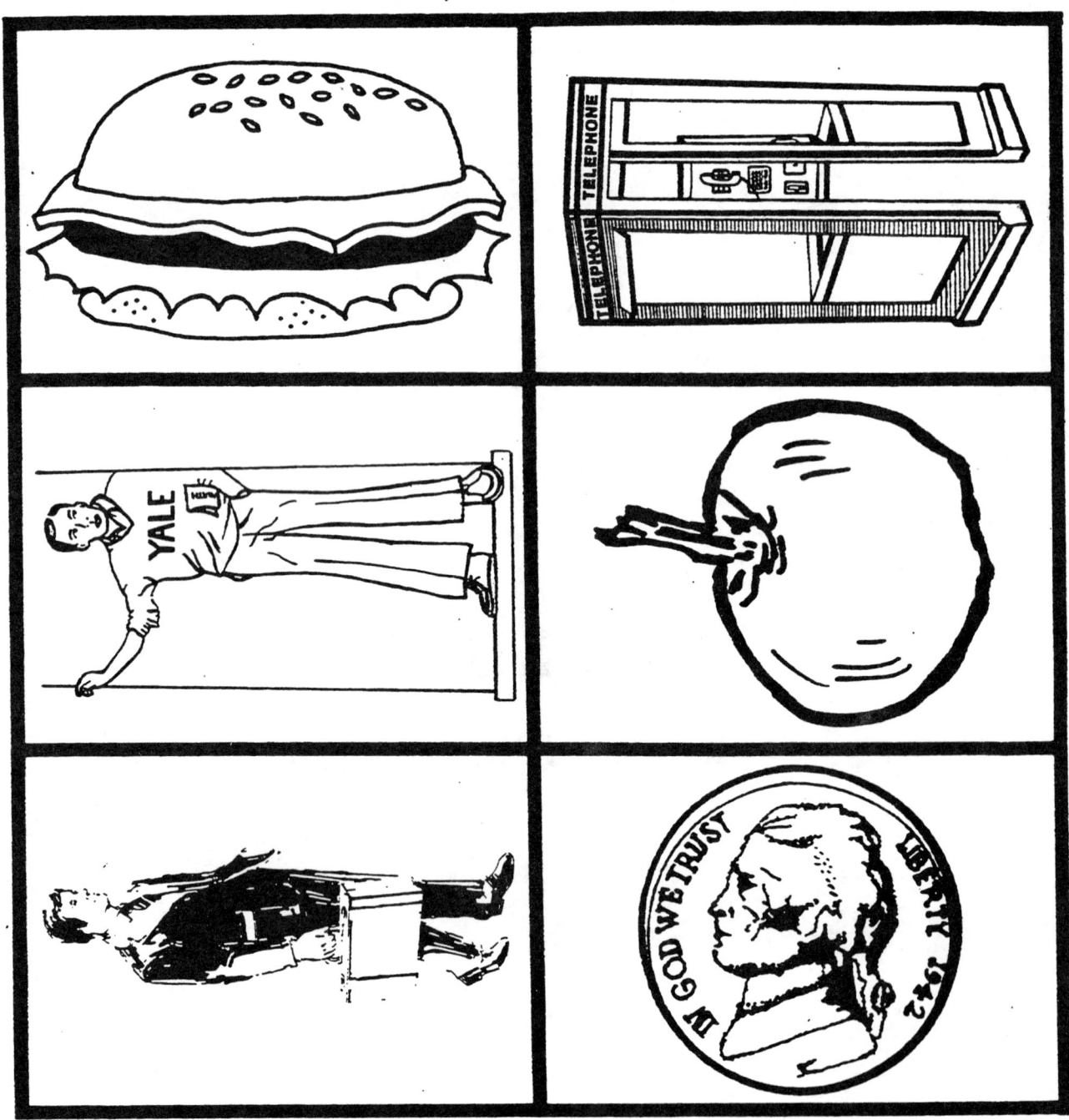

Visuals for Student Workbook p. 35

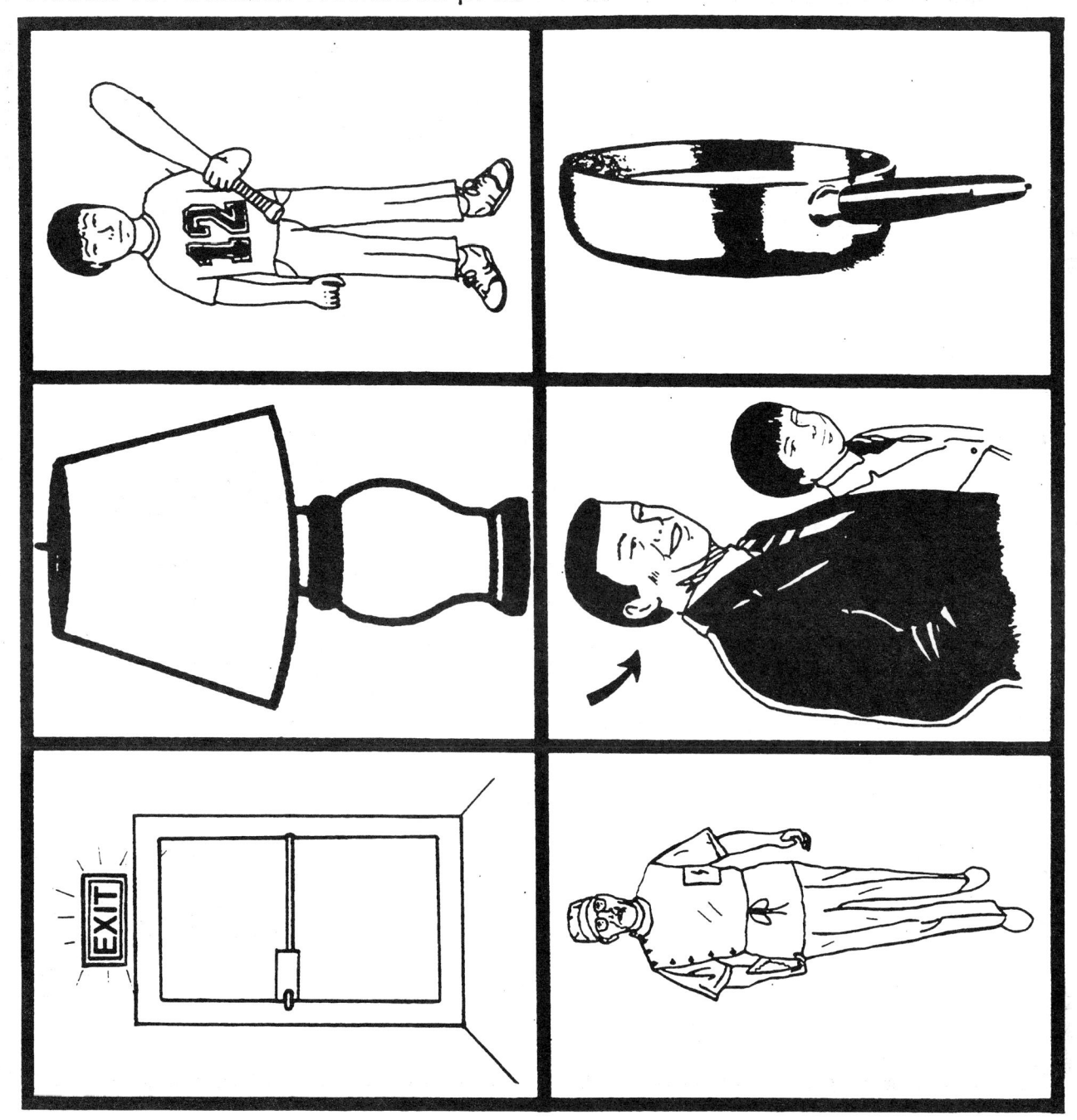

373

Visuals for Student Workbook p. 40

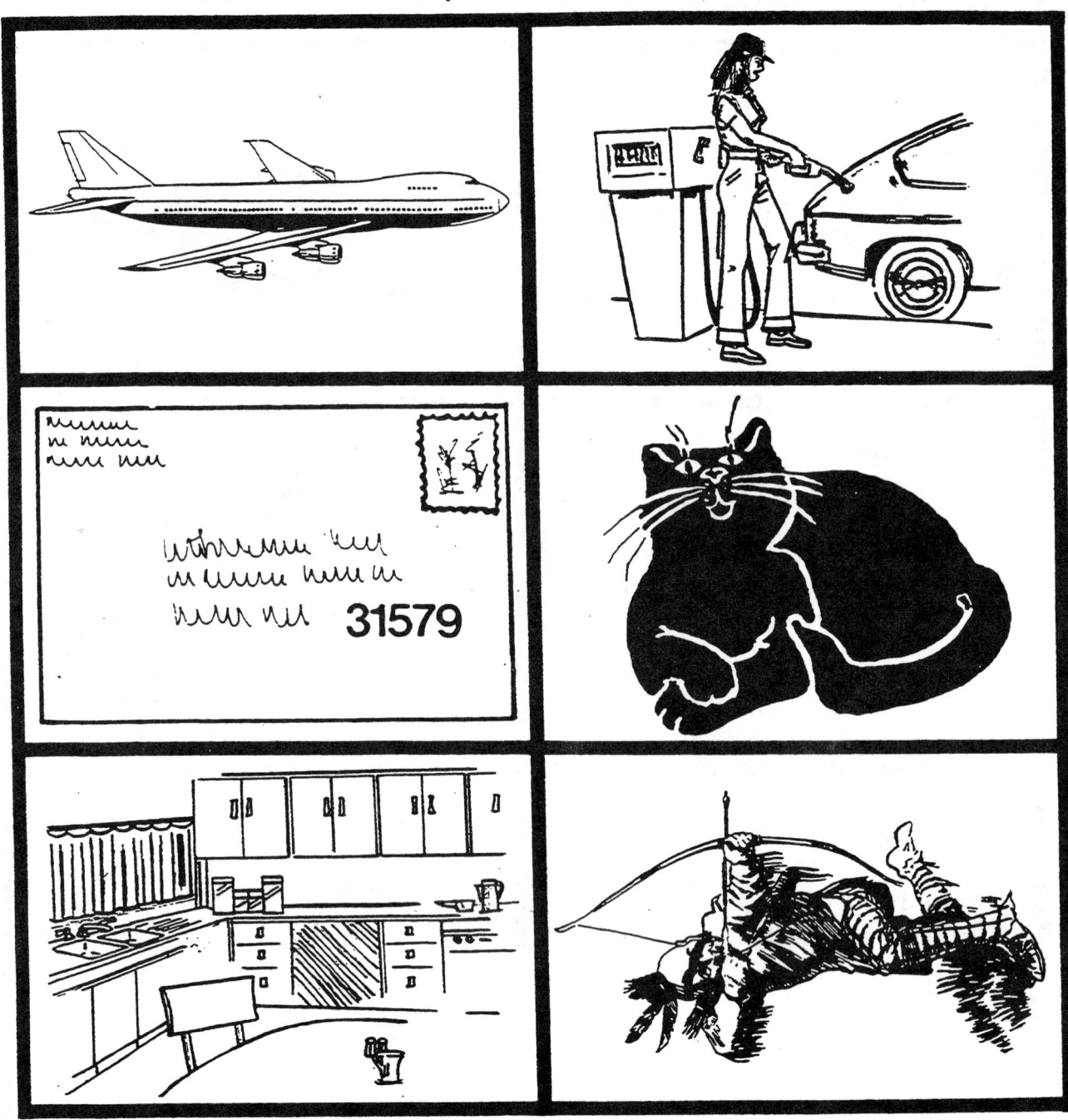

Visuals for Student Workbook p. 46

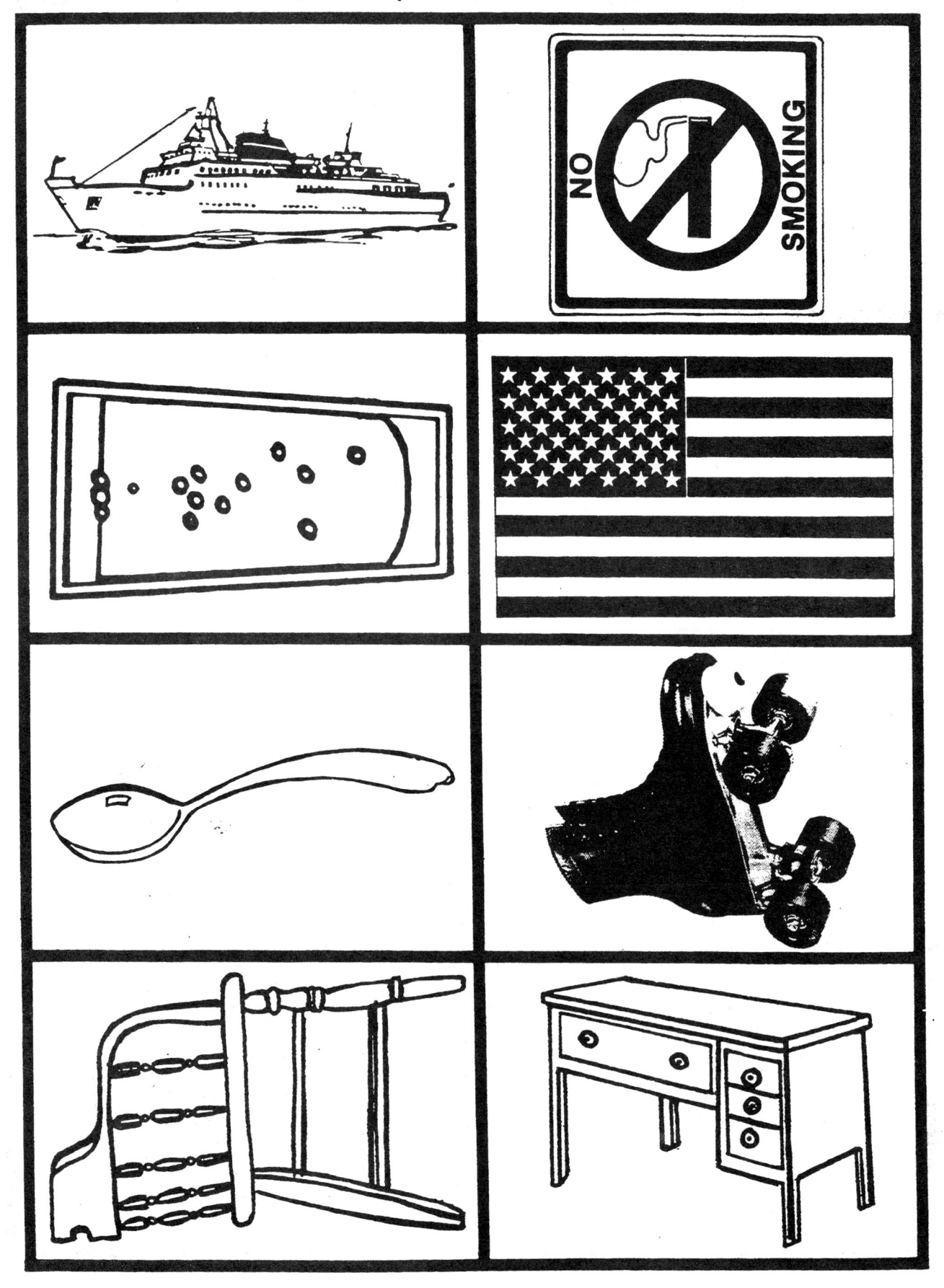

375

Visuals for Student Workbook p. 48

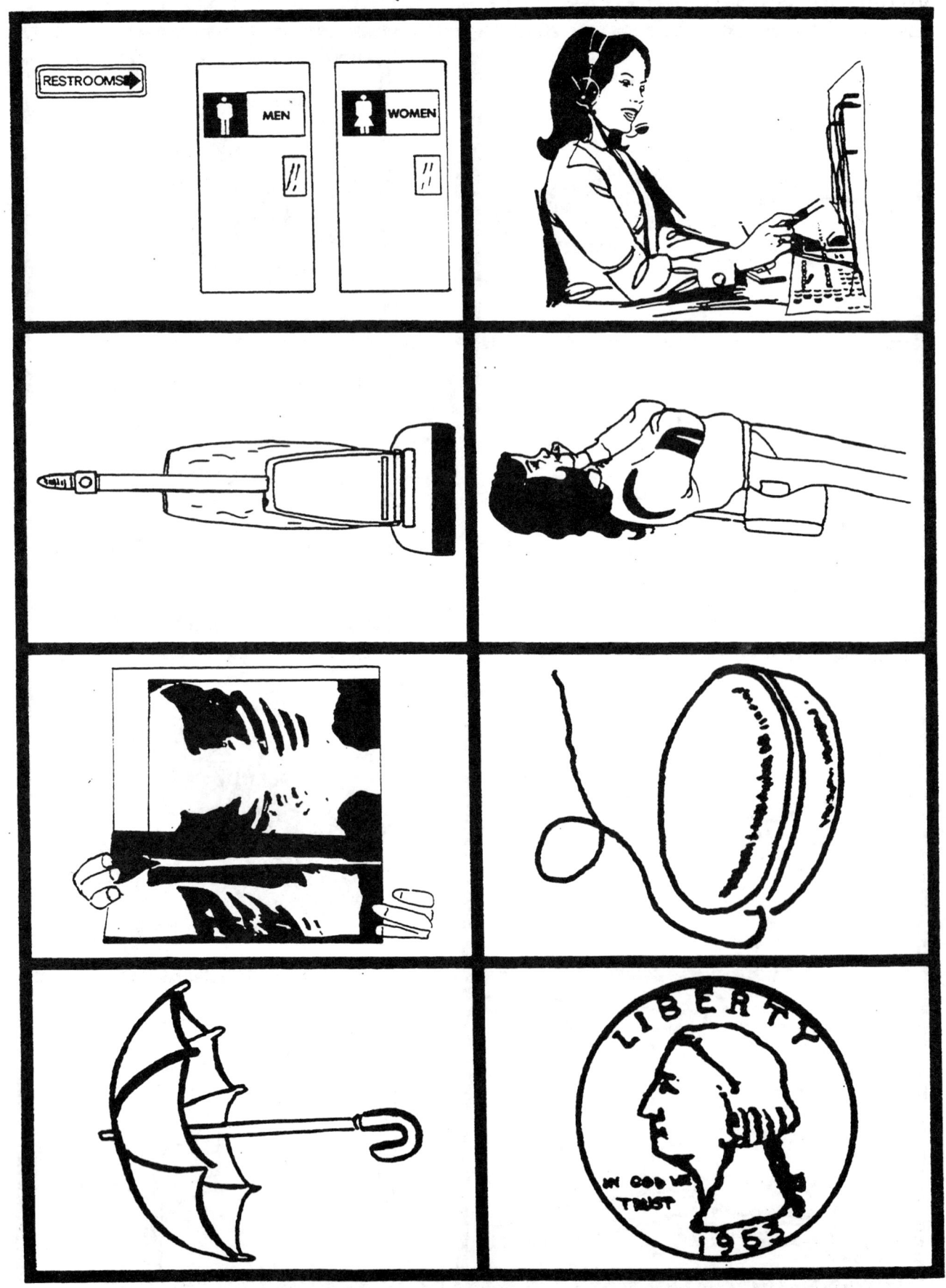

Visuals for Student Workbook p. 55

Visuals for Student Workbook p. 65

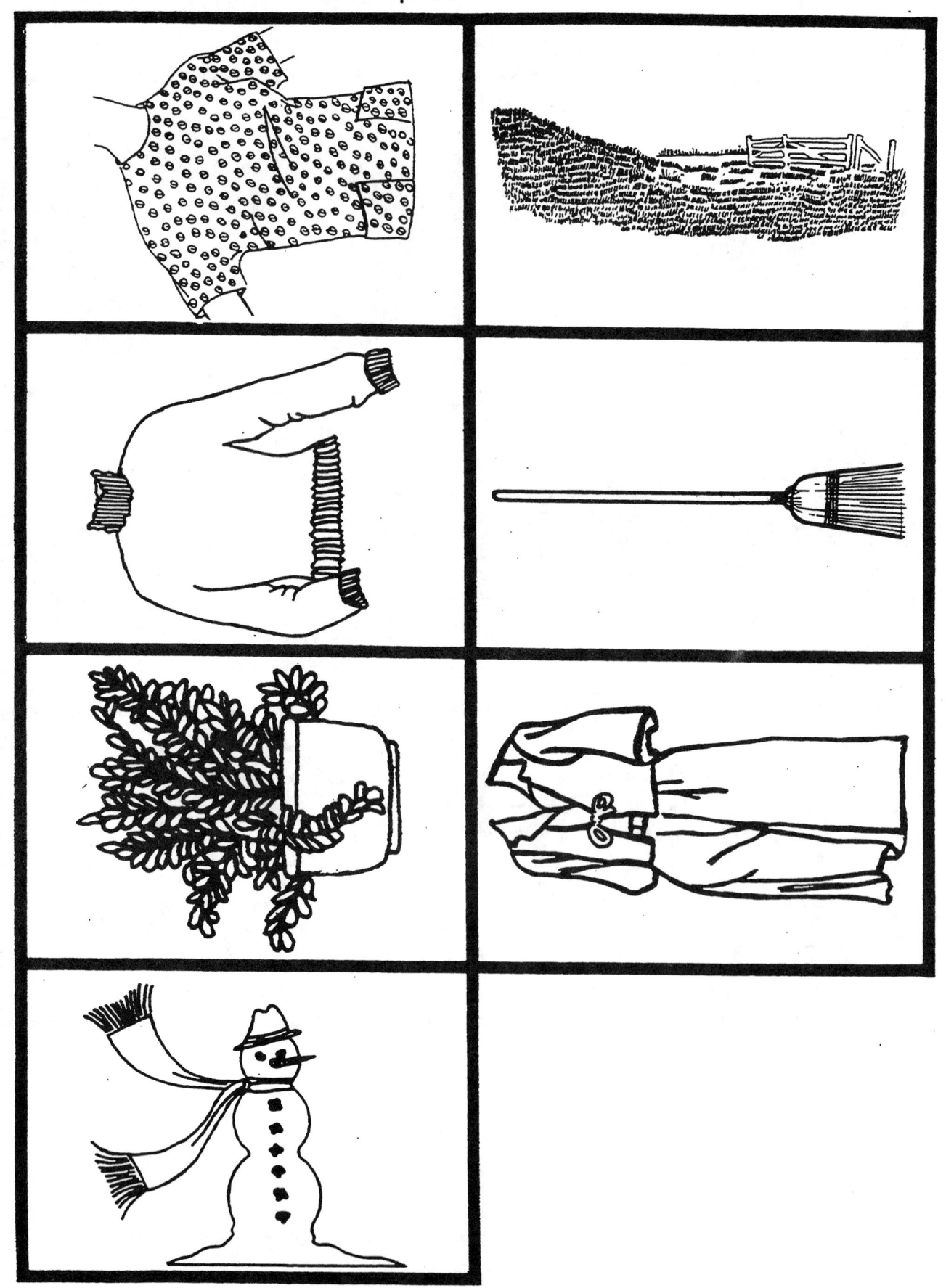

Visuals for Student Workbook p. 69

Visuals for Student Workbook p. 99

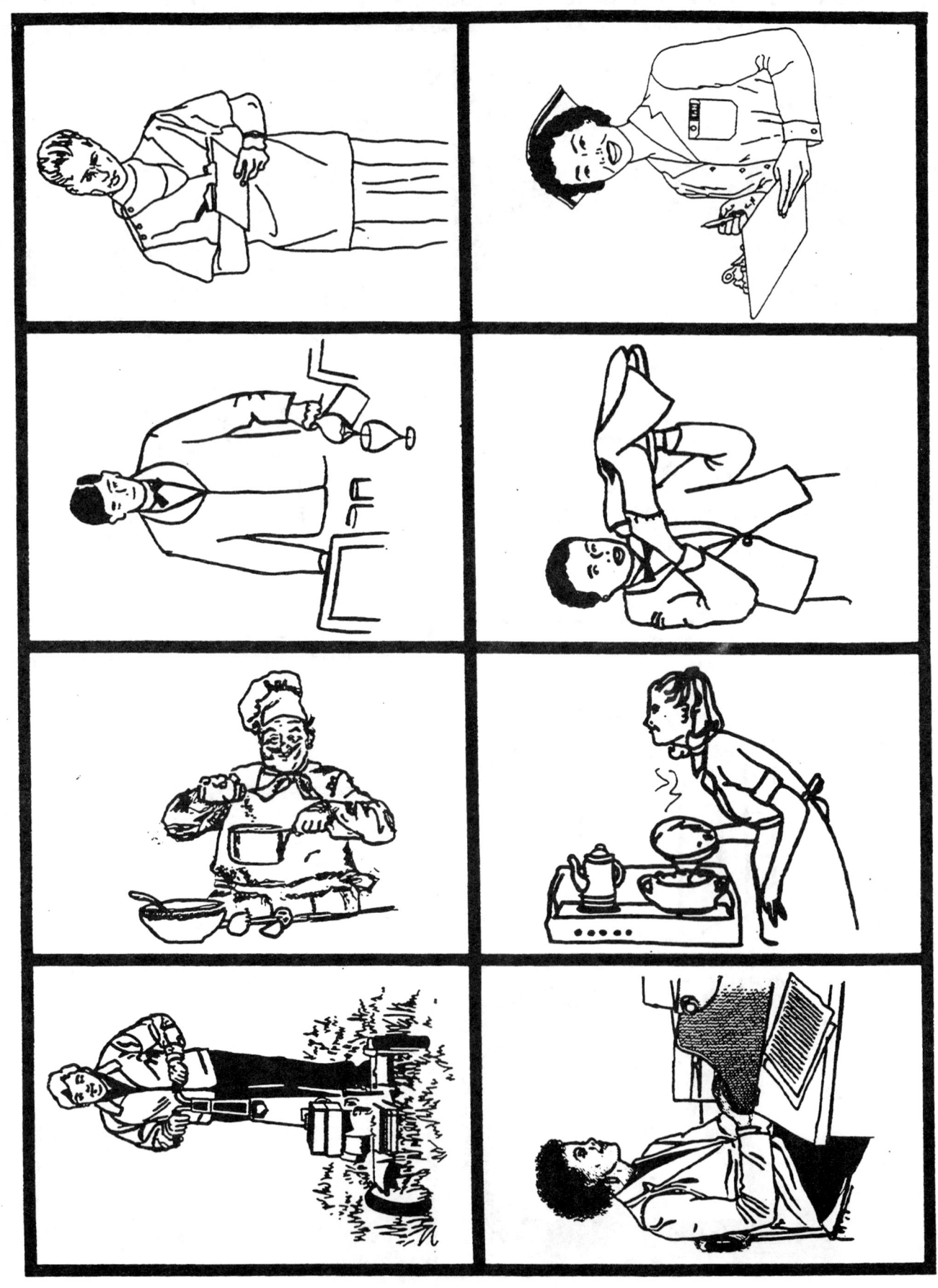

Visuals for Student Workbook p. 99 (continued)

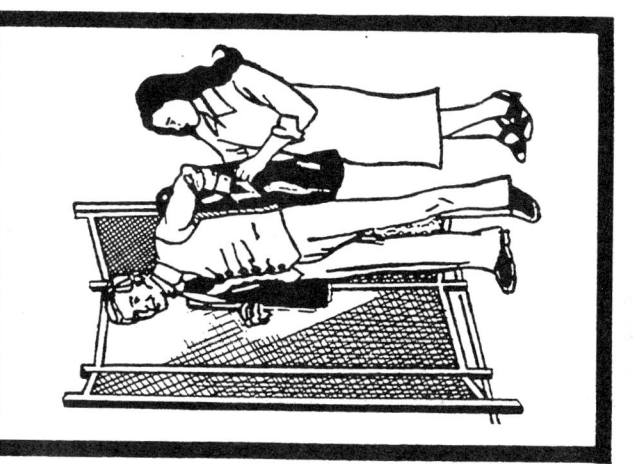

Visuals for Student Workbook p. 109

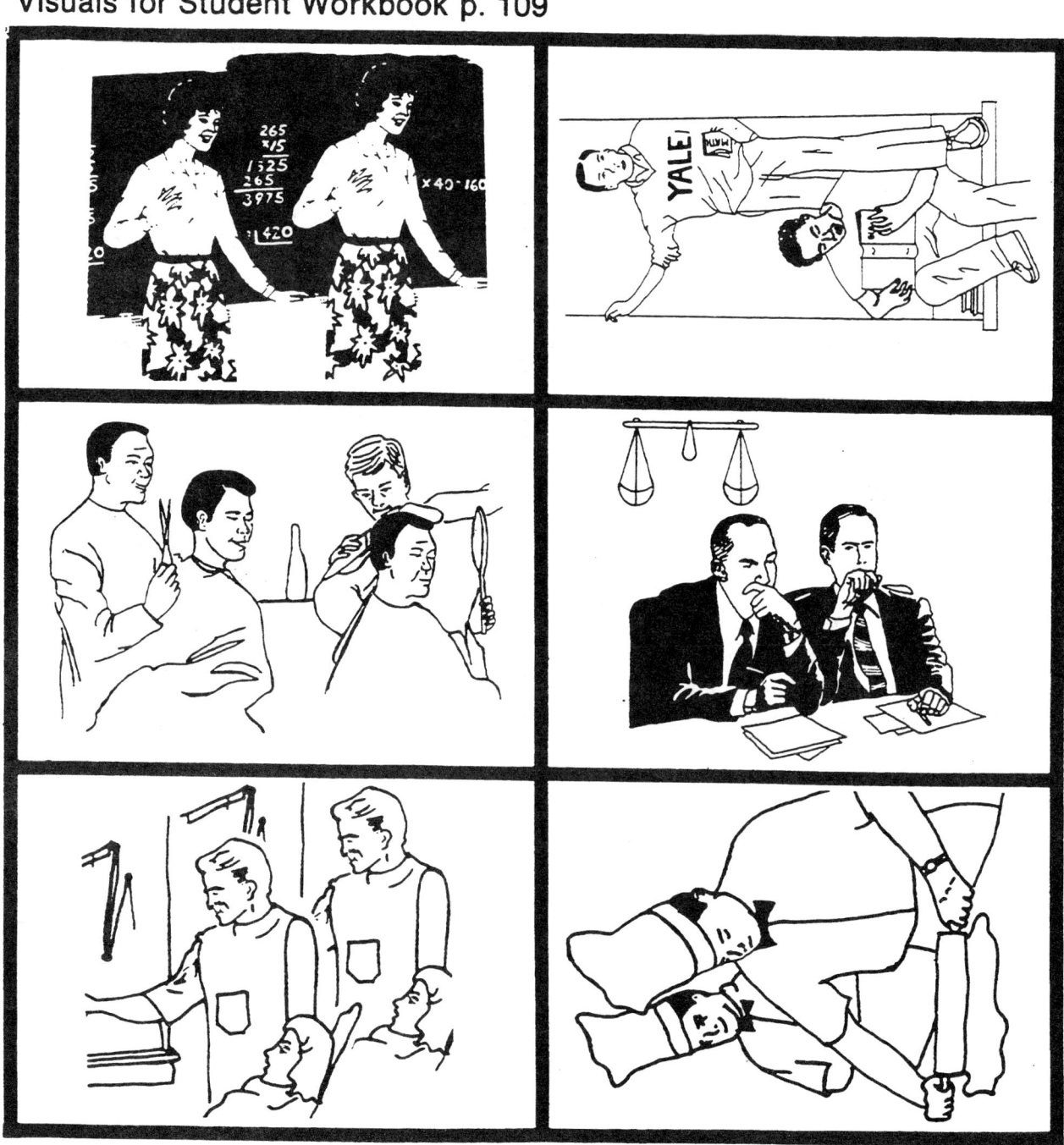

Visuals for Student Workbook p. 149

Visuals for Student Workbook p. 155-6

Visuals for Student Workbook p. 163

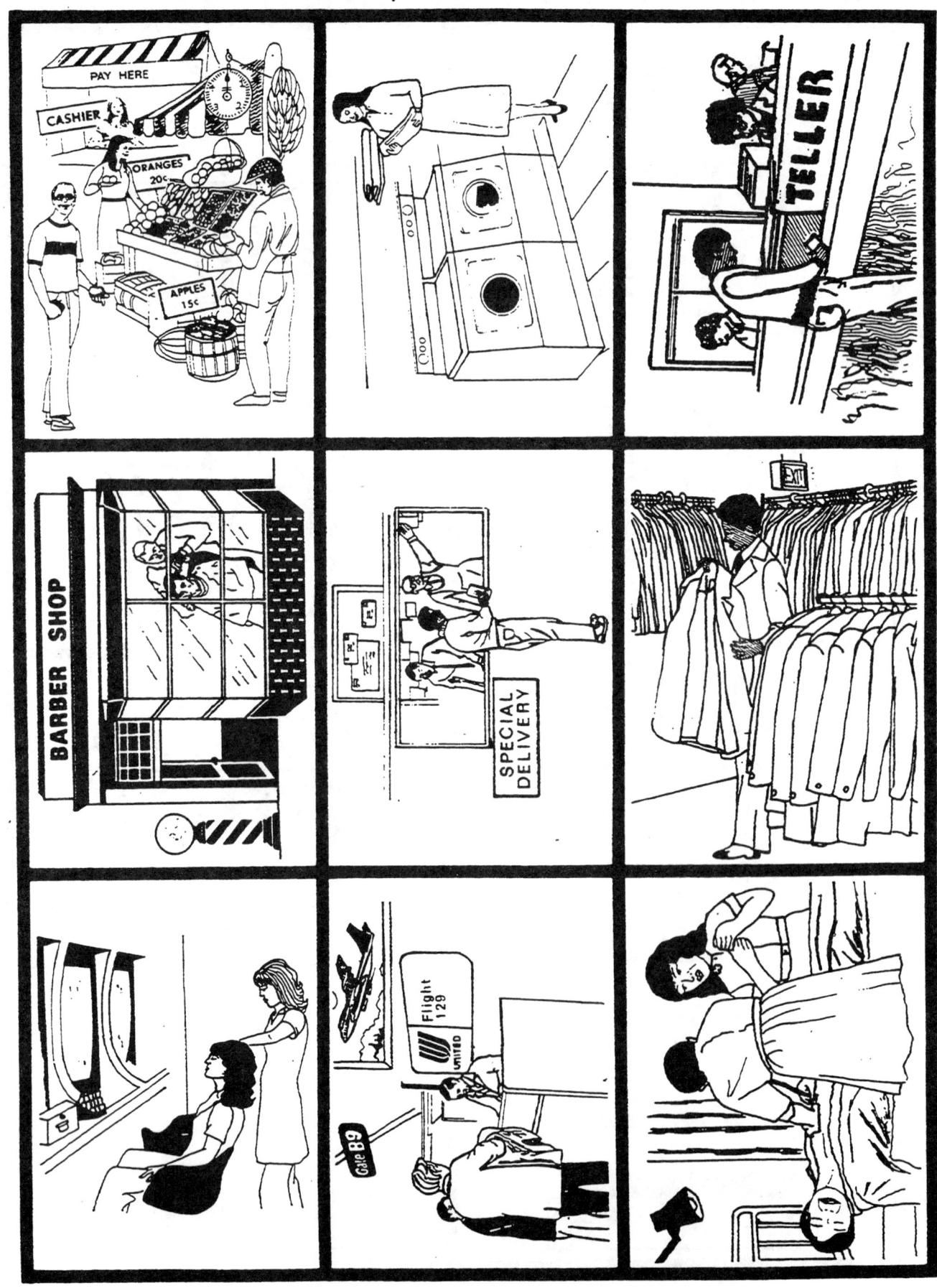

Visuals for Student Workbook p. 175

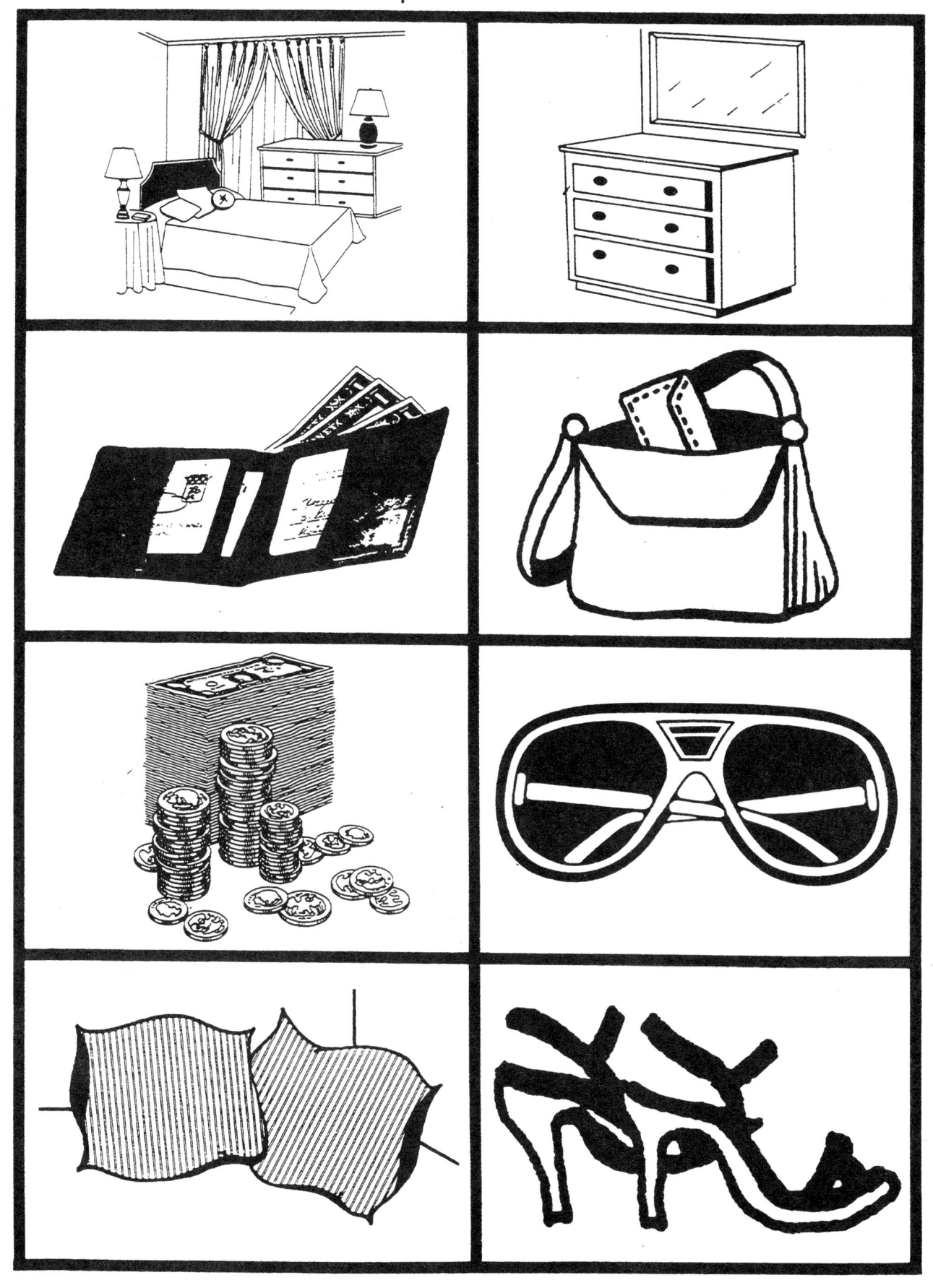

385

Visuals for Student Workbook p. 180

Visuals for student Workbook p. 185

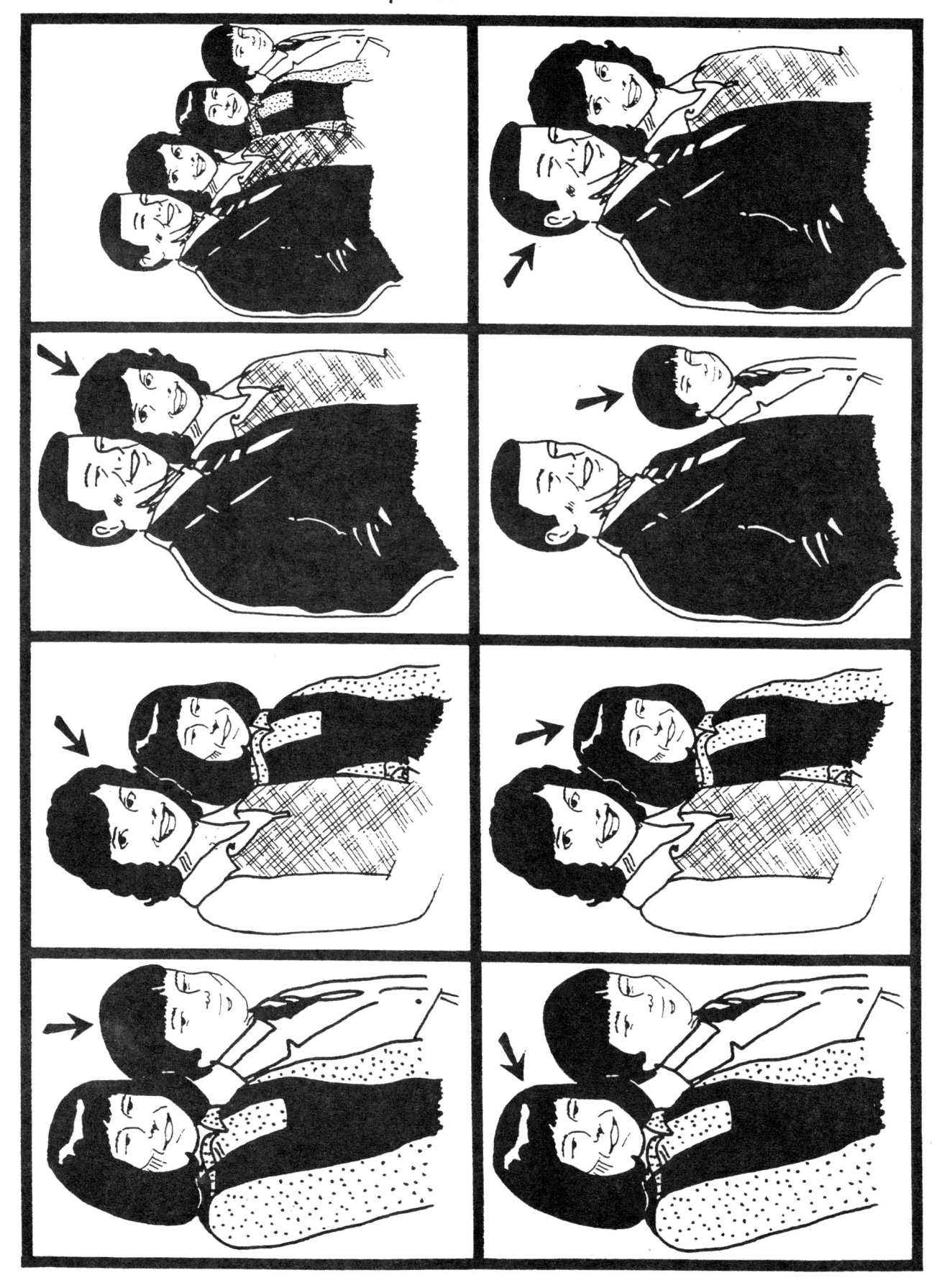

387

APPENDIX B

Visuals Corresponding to *Passage to ESL Literacy* from *Delta's Effective ESL for the 21st Century, Volume 3*

ESL instructors may already have a set of visuals entitled **Delta's Effective ESL for the 21st Century, Volume 3**. The following is a complete listing of visuals which can be used to teach the lessons in *Passage to ESL Literacy*.

Student Workbook   p. 1
- P1   Dialogue (How are you?)
- P2   Dialogue (What's your name?)

Student Workbook   p. 8
- P109 Telephone

Student Workbook   p. 31

P9	housewife		for Hh /h/
P10	hat	P50	hot dog
P49	hamburger	P79	hospital
		P113	house
			for Tt /t/
P24	teacher	P97	TV/television
P55	tea	P109	telephone
P84	table	P122	toilet
			for Ss /s/
P11	secretary	P92	son
P12	saleslady	P94	sister
P25	student	P122	sink
		P142	suit
			for Aa /ă/
P57	apple	P108	ankle
			for Mm /m/
P18	man	P93	mother
P80	map	P190	mailman
P81	mop		
			for Nn /n/
P6	nurse	P45	nickel

Student Workbook p. 35

			for Bb /b/
P18	Ben	P23	busboy
P20	baker	P72	bank
P21	barber	P86	bed
			for Pp /p/
P44	penny	P83	purse
P61	pepper	P124	pin
P73	post office, package		
			for Ll /l/
P3	letter	P76	laundromat
P22	lawyer	P120	living room, lamp
P60	lemon		

P48	fifty cents		for Ff /f/
P90	family	P108	foot
P92	father	P151	florist, flowers

for Ee /ĕ/
    P105 elbow

P18   B<u>e</u>n   P107 l<u>e</u>g
P60 l<u>e</u>mon

for Dd /d/
    P46 dime

P2   desk   P52 doughnut
P5   doctor   P93 daughter
P19 dentist

for Jj /j/

Student Workbook p. 40
    P137 Japanese food
  P42 jacket

for Gg /g/
    P94 girl

P10 gardener   P116 girls
P62 grapefruit

for Zz /z/

P42 zipper, zipping

for Cc /k/
    P55 coffee

P8   cook   P69 cabbage
P20 cake   P70 carrot
P28 comb   P144 coat
P43 calendar

for Kk /k/

P89 kitchen

for Ii /ĭ/
    P124 p<u>i</u>n

P117 li<u>c</u>k
P120 l<u>i</u>ving room

Student Workbook p. 41
                                  P86 bed
  P120 lamp

Student Workbook p. 46   for /sh/
  P16 shoe   P143 shirt

for /gl/
P41 glass   P87 glasses

for /fl/
P151 florist, flowers

for /sk/
P141 skirt

                    for /ch/
- P24 chalkboard   P121 chairs
- P90 children   P126 chicken
- P120 chair   P136 Chinese food

Student Workbook p. 48

                    for Rr /r/
- P150 restaurant

                    for Oo /ŏ/
- P58 orange   P84 on

                    for Vv /v/
- P169 vacuum

                    for Ww /w/
- P7 waiter   P127 wings
- P83 wallet   P150 waitress
- P91 wife

                    for Xx /x/
- P138 Mexican food

                    for Uu /ŭ/
- P85 under   P 172 umbrella
- P171 usher

                    for Qu /qu/
- P47 quarter

Student Workbook p. 51
- P1 How are you?
- P2 What's your name?

Student Workbook p.55

                    for/wh/
- P79 wheel chair

                    for /th/
- P122 bathroom   P133 thirsty
- P130 thighs   P171 theater

                    for /st/
- P25 student   P101 stomach ache
- P51 straw   P160 stamp

                    for /qu/
- P47 quarter

                    for /ph/
- P109 telephone

                    for /cl/
- P72 clock   P123 closet

Student Workbook   p. 65   for /bl/
   P168 blanket

                                 for /gr/
   P62   grapefruit

                                 for /br/
   P115 brothers   P128 breasts

                                 for /dr/
   P51   drink   P129 drumsticks
   P86   dresser   P140 dress

Student Workbook   p. 67
   P57   apple   P109 telephone

Student Workbook   p.69   for /sl/
   P168 sleeping

                                 for /cr/
   P117 ice cream

                                 for /kn/
   P107 knee

Student Workbook   p. 85-89
   P3   Dialogue (What's your address?)

Student Workbook   p. 90-92
   P4   Dialogue (Good evening.)

Student Workbook   p. 99-106
   P5   a doctor   P10   a gardener
   P6   a nurse   P11   a secretary
   P7   a waiter   P12   a saleslady
   P8   a cook   P13   a salesman
   P9   a housewife   P14   Dialogue (He's a doctor.)

Student Workbook p. 107
   P18   Ben

Student Workbook   p. 109-115
   P26   dentists   P31   busboys
   P27   bakers   P32   teachers
   P28   barbers   P33   students
   P29   lawyers   P34   cooks
   P30   waiters   P35   doctors

Student Workbook   p. 116-117 and 127
   P39   Dialogue (Where are your from?)

Student Workbook   p. 128-131
   P43   Dialogue (What day is it?)

Student Workbook   p. 137-143
- P44   a penny
- P45   a nickel
- P46   a dime
- P47   a quarter
- P48   a half dollar
- P49   a hamburger 50¢
- P50   a hot dog 30¢
- P51   a soft drink 15¢
- P52   a doughnut 15¢
- P53   Dialogue (The Vending Truck)

Student Workbook   p. 149-153
- P57   an apple
- P58   an orange
- P59   an onion
- P60   a lemon
- P61   a pepper (green)
- P62   a grapefruit
- P63   Dialogue (It's a lemon)

Student Workbook   p. 155-160
- P64   lemons
- P65   apples
- P66   oranges
- P67   onions
- P68   peppers
- P69   a cabbage and cabbages
- P70   a carrot and carrots
- P71   Dialogue (Are these carrots?)

Student Workbook   p. 163-168
- P72   at the bank
- P73   at the post office
- P74   at the department store
- P75   at the beauty shop
- P76   at the laundromat
- P77   at the airport
- P78   at the market
- P79   at the hospital

Student Workbook   p. 175
- P86   a bedroom

Student Workbook   p. 176-177
- P83   a wallet and <u>in</u> the purse
- P84   <u>on</u> the table
- P85   <u>under</u> the table

Student Workbook   p. 178-179
- P87   Dialogue (Where are my shoes?)

Student Workbook   p. 180
- P89   a kitchen

Student Workbook   p. 185-191
- P90   The Kim family
- P91   husband and wife
- P92   father and son
- P93   mother and daughter
- P94   brother and sister
- P95   Dialogue (This is my wife)

APPENDIX C

Exercises for Duplication

Name _____

last

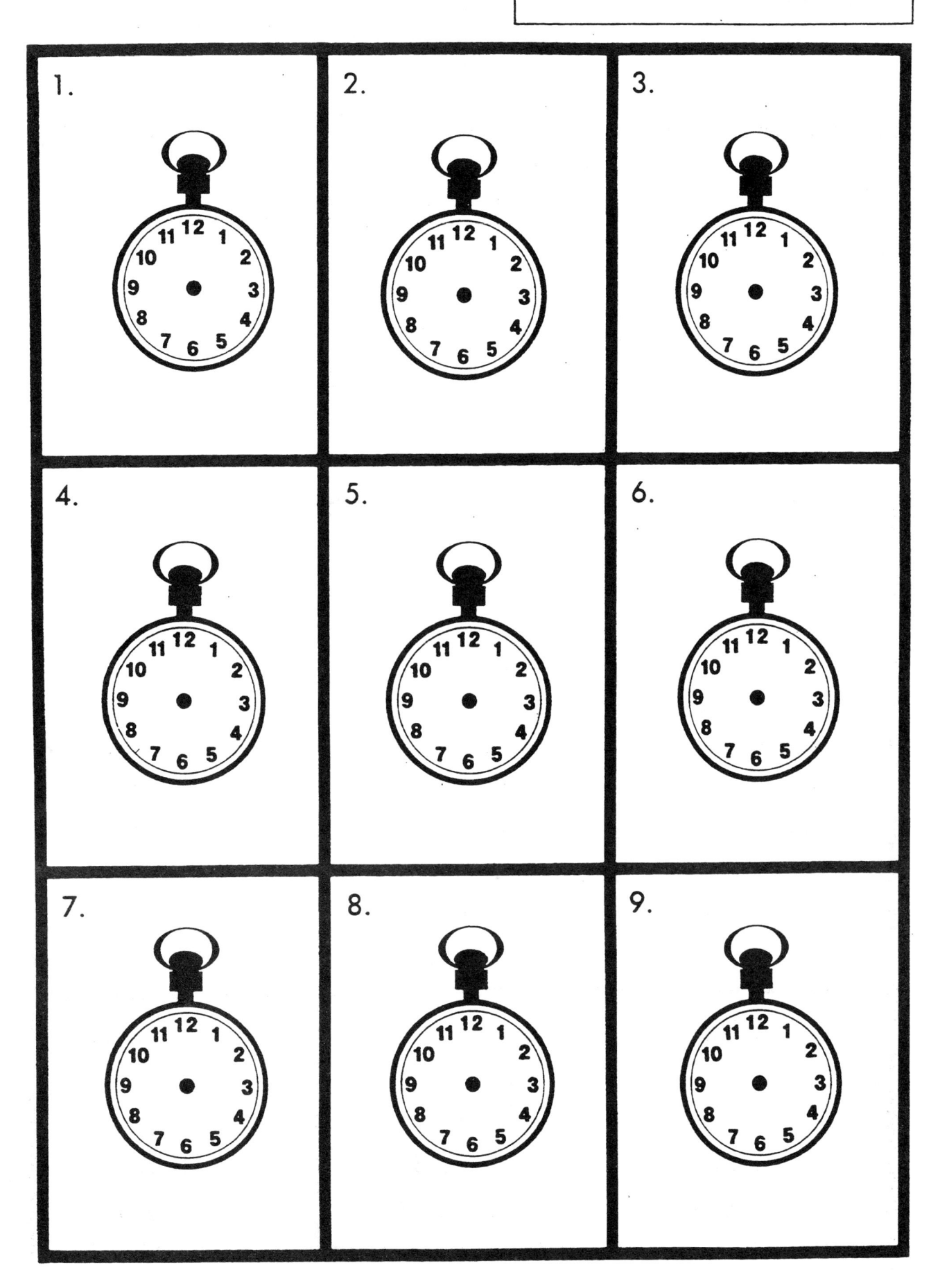

1.

2.

3.

4.

5.

6.

7.

8.

9.

397

Alphabetizing

Mr.
Mrs. _____
Miss   last   first
Ms.

DIRECTIONS: Put the words in alphabetical order by writing the number in the blank.

☺ _5_ zip code
_2_ city
_3_ state
_4_ telephone
_1_ address

___ name	___ brown	___ plant
___ first	___ white	___ pen
___ age	___ yellow	___ pan
___ hair	___ green	___ pill
___ last	___ red	___ push

___ slow	___ mall	___ cat
___ stop	___ mat	___ cashier
___ spoon	___ mast	___ cap
___ sex	___ mad	___ cab
___ sat	___ man	___ can

___ bat	___ desk	___ closed
___ Ben	___ down	___ you
___ blue	___ Ann	___ clock
___ black	___ dad	___ your
___ brown	___ hand	___ yes

DEPARTMENT OF HEALTH AND HUMAN SERVICES
SOCIAL SECURITY ADMINISTRATION

FORM APPROVED
OMB NO. 72-S79002

FORM SS-5 — APPLICATION FOR A SOCIAL SECURITY NUMBER CARD
(Original, Replacement or Correction)

MICROFILM REF. NO. (SSA USE ONLY)

Unless the requested information is provided, we may not be able to issue a Social Security Number (20 CFR 422.103(b))

INSTRUCTIONS TO APPLICANT ▶ Before completing this form, please read the instructions on the opposite page. You can type or print, using pen with dark blue or black ink. Do not use pencil.

NAA	NAME TO BE SHOWN ON CARD	First	Middle	Last
NAB / 1	FULL NAME AT BIRTH (IF OTHER THAN ABOVE)	First	Middle	Last
ONA	OTHER NAME(S) USED			

2 STT MAILING ADDRESS (Street/Apt. No., P.O. Box, Rural Route No.)

CTY / STE / ZIP — CITY | STATE | ZIP CODE

3 CSP CITIZENSHIP (Check one only)
- a. U.S. citizen
- b. Legal alien allowed to work
- c. Legal alien not allowed to work
- d. Other (See instructions on Page 2)

4 SEX
- Male
- Female

5 ETB RACE/ETHNIC DESCRIPTION (Check one only) (Voluntary)
- a. Asian, Asian-American or Pacific Islander (Includes persons of Chinese, Filipino, Japanese, Korean, Samoan, etc., ancestry or descent)
- b. Hispanic (Includes persons of Chicano, Cuban, Mexican or Mexican-American, Puerto Rican, South or Central American, or other Spanish ancestry or descent)
- c. Negro or Black (not Hispanic)
- d. North American Indian or Alaskan Native
- e. White (not Hispanic)

6 DOB DATE OF BIRTH — MONTH | DAY | YEAR
7 AGE / PRESENT AGE
8 PLB PLACE OF BIRTH — CITY | STATE OR FOREIGN COUNTRY

9 MNA MOTHER'S NAME AT HER BIRTH — First | Middle | Last (her maiden name)
FNA FATHER'S NAME — First | Middle | Last

10 PNO a. Have you or someone on your behalf applied for a social security number before? ☐ No ☐ Don't Know ☐ Yes
If you checked "yes", complete items "b" through "e" below; otherwise go to item 11.

SSN / PNS / PNY b. Enter social security number | c. In what State did you apply? | What year?

NLC d. Enter the name shown on your most recent social security card | e. If the birth date you used was different from the date shown in item 6, enter it here. | MONTH | DAY | YEAR

11 DON TODAY'S DATE — MONTH | DAY | YEAR
12 Telephone number where we can reach you during the day ▶ HOME | OTHER

13 ASD WARNING: Deliberately providing false information on this application is punishable by a fine of $1,000 or one year in jail, or both.
YOUR SIGNATURE

14 YOUR RELATIONSHIP TO PERSON IN ITEM 1
- ☐ Self
- ☐ Other (Specify) _____

WITNESS (Needed only if signed by mark "X") | WITNESS (Needed only if signed by mark "X")

DO NOT WRITE BELOW THIS LINE (FOR SSA USE ONLY) | DTC SSA RECEIPT DATE _____

☐ SUPPORTING DOCUMENT- SSN ASSIGNED OR VERIFIED
EXPEDITE CASE
☐ DUP ISSUED   SSN

NPN

DOC | NTC | CAN | BIC | SIGNATURE AND TITLE OF EMPLOYEE(S) REVIEWING EVIDENCE AND/OR CONDUCTING INTERVIEW.

TYPE(S) OF EVIDENCE SUBMITTED

☐ MANDATORY IN PERSON INTERVIEW CONDUCTED

DATE
DATE

IDN | ITV | DCL

FORM SS-5 (2-81)   PRIOR EDITIONS SHOULD BE DESTROYED

APPLICATION

Mr.
Mrs.
Miss
Ms.

1. Name — last | first | middle

2. Address — street / city | state | zip

3. Date of Birth

4. Sex ☐ Male ☐ Female

Age

5. Place of Birth

6. Wt.

7. Ht.

8. Marital Status:
☐ married
☐ single
☐ separated
☐ divorced
☐ widowed

9. Social Security No. ☐☐☐-☐☐-☐☐☐☐

10. home phone

11. hair color

12. eye color

13. name of spouse

14. maiden name

Sign your name here _____

It's a(n) _____ .   They're _____ s.
            or   or
This is a(n) _____ .   These are _____ s.

1.
2.
3.
4.
5.
6.

401

It's a(n) _____ .   They're _____ s.
   or   or
That's a(n) _____ .   Those are _____ s.

1.

2.

3.

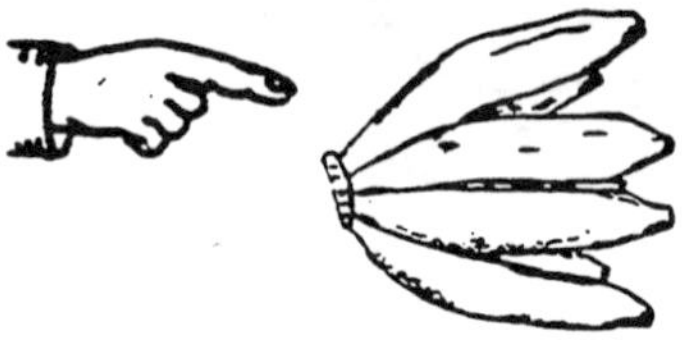

4.

5.

6.

402

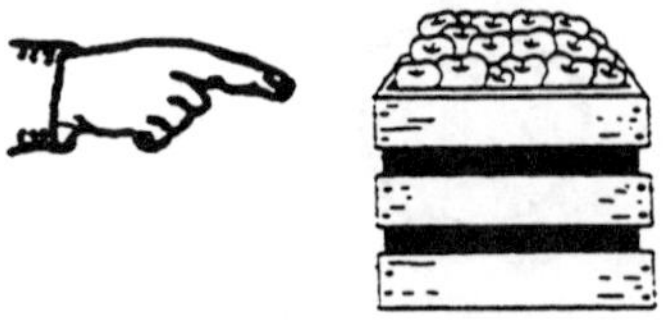

Directions: T: For each row call out a sight word.
St: Circle or underline the word.
T: Recopy the worksheet several times. Call out different words each time.

Name _____

Directions: Listen. Find the word.

☺ what	window	where	watch	what's

1. this	that	these	those	they
2. Please	plant	flag	Saturday	Sunday
3. are	aren't	alphabet	apple	at
4. there	hair	thanks	takes	here
5. He's	She's	isn't	It's	is
6. truck	black	city	student	orange
7. Sam	small	spoon	stop	slow
8. dime	time	sign	shop	sing
9. pill	mall	ball	tall	market
10. green	grass	glass	yellow	gray
11. weight	watch	height	late	date
12. Push	Pull	ill	well	Hill
13. quiet	quarter	color	dollar	closed
14. birthdate	birthplace	where	what	whale

403

Directions: T: Have students cut up these sight words and create as many and varied sentences as possible.
St: Keep the words in an envelope.

a	The	How	They	his
It	Those	I'm	the	from
student	50	orange	red	5
This	apple	It's	are	What's
You	dollars	an	is	The
much	is	That	cents	an
your	quarter	are	It's	here
lemons	They're	teachers	yellow	my
It's	airport	carrots	early	is
aren't	small	These	are	isn't
Where	not	there	dress	here
hot dog	dentists	single	married	a

APPENDIX D

Games for Duplication

Directions: T: Call out a word beginning with one of these letters. For this page, use the short vowel sounds and the soft "c" and "g" sounds.
St: Listen and say the number of the initial sound.

1. c	2. i	3. r	4. h
5. j	6. a	7. g	8. b
9. e	10. p	11. k	12. o
13. f	14. m	15. u	16. t

Directions:
T: Call out a word beginning with one of these letters. For this page, use the long vowel sounds and the hard "c" and "g" sounds.
St: Listen and say the number of the initial sound.

1. a	2. s	3. w	4. o
5. l	6. e	7. v	8. z
9. d	10. qu	11. i	12. g
13. u	14. y	15. c	16. n

Directions: T: Call out a word beginning with one of these blends or digraphs.
St: Listen and say the number of the initial sound.

1. br	2. dr	3. th	4. ch
5. pl	6. fl	7. sw	8. tw
9. sh	10. fr	11. pr	12. tr
13. sl	14. st	15. sp	16. sk

Directions: T: Call out a word beginning with one of these blends or digraphs.
St: Listen and say the number of the initial sound.

1. bl	2. gl	3. sm	4. sw
5. cl	6. cr	7. sn	8. gr
9. gl	10. qu	11. ph	12. kn
13. th	14. sh	15. ch	16. wh

L I N G O ! !

for any number of players up to 16

Components

Flash Cards: of the 27 common consonant blends and digraphs made by the teacher, to be used as a teaching tool and/or a review instrument before the Lingo game is played. Elicit free response from the students in discovering words beginning with the blends and digraphs. Note blends and digraphs can have an initial, medial or final position in a word. For example: "th" t<u>h</u>roat, ma<u>th</u>ematics, too<u>th</u>.

Lingo Consonant Blend and Digraph Sheet: on p. 412 gives a complete list of the 27 blends and digraphs used in the game and is used during the game (see instructions). It also lists what letter (L,I,N,G,O) the particular blend or digraph falls under.

Lingo Cards: 16 cards to be duplicated on 6 x 5 oak tag by the teacher. Sample card and cards for duplication are on p. 413-415.

Lingo Squares: 27 squares on p. 415 to be cut, placed in a container (small box or baggie) and scrambled. These are used by the "caller" to call out the blends and digraphs, for example, "N,/sm/".

Markers: teacher can provide beans to cover the blend or digraph on the Lingo card after it has been called.

Preliminary Preparation

In American culture, learning and leisure time are often spent in playing games. Bingo is a very popular game with Americans. Lingo is very similar to Bingo except that blends and digraphs are used instead of numbers. Bingo players pay for their cards and win the money in the "kitty".

This game can be played in beginning level elementary, secondary or Adult ESL classes providing it is used as a culminating and reinforcement exercise rather than as a teaching tool. Use of this game assumes that the player has a good working knowledge of the American alphabet and the common blends and digraphs. Lingo can also be used as a review exercise in an intermediate and advanced ESL class.

The target language background is non-specific in that the game has universal application and can be used by any ESL class regardless of the student's native language. Evaluation can be based on the player's ability to read the blends and digraphs from the flash cards, spell them, produce words containing the blends and digraphs and locate them on the game card.

Instructions For Use

1. Teach students how to play Lingo. Duplicate a card on the board/overhead. Place a marker in the free space in the center.

2. Call the blends and digraphs as would be done during a regular game, for example "L, /cl/". Continue to call blends and digraphs and mark spaces until there are 5 squares marked in a row vertically, horizontally or diagonally. Be certain to demonstrate all the possible ways of winning.

3. Upon winning, the instructor should call out "Lingo!" enthusiastically. Teach the students to call out "Lingo!"

4. Remove the markers from the winning row one by one, reading each blend or digraph and giving a word for each one. Continue instruction until students are familiar with game procedures.

5. Choose one person to be the "caller" of the game. It should be the teacher, teacher aide or a very good student to assure correct pronunciation of the blends.

6. The caller shuffles the 16 Lingo cards and places them face down on the table. The caller then allows each player to draw a card. The markers (beans) are then distributed to the players.

7. The students place their Lingo card face up in front of them. To begin, each player places a marker on the free space in the center of his card marked ★.

8. The caller places before him the Lingo Consonant Blend and Digraph Sheet which gives a complete list of blends and digraphs used in the game and shakes the container of Lingo squares.

9. The caller draws a Lingo square randomly from the container and says it twice, naming the letter and the blend, or digraph, for example: "G, /bl/". The caller places the square on the Lingo Consonant Blend Sheet in the "G, /bl/" space. The player(s) having a card with "G/bl/" place their markers over the "bl".

10. The game proceeds in this way with the caller calling the blends and digraphs and players covering those called until a player has covered five blends in a row in any direction. At this point, the player calls "Lingo" and the game stops. The other players **should not** remove their markers until that person has officially won.

11. To officially win, the player must (a) call back the five blends while the caller notes if they are on the Lingo Consonant Blend Sheet, meaning that they have indeed been called. If the blends do not correspond, the game continues. If they do correspond, the player must (b) give a word for each of the 5 blends or digraphs. If the player cannot give a word for each, the player wins only half the "kitty"* and the game continues. If he can perform this task, the player wins the entire "kitty" and a new game begins.

*12. Lingo can be played for stakes in the Adult ESL classes. Each player may buy from the "Banker-caller" as many cards as he wishes at a set price (a penny or nickel is suggested). The pennies are put in the "kitty" and the stakes are won accordingly. In non-adult classes, the teacher should provide some inexpensive prizes.

LINGO CONSONANT BLEND AND DIGRAPH SHEET

L	I	N	G	O
cl	pl	gr	bl	ch
cr	pr	qu	br	dr
gl	ph	sh	sn	st
wh	sk	sm	kn	sw
fl	sl	sp	tr	tw
fr	th			

LINGO CARDS

L	I	N	G	O
gl	th	sm	br	tw
fr	ph	gr	kn	st
fl	sk	*	tr	ch
cl	sl	sp	sn	sw
cr	pl	sh	bl	dr

L	I	N	G	O
wh	pl	sh	sn	dr
fl	ph	gr	br	tw
gl	pr	*	kn	sw
cl	th	qu	bl	ch
fr	sk	sp	tr	st

L	I	N	G	O
cl	sk	sp	tr	st
cr	ph	sh	kn	dr
gl	sl	*	bl	tw
wh	pr	sm	sn	sw
fl	th	gr	br	ch

L	I	N	G	O
cl	th	sp	bl	ch
cr	sl	gr	tr	sw
fl	sk	*	br	tw
wh	pr	qu	sn	dr
fr	pl	sh	kn	st

Card 1

L	I	N	G	O
cl	ph	gr	sn	st
wh	sk	sh	kn	dr
fr	pl	*	bl	ch
fl	pr	qu	tr	tw
cr	sl	sp	br	sw

Card 2

L	I	N	G	O
fr	sl	gr	tr	sw
fl	th	sm	bl	ch
cl	pr	*	sn	dr
cr	pl	sp	br	tw
gl	sk	qu	kn	st

Card 3

L	I	N	G	O
cr	th	sm	tr	sw
gl	pr	qu	sn	st
wh	sk	*	kn	ch
fl	pl	gr	br	dr
fr	sl	sp	bl	tw

Card 4

L	I	N	G	O
gl	pl	sm	kn	dr
wh	sl	gr	tr	tw
fr	pr	*	br	st
fl	sk	sp	bl	ch
cr	ph	qu	sn	sw

Card 5

L	I	N	G	O
fl	sl	gr	br	st
wh	sk	sp	sn	sw
fr	th	*	tr	ch
cr	pr	sm	kn	dr
cl	pl	sh	bl	tw

Card 6

L	I	N	G	O
wh	pl	gr	bl	tw
cl	th	sh	sn	dr
fl	sl	*	br	st
cr	pr	qu	kn	sw
fr	sk	sm	tr	ch

Card 7

L	I	N	G	O
wh	ph	qu	kn	tw
cr	sk	gr	br	ch
fr	sl	*	sn	sw
fl	pr	sp	bl	st
cl	pl	sm	tr	dr

Card 8

L	I	N	G	O
gl	ph	sm	kn	st
cr	pl	qu	bl	sw
fr	th	*	tr	dr
wh	sl	sh	br	tw
fl	pr	gr	sn	ch

Card 9

L	I	N	G	O
cr	pl	qu	sn	ch
wh	sl	sh	kn	sw
cl	ph	*	br	st
fl	sk	gr	tr	tw
gl	pr	sm	bl	dr

L	I	N	G	O
cl	ph	qu	tr	sw
gl	pl	sh	br	ch
fr	pr	✽	sn	st
wh	sk	gr	bl	tw
fl	sl	sm	kn	dr

L	I	N	G	O
gl	th	sp	br	dr
cl	sl	gr	bl	ch
wh	pr	✽	kn	tw
cr	pl	qu	sn	sw
fl	sk	sh	tr	st

L	I	N	G	O
fr	pr	sm	sn	ch
cr	pl	qu	br	tw
cl	sl	✽	kn	dr
gl	sk	sh	bl	st
fl	ph	gr	tr	sw

LINGO SQUARES

L	I	N	G	O
/cl/	/pl/	/gr/	/bl/	/ch/
L	**I**	**N**	**G**	**O**
/cr/	/pr/	/qu/	/br/	/dr/
L	**I**	**N**	**G**	**O**
/gl/	/ph/	/sh/	/sn/	/st/
L	**I**	**N**	**G**	**O**
/wh/	/sk/	/sm/	/kn/	/sw/
L	**I**	**N**	**G**	**O**
/fl/	/sl/	/sp/	/tr/	/tw/
L	**I**			
/fr/	/th/			

← cut

↑ cut

APPENDIX E

Sight Words

It is suggested that students number their sight word flash cards in the upper right hand corner for easy retrieval and organization. Note that some of these words are "optional".

1. name	26. ham	51. man/woman
2. first	27. an	52. last/first
3. last	28. man	53. dad/mom
4. circle	29. Nan	54. fat/thin
5. address	30. tan	55. fast/slow
6. city	31. Ann	56. sad/glad
7. state	32. bat(s)	57. sad/happy
8. zip code	33. pan(s)	58. jet
9. telephone	34. lamp	59. jam
10. number	35. small	60. get
11. phone no.	36. ball	61. gas
12. home phone	37. fat	62. flag
13. social security number	38. fast	63. zip
14. soc. sec. no.	39. ten	64. cat
15. same	40. men	65. cap
16. different	41. Ben	66. Ken
17. How are you?	42. pen	67. kiss
18. Fine, thank you.	43. pet	68. ill
19. at	44. he	69. it
20. hat	45. Lee	70. in
21. hats	46. dad	71. age
22. sat	47. sad	72. bed
23. Sam	48. mad	73. It's
24. mat	49. and	74. is
25. mast	50. hand	75. isn't
		76. Hi.

77. Jan
78. OK
79. She's
80. not
81. well
82. sick
83. He's
84. tall
85. sing
86. ill/well
87. sick/well
88. fine/OK
89. sick/ill
90. the
91. mall
92. takes
93. pill
94. Mr.
95. Mrs.
96. Miss
97. Ms.
98. ship
99. glass
100. spoon
101. desk
102. watch
103. chair
104. red
105. on

106. open
107. very
108. walk
109. what
110. What's
111. exit
112. yes
113. you
114. up
115. us
116. quiet
117. Hello
118. thank
119. your
120. are
121. sex
122. how
123. Watch your step
124. store
125. closed
126. No U Turn
127. stop
128. check out
129. Male
130. Female
131. whale
132. three
133. quarter
134. clock
135. Speed Limit 45 MPH

136. Hill
137. Push
138. Pull
139. Cashier
140. No Smoking
141. Restrooms
142. women
143. push/pull
144. no/yes
145. men/women
146. white
147. black
148. brown
149. green
150. blue
151. color
152. yellow
153. orange
154. gray
155. plant
156. sweater
157. dress
158. snowman
159. My
160. hair
161. eyes
162. slow
163. truck
164. credit card
165. fries

166. present
167. knife
168. twenty
169. fast/slow
170. up/down
171. alphabet
172. before
173. after
174. pencil
175. book
176. notebook
177. door
178. window
179. chalkboard
180. table
181. your
182. Street (St.)
183. Avenue (Ave.)
184. area code
185. height
186. Good morning
187. Good afternoon
188. Good evenining
189. time
190. Thanks
191. o'clock
192. I'm
193. early
194. on time
195. late
196. sorry

197. doctor
198. nurse
199. busboy
200. waiter
201. cook
202. housewife
203 gardener
204. secretary
205. salesman
206. saleslady
207. doctor/nurse
208. salesman/saleslady
209. weight
210. his
211. her
212. his/her
213. they
214. They're
215. teachers
216. barbers
217. lawyers
218. students
219. bakers
220. dentists
221. is/are
222. aren't
223. where
224. from
225. I'm
226. Japan/Japanese
227. Mexico/Mexican

228. China/Chinese
229. country
230. We're
231. birthplace
232. Excuse me
233. middle (name)
234. Good night
235. How time flies.
236. married
237. single
238. month
239. day
240. date
241. March
242. Sunday (Sun.)
243. Monday (Mon.)
244. Tuesday (Tues.)
245. Wednesday (Wed.)
246. Thursday (Thur.)
247. Friday (Fri.)
248. Saturday (Sat.)
249. today
250. divorced
251. widowed
252. date of birth
253. birthdate
254. penny
255. cent(s)
256. much

257. nickel
258. dime
259. half dollar
260. dollar
261. signature
262. separated
263. marital status
264. this
265. that
266. place of birth
267. orange
268. lemon
269. banana
270. pepper
271. apple
272. onion
273. sign here
274. food
275. drink
276. coins
277. out of order
278. carrots
279. cabbages
208. peppers
281. oranges
282. onions
283. lemons
284. these
285. those
286. give

287. me
288. one
289. please
290. apples
291. 50¢/lb.
292. all right
293. You're welcome.
294. bank
295. barber shop
296. post office
297. department store
298. beauty shop
299. laundromat
300. airport
301. market
302. hospital
303. Ht.
304. Wt.
305. here
306. there
307. egg
308. grow
309. Yummy!
310. good
311. bedroom
312. dresser
313. wallet
314. purse
315. money

316. glasses
317. pillows
318. shoes
319. under
320. box
321. kitchen
322. sink
323. stove
324. cabinet
325. counter
326. refrigerator
327. maiden (name)
328. United States
329. family
330. husband
331. wife
332. father
333. mother
334. son
335. daughter
336. brother
337. sister
338. spouse
339. How do you do?